KIDS IN THE JAIL

KIDS IN THE JAIL

Why Our Young Offenders
Do The Things They Do

By Paul Vasey

Black Moss Press

©Copyright Paul Vasey, 1995

Published by Black Moss Press
2450 Byng Road, Windsor, Ontario, N8W 3E8.

Black Moss books are distributed by Firefly Books,
250 Sparks Avenue, Willowdale, Ontario, M2H 2S4.
All orders should be directed there.

Financial assistance toward the publication of this book
was provided by the Canada Council and the Ontario
Arts Council.

Cover design by Richard Withey
Layout and page design by Kristina Carroll

Canadian Cataloguing in Publication Data:

Vasey, Paul

Kids in the jail : why our young offenders do

the things they do

ISBN 0-88753-257-8

1. Juvenile delinquency--Canada. I. Title.

HV9108.V39 1995   364.3'6'0971   C95-900227-8

All of the names of the young offenders and jail staff members in this book have
been changed to protect their identities.

For Marilyn, once more
and
For Kirsten and Adam

The child is father of the man
*   - Wordsworth*

A First Word

One long September night a year ago, our city held its breath. A nine-year-old boy vanished from a factory-district field, seemingly without a trace. The missing boy and a pal had been searching the field for snakes when an older boy approached. The teen told them he knew of a better spot to find snakes and the three of them headed across the field together.

The missing boy's friend became separated from the others, quickly looked around for them, couldn't see them and ran home to tell his parents. The boy and his father returned to the field but found no sign of the missing boy. The father called the cops.

For twelve hours, everyone hoped for the best and feared the worst. This incident happened not long after two boys kidnapped and murdered a child in England, and that murder was not far from the minds of everyone searching for the missing kid.

A little after four the next morning, the nine-year-old was found, badly beaten, almost blind, freezing cold and left for dead. Somehow, he had survived the beating and the night.

Police arrested a teenager and charged him with abduction and attempted murder.

They said there was no known motive.

That incident certainly got me thinking, and wondering. Mostly what I wondered was: how could someone beat up a little kid and leave him in a field? After that case made the headlines in my town, I started looking for and collecting news stories about kids charged with crimes, kids convicted of crimes. No shortage of stories: I've got a file folder three inches thick, kids and crimes coast to coast. I also started clipping stories quoting people demanding something be done to put an end to all this kid crime. Mostly, what these people wanted was for the kids to go to jail for a long, long time. The longer the better. And adult prison, if possible.

After a year of collecting news stories I was still asking myself the same questions I asked myself the morning they found the nine-year-old bloodied, but still breathing, in a field not far from my home:

Why are criminal kids doing what they're doing?

What happens to them once they're caught?

How does 'the system' work and how could it be improved to deal with these kids more effectively?

I like kids and spend a lot of time with them. I was once a Big Brother. When my wife and I had kids of our own I became involved in the usual parental activities: I was a Cub leader for a couple of years, I coached my daughter's softball team and my son's baseball team. Though I still devote a lot of my spare time to coaching kids, I'm certainly no expert when it comes to teenagers. Particularly troubled teenagers.

But a working life as a journalist has taught me where to look for the answers to the questions that intrigue me. In the news business, a good rule of thumb is 'go to the source.' If you want insights into the behaviour and motivations of troubled kids, you turn first to the people who work most closely with them. Over the years, I've done a number of stories about troubled teenagers and I came to know the director of a maximum security jail for young offenders. It was to him — I'll call him William B. — that I first turned. I told him I would like to spend some time in his jail, observe the kids and the way in which they were treated, talk to the staff and get their answers to my questions.

William B. took my proposal to his superiors and, after several months thinking it over, they agreed to give me access to his jail. There were conditions: I could not name the jail; I must use assumed first names for its employees and its inmates; I could not interview any of the kids without William B.'s approval; I could not be alone with any of the inmates at any time; and when I was finished writing the book, both William B. and his superiors were to have access to the manuscript to ensure I had not inadvertently identified any of the kids in their charge. Journalists never like to relinquish their freedoms and I gave a lot of thought to these conditions. In the end, I felt it was worth it to allow you, the reader, access to a jail you'd otherwise never visit and meet the people who work there, people who know — perhaps better than anyone — what makes criminal kids tick and what needs to be done to make the 'system' deal with these kids more effectively.

So, late last spring, I began visiting the jail on a regular basis, spending two or three hours a day watching the kids do what kids do in a jail, watching the staff work with them, interviewing staff, making notes. Over a period of several months I spent dozens of hours observing the routine in the jail from the time the kids woke up until the time they went to bed. I was allowed access to all the programs the kids engaged in and many of the staff meetings.

I also sought out people in my community who deal with young offenders on a daily basis. I talked at length with judges, Crown prosecutors, cops, child-care workers, social workers, child psychologists, criminologists, and those who run other facilities which care for troubled and criminal kids. I was looking for a wide spectrum of answers and, as you will shortly read for yourself, a spectrum is what I got.

Many of the people you will encounter in this book are from Windsor, Ontario and they talk about the kids they've arrested, prosecuted, jailed, and treated in this community. These professionals and the people you'll meet in the jail represent only a fraction of those who work with young offenders across the country. But what people in my community, and in this one Ontario jail, say about criminal kids is much the same as what the professionals in your community or in a jail near you would say if you sat down with them and asked them some basic questions.

Crime is crime no matter where it's committed. The criminal kids in my town, and in this jail, are no different than criminal kids in your community or in jails anywhere in Canada.

7:16 a.m. ────────────────────────────────

In the early light of dawn it doesn't look much like a maximum-security jail. It looks more like a college dorm, or one of those cut-rate freeway motels: two storeys, sandy brick, a row of narrow upper-storey windows, some curtains closed, some not; more windows, wider and taller, on the lower floor. No bars. No barbed wire. But there are a couple of tipoffs. Between the parking lot and the building there's a triangular asphalt exercise yard: net-less basketball hoop, a couple of picnic tables, a couple of benches. The fence is eighteen feet tall. You could scale the first twelve, if you were nimble. Or desperate. Or high on your own adrenaline. The lower part of the fence is regulation school-yard chain-link. But twelve feet is about as far as you'd get. The mesh from there to the top is smaller than the tips of your fingers. The only escapees from this yard are the birds — sparrows and finches, wrens and starlings — which swoop down from the nearby trees, loiter, flutter aloft and dart away into the distant blue. Attached to the outside of the fence at the end nearest the parking lot is a small sign, white letters on a navy background: 'Please Remember To Lock Your Car.' Screwed to the wall near the front door is another metal sign: 'Police Parking Only.'

So, it may not look much like a jail for young offenders, but go through the double doors into the lobby (the first door is

10

unlocked, the second controlled by the receptionist) and it certainly starts to feel like a jail. The receptionist's area is partitioned from the lobby by glass walls. The glass in the doors and elsewhere throughout the building is shatterproof. The door to the receptionist's area, like the front doors and the steel door which leads to the jail itself and the steel doors which separate one area of the jail from another, is secured by a magnetic lock, two tons of force. There are two tiny lights at the bottom of each lock: green for locked, red for open. The people who work here — they call themselves "staff," not guards — look up at those lights out of habit every time they close a door behind themselves.

"We think about security, first and foremost." Patricia P. is a supervisor at the jail. She's not understating matters. Before allowing me to enter the jail, Director William B. asked Patricia to give me a security primer, a kind of shorthand version of the course all new staff members must go through. The session lasted almost an hour.

Rules of The House:

When staff members arrive for work they drop their car keys in a drawer in the receptionist's area and pick up a jail key which is on a plastic spiral cord they clip to their belts. One key fits all the locks except those in the doors leading to the outside. There are only three of those keys in the place, and the kids don't know who has them. So, if the kids overpower staff and grab the key, they can get only as far as the lobby or the playpen. Staff carry nothing that could be used as a weapon: no pens, no nail files, no nail clippers, no sets of keys, no penknives. They do carry two-way radios strapped to their belts. Help is a call away.

The jail is a Phase One Young Offender Secure Detention and Custody Facility. Translation: it's a 14-bed jail for kids aged 12 to 15. The jail is funded — $1.5 million a year — by the Ministry of

Community and Social Services. Older young offenders — those 16 to 18 — are held in Phase Two Young Offender Secure Detention and Custody Facilities. Those facilities, you figure the logic, are funded by the Ministry of Corrections.

However, not all the kids in the jail are 12 to 15. "Some could be older," says Patricia P. "If they've been convicted when they're 15, we could have them until they're 17. The maximum sentence is three years, but few stay three years. We had one for two years, and we've had one in here for two hours. The majority are here for 60 to 90 days. Some are here for a year, but just a few. Very rarely do we have them longer than that." Just now, though, one kid is serving a year and a half. Not all of these kids have hurt people, but some have. Kids have been sent here for assault, aggravated assault, sexual assault, rape, attempted murder and murder.

The motto here: never be too trusting of the kids. "I always have it in the back of my head, 'jeez, I don't know about this kid.' Some of them, I honestly believe they'd never hurt me. But I wouldn't trust any of them not to run away if they got the chance. You don't trust them, completely, ever." Stable is not an adjective to describe any of them.

"Some of these kids are so emotionally disturbed you just never know what they're going to do." An example? Just the day before, Patricia was working with one boy. He was distraught, in tears, and Patricia thought to herself 'poor kid' and began to talk to him, trying to comfort him, find out what was bothering him. She snaps her fingers: "Just like that, he came right at me. I was backing up when he hit me, luckily, or he'd really have hurt me." As it was, she has bruises. Two other staff were on duty on the floor. They ordered the other kids into their rooms, hit the locks, and then they and Patricia went into the boy's room. It took all three of them to control the kid, though there was not much to him: he weighed, maybe, a hundred pounds. "So it went from 'oh, the poor kid' to 'oh oh, he's coming at me' in the space of a couple of seconds."

So, never forget it's a jail you're in. And never forget there's a very good reason the kids are here. And never forget the rules of the house.

The inmates, or 'residents' as they're called, are grouped in sevens, two staff members per group. When the kids are in a room — classroom, dining room, rec room — one staff member is against one wall, the other is near the door. They're always positioned so they can see all the kids in the room, and see everything that's going on. Staff never allow themselves to be alone in a room with a kid: they don't want the kids to be able to allege abuse, and they don't want to be in a position where they can be overpowered.

Never let a kid get behind you. When the kids are moving from one area to another, they walk single file down the right side of the hall. One staff is at the head of the line, walking backwards, the other is at the back of the line, walking frontwards. The two groups of kids are never in the same room or on the same floor at the same time, except at night, when they're in their rooms. If one group is out in the playpen, the other is in the rec room. If one group is having supper downstairs, the other kids are in their rooms, quiet time.

When the kids are eating, they are issued plastic utensils and dishes. When they're finished eating, the staff count the utensils. If the kids are given popsicles, the staff gather up the sticks and count them. When the kids are in school, they are issued plastic cups with pen, pencil, ruler, glue; when class is over, they hand the cups back. Everything is counted. If anything's missing, staff freeze the room: no one moves until the missing piece is found.

The kids are not allowed to keep anything in their rooms. Their books, photo albums, Walkman sets, and other personal items are kept in a cart. During quiet time, staff roll the cart from room to room. The kids can take one item each. The staff keep a log of who's got what. When quiet time is over, the item goes back on the cart. Check mark on the log.

Clothing is restricted: no belts, no string in the waistband of sweatpants, no buckles on the jackets. No necklaces, no earrings, no rings. The kids wear running shoes with Velcro fasteners or they wear slippers or they go in stocking feet.

One kid per bedroom. Concrete-block walls, no pictures allowed (things can be hidden behind pictures). The floor is tiled. The window won't open and won't break. The curtains are hung from a Velcro strip. There's a single bed, a desk, a stool. All the bedroom furniture is bolted to the floor. The pillow and mattress are covered with thick grey plastic, zippered at one end. The tabs of the zippers are sewn shut, so nothing can be tucked inside. Every morning the kids strip the two sheets and comforter from their beds and roll them up. Staff do a security check of the bedrooms twice a day. "We check every nook and cranny. We check under the mattresses, under the beds, the whole floor area, in their desks, in their closets (which are outside the rooms)." The curtains over the window in the door are on the outside, so staff can check the room at all times. Staff check each room every fifteen minutes throughout the night.

Each child is allowed to have a comb, a brush, a toothbrush, shampoo and conditioner, all of which are kept in a plastic container locked in his closet. When the kids come out each morning to have a shower, the staff unlock the closets. All the items are counted before the tray is returned and the closet locked.

If the kids have to leave the jail to visit a doctor, psychiatrist, probation officer, or go to court, they're transported in the grey, seven-seater Chrysler mini-van parked out front. The kid rides in the back seat, left side. A staff member sits on the middle seat, between the kid and the sliding side door. If two kids are being transported, there'll be two staffers on the middle seat. When the kids return, they leave their shoes in the lobby. They're taken down the ramp and into a windowless room. A staff member stands in the doorway where he can see the kid. Another stands down the hallway where he can see his colleague. Female inmate, female staff members. Male inmate, male staff members. The kid is told to undress and shove his clothes out into the hall. The staff member in the doorway asks the naked kid to turn around, then gives the kid a robe. The pile of clothes goes to the laundry where it's given a security check. The kid is taken upstairs for a fresh set of clothes from his closet. "Any time a kid leaves, you can't be assured they haven't picked up something or been slipped something. You can't watch them every second, so they're always searched when they come back."

There's a security sweep of the building and the playpen at least twice a day. "We check for weapons that have been left at the bottom of the fence. Or matches, or cigarettes." The chain link is inspected to make sure no one has cut it, and to make sure the lower edge is secured.

"Some people say 'wow, this is extreme.' But it isn't. It's preventive. It's our way, and it works, so we'll keep doing it. We want to make sure they stay safe and that we stay safe. Very early on, a group overpowered a staff member. It's never happened since. And we want to make sure it doesn't happen."

Welcome to the jail.

7:31 a.m. ————————————————

The kids' bedrooms are on the second floor. The doors open, left and right, off a long hallway of grey-painted concrete block walls and grey carpeting. At either end of the hall there's a staff office and a kids' lounge. There's a bathroom at one end of the hall, two at the other.

First thing in the morning the lights are low. It's the absence of sound you notice: no radio, no chatter, no laughter. Down at the far end of the hall, a couple of staff members are filling out reports which detail, quarter hour by quarter hour, what happened overnight: who couldn't sleep, who was fidgety, who was troubled, who slept straight through. The reports will give the day staff their first clue about how the day is likely to unfold.

Knock, knock.

"Who's knocking?" Frances E. lifts the curtain covering the window of George's room. "Were you knocking, George?"

George wants to have a shower. She tells him to come out. "Number 2 is open." She unlocks his cupboard door, he takes out his plastic tray: toothpaste, toothbrush, shampoo, conditioner. Holding his beltless robe together with one hand, he heads down the hall to Bathroom Number 2. He knocks, pushes the door open, and enters.

All along the hall, small piles of bathrobes and slippers. They're left outside the doors, in the event the fire alarm might go off in the night. "It's happened. In winter."

Someone is knocking.

"Is that you Grant?"

It is. "Come on out." Grant opens his door, bends down, snatches the robe up off the floor and goes back into his room. When he comes out a moment later, he asks, "Could you let me into my closet?" She does, and tells him, "Number 1 is open."

Early risers get the showers. Everyone else has to wait his/her turn. There's one washroom for the females and there are two for the males. Once the early risers have showered, they return to their rooms, dress, and wait until the late comers are washed and combed. Once the members of one group have showered and dressed, that group can head down for breakfast. Then the other group can get cleaned up.

Frances closes Grant's closet door and turns the key. "Do you have good news for me today?" "Yah." "Excellent news?" "Yah." "Keep it going, eh?" "Yah." He flaps down the hall in too-large slippers, the sandal type.

Grant's excellent news? He's trying for another 50 day. Fifty is the highest number of points you can earn in a day. You have them when you wake up. You lose them, one by one, for things which you do that you ought not to have done. Fifty earns you a tag on your door and an invitation to a 50s party on the weekend. You get to go to the honours lounge, shoot pool, listen to music, watch a movie, buy a pop, if you want, from the lounge machine. It's the jail equivalent of a happening Saturday night, all things being relative.

Grant passes me on the way to the shower. "Hi Paul. How you doin' today?" "Fine. How about you?" "Good. Except I need a cigarette." Sorry about your luck. No smokes are allowed.

"Come on out, Elizabeth." Elizabeth is the first of the three females to come out into the hallway, which means she gets the shower first. "Can I have a twenty-minute shower today?" Not today. Not tomorrow. Not until you get home again. "Fifteen?" "You know the rule."

The shower rule, and the other Morning Routine rules, are printed out for all to see and taped to the wall:

Morning Routine:
1. Once you are awakened, fold sheets then knock
on door and wait patiently for staff to get to you.
2. No stalling while out of room. Reasons to be out of room:
showers, meds, cleaning bathroom.
3. Showers are to be no more than 10 minutes.
4. No knocking once all your morning tasks have
been completed.

5. Bed should be neatly made before leaving room.
6. If you need to request phone calls to lawyer,
probation officer, social worker, this is to be
done before school, during recess, at lunch time
or at quiet time.

Elizabeth: "Can I have a razor, Frances?" Frances says she'll get one. A few minutes later, she hands Elizabeth the razor and stands in the bathroom doorway while Elizabeth shaves her legs. Once the razor's been rinsed, Frances takes it back to the staff office. "Everyone's supervised when they're using razors. And if they're on a suicide caution or a suicide alert, no shaving is allowed."

"Who's knocking?"

It's Bob. Larry R. lifts the flap covering the window of the door. "You'll have to wait, Bob, both bathrooms are in use." Bob doesn't want to shower. He wants to get his clothes from the basket in the hall and fold them. "Come on out." Bob picks up the basket and takes it into his room. The day before was laundry day. Put your clothes into the basket dirty, you get them back clean but you do your own folding. A few moments later Bob knocks again. "Come on out." Larry unlocks Bob's closet, waits until all the clothes are neatly placed on the shelves, locks the closet door. "How are you this morning, Larry?" "I'm fine, Bob. You?" "Good. I actually had a good sleep." "Good for you. Back inside. You're next in line for the shower."

"Hey Larry?" "Yes, Walt." "You got a nail clipper?" Larry goes into the office and gets one. "You know how to work one of these babies?" The kid looks at him, puzzled. Then smiles. "Yah." "That's good, because I can't find the owner's manual." Walt smirks, and goes to work on his nails. Larry watches, waits, and then holds out his hand, palm up. "Thanks."

Larry checks his watch. "Jeez. Better get going on the meds."

Medications are given twice daily, once in the morning, again at night. It's the supervisor's job to open the medication closet, get out the tray, put the right pills in the right containers and get them to the right kids. What kind of medications do they dole out? "A lot of face stuff. I'm telling you, if they'd had all this stuff when I was a kid, I wouldn't have been a pizza face." The stuff works. Zits disappear. "Which is great for their self-esteem, their self-image. They want to look good. Which is great." But zits aren't their only concern. They get lots of aches and pains, especially on Tuesdays. Why Tuesdays? "The doctor's in on Tuesday." And there's generally a line-up: aches, pains, spots, rashes, you name it, though generally there's nothing very serious. For a lot of these kids, a doctor is a novelty. Few have made regular visits to a family doctor. Few have had a family doctor. "So they like to go to the doctor. They'll go to the doctor for some little spot on the back of their hand that you can hardly see. They'll go for something you and I wouldn't think of going to a doctor about." Novelty is novelty and attention is worth its weight in gold.

George is out of the shower and dressed and coming back down the hall with his brush in one hand, a bottle of gel in the other. "Frances, will you help me with my gel?"

Frances is going to be busy for a few minutes at the far end of the hall, but if George can wait, she'll be glad to help him when she's free. George will wait. He goes into the lounge, takes the chair nearest the door, starts waiting (sticking his head out every so often to chart her progress). "I can give you a hand with that if you want." George looks up at Larry. "No thanks. I'll wait for Frances." "You could do it yourself, George. I'll show you how." "No. I want Frances to do it."

Knock knock.

"Come on out Bob. Number 2's clear."

Knock knock.

"Come on out Sandy. Number 1's clear."

Sandy pads down the hall, slippers slapping.

Here comes Frances. George is all smiles, hands her the bottle of gel, then the brush. "You hold onto the brush for a minute." He takes it back. She puts a little dab of gel on her palm. "About this much, see?" George nods. "You watching?" "I'm watching." "Then you rub your hands together and then rub your hair. Like this." She starts rubbing his hair. "Okay?" "Okay." Then she looks up at me: "He's being released soon, so we're showing him how to do these things." She looks down at George "Aren't we?" "Yah. Because nobody's going to be there to do it for me, eh Frances?" "How are you feeling. You feeling anxious?" "No." "About your meeting?" "No." It's a plan-of-care meeting they're talking about, one of a series they'll have during which social workers and probation officers and Children's Aid Society workers get together to talk about what will happen to George when he walks out the door in three weeks' time, there being no particular place for George to go. The door shut behind him after he left home and nobody's willing to open it. Certainly not George.

"They'll ask you questions, George." "Like where I'll be comfortable going?" "Yah. That's a good question. And they'll ask you other questions, too. And don't you be embarrassed to ask questions. If you have questions, you ask them, all right?" "All right." "If you ask the questions, then you'll get answers and once you get the answers to your questions, then you'll feel less anxious." "All right." "These are all professionals, George They're there to do a service for you. You understand that? They're there to help you. They all want to help you and they have the knowledge to help you. Understand?" Frances is now working the brush and the blow dryer. George nods.

"You know what it'll be like George?" "No. What?" "It'll be like you're the president of a big corporation. The boss. And you'll come into the room and all these people who work for you will be sitting around the table. And they'll want to know what you want them to do next. And you can tell them. Understand?" George's smile says it all. Frances says she'll find out what time the meeting will be held. "I want you to know right now so that you're not anxious waiting around all day." "William (the jail's director) already told me." "Oh. That's good." Frances switches off the dryer. "You remember. These people are performing a service for you. You're the boss. Remember?" "Yah. I'll remember."

Out in the hall, Larry takes a look at Stew's hair. "Bad hair day?" Stew is definitely having a bad hair day, curls gone wild. "I was trying to brush it and whole handfuls came out." Larry smiles one of those 'yah, right' smiles. "I'm serious. Handfuls." "Ever heard of conditioner? Works miracles." Stew heads down the hall toward the lounge. "Can I use the dryer?" "Yup. Be my guest."

Walt wants to know if he can take his Walkman into his room while he waits for everyone else to finish their routines.

He can have his Walkman or book, his choice.

"Do I have chores today?" Norm is standing about two feet from the Chore Chart on the wall. "Have a look." Norm looks at the chart. "What day is this?" "This would be Thursday," says Larry, "all day." Norm checks the chart, again. Lucky him: no chores until tomorrow. Tomorrow, he'll be cleaning Bathroom Number 1.

Stew is having trouble with the brush and the tangles. Frances, passing by the lounge door, stops to investigate. "Here. Let me help." A quick lesson in rolling the brush and working the dryer to kill curls. "Get it?" "Oh. Now I get it." She watches as he gives it a whirl. "Hey, that works."

Off she goes. "Mary, don't forget your medications."

"I won't."

"Who's knocking?" It's Elizabeth. She wants the hair dryer. "You're next, after Stew."

John is knocking. "C'mon out." John is sleepy and surly. He's not happy that his room has been painted. "I'm gonna wreck it tonight. I'm gonna write all over the walls." Staffer Helen S. catches the comment. "Do you think that's a very good choice?" John doesn't answer. He heads for the shower.

Frances is still thinking about George and his meeting. "At first, he refused to go to any of the meetings where he was being discussed. Now, he insists on going." She smiles at the transformation. "If you could only have seen him when he first came in here. He was just a little peanut of a thing. He's grown so much. And he's changed so much. You'd be amazed." She shakes her head at the thought. "He's extremely intelligent. He learned pool in one day, and now he beats everyone. He's the best at ping pong, and he never played it before he came here. He's the best speller. He's the best one during question and answer. When he first came in here, he was never very good with his peers. But now he's a leader in his group." Proud smile. "But there's still that little dark spot in there. The little boy we still don't know."

"Frances?" "Yes, Stew." "How's that?" "That's great. You did a great job." Stew heads back to his room. "Elizabeth, the dryer's free." Elizabeth comes down the hall, in a hurry. "Remember, other people will want to use it." "Yah." Elizabeth is also not in the best of humour this morning, apparently.

"Frances?" "Yes, Mary." "Can you get me a bandage?" Frances can, and does. She comes back, peeling the wrapper. "Thank you Frances. I can do that." Mary takes the bandage and heads down the hall.

John emerges from the shower, gel slathered in his hair. His head glistens. Larry takes one look at him. "Gel got away from you, eh?" John looks at him, but doesn't answer. "May have to do something about that, John." John still doesn't answer. Larry is making mental notes. The mental notes have to do with security. Even hair gel can be a security risk: kids can momentarily blind a staff member by smearing gel in his eyes; kids can jam it into key locks or smear it on magnetic locks. Ingenuity knows few bounds.

Norm asks Helen to open his closet door. On the back of the door he's taped a hand-drawn calendar, neat numbered squares on yellow foolscap. There's a big star on Saturday's square and the letters TR. He's got a temporary release that day. There's a bigger star the following Thursday. He taps the star with his fingernail. Big smile. "That's your release date?" "Yah. I'm outta here." Norm puts his tray on one of the shelves, gets his clothes, heads for his room.

John comes out, dressed. No appreciable improvement in his mood. Shift supervisor Patricia P. takes one look at his T-shirt. "How'd that get ripped,?" John doesn't answer. Patricia says he should change his shirt. "I'm gonna wear it." Patricia thinks he should think about that decision. "I'm gonna wear it." He's got two choices: change shirts, or spend a few minutes in the time-out room thinking about why he should make himself presentable in the morning.

As Helen says, watching from a distance, "He's quite low-functioning." The staff will go an extra step with him, explaining his options, trying to direct him to make suitable choices. They won't let him get away with anything, but they do make allowances. He's slower than the others to see the direction his actions are leading him, so they give him a little more time than the others to make his decisions. But with him, as with all the others, there are lines it's better not to cross.

"I'm not takin' it off."

Time-out room is this way.

23

The time-out room is eight feet by eight with concrete-block walls, cement floor, a ceiling light shielded by shatter-proof glass. In goes John. Larry stands just outside the door.

Fifteen minutes later, the showers are done, the bathrooms are mopped, the meds have been distributed and John, head still glistening, is wearing a new T-shirt.

"Let's go."

No need to ask twice. The kids line up: John, Mary, Walt, Fred, Rick, Norm and George. They're perfectly normal-looking kids: only one tattoo, no missing teeth, no attitude. Some of them smile, others are shyly friendly. They don't look or act like thugs. They're polite, please and thank you, at least for the most part. Some of them have pimples, some the skin of angels. Some of them are blonde, some of them brunette, some have black hair. Some like their hair clipped short, some like it to the collar, or longer. Some of them have brown eyes, some blue. Some like blue jeans, some prefer sweatsuits. Some are quick with a quip, others quiet and watchful. They look like the kids who hang out at the mall, the kids you pass on the street downtown. Or, as I say to one of the teachers a little later, "They look like they could live on my street." "They do," she says.

Helen is at the head of the line, walking backwards, Larry is at the back of the line walking forwards. Left, right, left, right. We stop at the metal door at the end of the hall. Helen looks up, checks the light. Turns her key in the lock, watches the light go from green to red, backs out into the rampway. Down to breakfast we go.

Larry checks the light as the door silently shuts.

What, exactly, have these pleasant-looking, not in the least out-of-the-ordinary-looking children done to wake up this morning in a maximum-security jail? I wish I could tell you, but nothing

24

which might identify any of these children can be put between the covers of this book, or in the pages of a local newspaper, or be broadcast on radio stations like the one where I work. I can't give you specific descriptions of the kids or detailed accounts of what they've done. However, you don't need much imagination. Rare is the day you pick up the paper and don't read about kids causing trouble. Kids, some as young as 10. Some of the trouble they cause is pretty minor. Much of it is anything but.

VICTORIA — A retired navy man who extended a helping hand to a teenager had that hand smashed with a pipe.

OYAMA, B.C. — A 44-year-old tree-planter remains in critical condition in hospital after a gang of axe-wielding youths caved in a portion of his skull.

EDMONTON — An abused child, who became an abuser, took a knife to his stepsister while molesting her. He was sentenced to 18 months in secure custody.

NORTH BATTLEFORD, Sask. — A 15-year-old boy pleaded guilty to assaulting a fellow student with a drill bit.

WINNIPEG — A 14-year-old girl living in a group home was forced into prostitution by two other teenaged girls, police say.

CORNWALL, Ont. — A 17-year-old youth accused in the slaying of a 16-year-old girl now faces a second first-degree murder charge in the death of another teenager.

OTTAWA — A 10-year-old boy described by police as a gun expert was suspended from school Wednesday after he showed up with two loaded handguns.

HULL, Que. — A 16-year-old boy was stabbed to death by another teen when he tried to defend his girlfriend.

MONTREAL — Three boys, ranging in age from 11 to 15, have been arrested after a 17-year-old girl was raped.

SUSSEX, N.B. — A teenager is going to jail after hosting a

bash at a farmhouse he rented. Fuelled by liquor and drugs, revellers tore light fixtures from the walls and threw furniture through windows. Damage was $25,000.

MILL COVE, N.S. — Three youths have been charged with setting a fire that badly damaged an elementary school.

CHARLOTTETOWN — A 14-year-old boy has been charged with stabbing a girl in the hand because she wouldn't give him a basketball during a schoolyard game.

I've been collecting stories like these for more than a year. The file folder is twice the thickness of this book. The more stories I stuck in the folder, the more grimly fascinated I became.

These are kids we're reading about.

Children.

In his six years as director of the jail, William B. has dealt with kids who've committed just about every kind of crime you can imagine. "We've had second-degree murder and two attempted murders, a whole litany of serious sexual assaults, a lot of non-violent sexual assaults, if there is such a thing, and I don't mean to use the wrong words here, but sexual assault where there is no other violence. We have very few drug-dealing kids."

The road to the jail can start at the corner store. A kid pockets a pack of smokes while the clerk has her back turned. Check the odds: the clerk is bound to turn around, this time or the next time or the time after that. If the kid gets caught often enough, he can wind up sentenced, a week or a few, to an open custody facility: go to school during the day, check in at night. For these kids, that open door can be irresistible. "A lot of these kids are street kids and with these kinds of kids there's not a lot of respect for the law, or for any kind of authority," says William B. "If they see an open door, 'I'm outta here.' Once they go through the door, that's a serious offense."

It's what's known as 'escape lawful custody.' Definitely frowned upon. "They can be sent here for thirty days and it's the beginning of the spiral. So you can get someone here in secure custody for stealing a Bic lighter from Woolco. We have a lot of 'escape lawful custody' kids. Some of them flaunt the system. We had a kid in here once, spent 18 months here, and it all started with shoplifting. So it can get pretty silly. In some cases, kids could end up in here after being truant from school, if it's serious enough, recurs often enough. They could get sent to open custody, run from there and wind up in here for escape lawful custody. And with a lot of these kids, it could happen. It could just spiral out of control."

Spiralling out of control, kids can get ugly, especially if they get cornered. One of William's kids wound up in the jail after breaking into a house. He'd been armed with a knife. No one was home, no one got hurt and the kid got caught with an armful of stuff. One of the staff, hearing the details, was curious. What would have happened if the owners had come home while the kid was inside? "He said, 'I would've stabbed them, if I had to.'" The key thing was to get what he wanted and he was prepared to do whatever it required, even if that meant stabbing the homeowners. He wasn't out of control, he wasn't even angry. It was a sort of first-degree B&E. He was prepared to use the weapon if he felt he needed to.

"So. Breach of probation. Escape lawful custody. Violent assaults. Sexual assaults. That's our largest group of kids. And then we have a very small percentage of extremely violent crime."

It's the violence Mike Wilson can't help but notice. Mike's a cop. He started walking the beat in 1966 and, as he says almost as soon as we sit down to talk, "There's been quite a change in the generations" since he first pounded the beat. Kids back then got into the usual "fights and scraps. There were assaults, sure. But the fights were schoolyard fights. The kids would duke it out. They'd push and shove and a kid would take a swing and maybe connect, maybe knock the other kid on his ass and then he'd say 'had enough?' and that'd be that." That was then.

Now? What Mike Wilson sees as the reports cross his staff sergeant's desk in the Windsor Police Youth Bureau is this: "There aren't that many more violent assaults, probably. But the violent assaults are much more violent and the kids are using any kind of weapons of convenience: baseball bats, hockey sticks and real weapons — guns and knives. I'd say the general intent today, in a violent assault, is to inflict hurt on someone. Shootings and stabbings are much more prevalent today than back then."

And here's something completely different (and Mike Wilson won't be the last person to point it out): "The number of young ladies involved in violent crime these days." How young? "Thirteen, fourteen, fifteen." Ladies? "I just had three of them sitting in those chairs right there, sweet-looking kids, nice-looking little girls." The reason these sweet-looking, nice-looking little girls were sitting there? "The three of them were walking along and came upon another young lady and two of them grabbed her and held her while the third one beat her. Really beat her. It was extremely violent, to the point where the victim needed treatment." The reason for the beating? The one doing the beating summed it up, succinctly: " 'She was looking at me. Like I was a 'ho.'"

Then there was the time a girl was beating another, really beating her, "an unrelenting attack." The attack ended only when the victim was able to reach down into her ankle sock, pull her knife, and stab her attacker. "So, we had two to charge." Reason for this one? "She was lookin' at my man."

Then: a young girl and two male friends came up to a lone male. The girl pointed to him and said 'that's him.' "Her two buddies beat the shit out of him." Reason? The girl didn't like the way the victim had looked at her earlier in the evening.

"Some of these girls are very aggressive and very violent. They travel in two-somes and three-somes and four-somes." And they're quite willing to fight at the drop of a hat, or an eyelid, or a name. In 1993, the last year for which Mike Wilson has statistics, Windsor cops laid 981 charges against young male offenders, 302 charges against young females. Three males charged for every female. But Mike Wilson says consider this: females committed just about as many violent crimes as males.

Judge Saul Nosanchuk: "We have many more girls assaulting other girls. Vicious attacks in the street against other girls because of arguments in school. It seems there are vendettas going on with young women, and some young men too, but there are many, many more young women involved. It's so remarkable because it's so different than it was, so different from what I can remember as a youngster. We've had some very, very violent attacks done just out of spite."

Example? "One outside (a local high school) where these two girls were just doing it, I think, for another young woman who was angry at the victim for some reason. They were playing the enforcer. They just basically attacked her. One of them got on the bus and followed her, harassed her, and terrorized her. I couldn't imagine anything as nasty and vicious as that. They were 15."

Mike Wilson has seen his share of nasty and vicious and scary kids on the streets of Windsor.

Kid One: He started his career with a B&E. "He broke in, fed the dog, set the house on fire and took off. The dog died." The cops had a pretty good idea who'd done it and they turned up at the kid's door to ask some questions. The kid's mother said he wasn't home. The cops said they'd be back. Mom said she'd be moving before they came back. The cops asked for a forwarding address. She didn't want to give it out. She didn't want her kid to know where she was going.

Anyway, to cut the story short, the kid wound up in jail and was eventually released, at 15, in order to get psychiatric treatment. Before he could get his treatment, he torched another house. Nine people were inside, two of them died. The kid got three years. "Everyone figures, with the Young Offenders Act three years is three years, because there's no parole. But every year there's a review." After the kid's second review, he was back on the street. Wilson turned up at the review hearing. He went over to the kid. "I asked him if he ever thought of the guys who died in that fire. He just shook his head. 'Nope.' If nine guys had died in that fire, it would-n't have made any difference to him. Then I asked him where he was going to go if they let him out and he said he was going back to live with his mother." The same mother who'd given him the slip, years back? "That's the one. And this gets better. Because of the fact the kid has a psychological disability, he's going to be put on a disabili-ty pension." Some time before that hearing, the kid got on the phone to one of the detectives who'd worked on the arson case and made death threats. During the hearing, Wilson asked the kid's psychia-trist about the threats. "He said 'oh, he was going through a tough time. But we've dealt with that'. I urged them to keep him in, until the end of his sentence, to give him counselling and treatment. But they let him go."

Kid Two: A boy, 13, went to a neighbourhood park. There were some bikes against the fence. He got on one and started riding. The kid who owned it stopped him and told him to give the bike back. The would-be thief did, and left the park, came back, went up to the youngster who owned the bike, shoved a knife in his abdomen, pulled it out, wiped it off and walked out of the park. With the bike.

Kid Three: A young kid fiddled with the natural gas leading to the furnace in his basement, lit a candle and took off leaving his father, his sister and the sister's friend sleeping upstairs. The place went up like cheap fireworks. Fortunately, neither the father — the kid's target — nor the sister nor the sister's friend was injured. Regrets? None Mike Wilson could see when he interrogated the kid.

Kid Four: A kid, 16, meets a kid, 19. They conspire to break into the house of a man who lived near the 16-year-old. The kid knocked on the door and the neighbour let him in, then the 19-year-old pushed his way inside. They wrestled the homeowner into the bathroom and got him in the tub where they tried to suffocate him with a pillow. "That didn't work, so they tried to strangle him with an electrical cord, but that didn't work because the cord broke. So the 16-year-old got a butcher knife and shoved it right into his gut and that didn't work either and the guy started yelling 'please don't kill me' and the 19-year-old said 'that's not the way to kill him, this is the way to kill him' and he pulled the knife out and shoved it back in a few inches higher, right through the man's heart. Then they cleaned themselves up and helped themselves to some of the dead man's belongings and fled in his car."

You want to talk about violent kids, Mike Wilson has no shortage of stories. But he's quick to point out that though the violent stories are the ones which grab you, the ones you remember, the ones you tell your neighbours and friends, the ones which make the headlines, violent crimes are not the majority of the crimes the kids are committing. "The main crimes are thefts and B&Es. Those are number one and number two. Then there's assault and sexual assault and so on." Mike Wilson looks at the stat sheets. In April and May of 1993, for instance, Windsor cops laid about 130 charges under the Young Offenders Act. Of those, only 16 related to acts of violence. The numbers may go up or down, but the percentages stay about the same. And the numbers do go up and down. In 1993, police had more than 3,400 contacts with young offenders, a 5.4%

31

increase over the year before. "But the year before represented a big increase, 19.9% over the year before that. It seems to go in cycles. You say 'well, things seem to be calming down' and the next thing you know the numbers are up again."

Whatever the numbers, Mike Wilson would like to get this on the record: the vast majority of kids who come into contact with the cops come into contact only once. In 1993, police laid 1,283 charges under the Young Offenders Act, but almost twice as many incidents — 2,182 — were dealt with in other ways: warnings, talks with parents, recommendations for treatment and counselling, diversion to community service projects. For most kids, even the ones who are charged, one good scare is good enough. "Eighty percent of them, we won't see again. They're good kids who did dumb things and they got caught and they were scared shitless and their parents had a talk with them or maybe cuffed them and told them to smarten up." On the other hand, some of them will get anything but a cuffing, or a dressing down.

Janet Orchard is a child psychologist at Windsor's Regional Children's Centre. She works with adolescent sex offenders, some of whom wind up in jail. "We have families we work with that are really criminal families, where there's a long family history of one person after another being in jail."

Mike Wilson: "Twenty percent we'll see again. And ten percent percent we'll see a lot. They're our hard-core chronic offenders." Those kids are a minority, to be sure, but they're a violent and a dangerous minority. These are the kids who are doing drugs, serious drugs, and are in constant need of easy cash to buy more of what it is they're taking to make them feel the way they want to be feeling. Kids have always managed to get their hands on alcohol. And marijuana wasn't much more elusive, for those inclined to spark up. But these days the drugs of choice include crack cocaine, which can drive

32

you crazy. "Kids as a whole have gained access to a sophisticated range of drugs that weren't around back then."

Randy Semeniuk sees them all, from the shoplifters to the murderers. He's a Crown prosecutor for the County of Essex. "I think the change has been that young offenders are committing more serious crimes and they're committing them in a more vicious style. That's what I see."

Examples aren't far from the tip of his tongue:

Case One: The arsonist Mike Wilson had referred to. "The kid was walking down a street, walked by a house. Somebody sitting on the porch referred to his mother as a slut. The next day he went back and torched the house, killed two people. Two others were seriously injured, suffered severely broken legs, when they jumped out the upstairs windows. Just because a comment was made."

Case Two: "Another prosecutor was involved with young offenders who were involved in a rape. One of the young offenders was dating this 35-year-old prostitute. A couple of other young offenders meet up with her, take her to an apartment, and rape her with a broomstick. Then they insert a wine bottle into her vagina and pour the wine in. These are young offenders. These are 15- and 16-year-olds. It's mind-boggling at times."

Case Three: "I did a case a couple of years ago with a young offender who was 15. He was with his 70-year-old drinking buddy. Last bottle of beer in the case, they got into an argument over who would take it. The 15-year-old wanted it, took the old man's head and shoved it through a window, slicing his neck and then kept beating him until he was dead. A senseless brutal crime."

Case Four: A 66-year-old woman answered her door during a thunderstorm and a youngster asked if he could come in and use the phone to call home and get a ride. She let him in, and suddenly six others followed him inside. "A group of seven, the majority young offenders, tied her up and robbed her. Just unbelievable. And the one female who tied her up, when she was arrested by the police, made some very sick comments, one of them being 'who cares about a 66-year-old lady?' "

Which is not the least of it. Not by a long shot. Read on. Here's a passage from the police report, describing the arrest of two of the young offenders: "When advised of her charges, _____ started to laugh and said 'Lick my clit,' 'Suck my fucking tit,' 'Who cares about a 66-year-old lady?.' At this, she and _____ started laughing hysterically, jumping around on the couch (where they were seated, handcuffed), bumping into each other. They started to tell us to 'lick our clit' and 'suck our tit' and 'You guys want to fuck us, don't you?' _____ looked up at Detective _____, saw his wedding ring and said 'You're married, eh? Wouldn't you like to fuck me instead. I'm a good fuck.' The girls were asked to refrain from this type of language, to sit quietly. At this point in time _____ said 'it's my house. I can fucking say whatever I want. You guys are both old men and you're both assholes. Just shut the fuck up and don't tell us what to say, what to do or how to act.' The girls were again asked to refrain from this type of language. _____ looked up and said 'why don't you suck my tit. Lick my clit.' This appeared to be her favourite saying and she must have repeated it 15 to 20 times.

"At one point she stated to us, 'Wouldn't you like to have 12 kids just like me?' She was told she was facing serious allegations to which she started to laugh hysterically and said, 'Nobody cares about this shit. What are you going to do to us? We're just kids. Are they going to send us up to the Big House? Are they going to send us to the Pen? Ooooooh. Big deal. We'll be out. There's nothing nobody can do to us.' Again both girls laughed hysterically. 'We're just kids. Nobody will do anything to us. We'll be out. Just wait and see.' Again, both laughed hysterically and bounced around on the couch."

And just what does a young Crown prosecutor think when he reads reports like these and sees these kids in court? "You have mixed emotions. In this case, with the elderly lady, they're just vicious criminals and they deserve no sympathy whatsoever. And then on the other hand you think one of them who was involved, she was only 13 years of age and you wonder because of the age, they're kids, don't they deserve a break? So you're sort of torn. Because they're kids, treat them as children? And yet they've committed very criminal acts, should we treat them as criminals?

"Most kids who come in, who've committed their first shoplifting, I have sympathy for. But kids who commit serious crimes, at some point you have no sympathy. You treat them harshly. These kids who were involved in the robbery of the elderly lady, I have no sympathy for them. I'm just trying to make their lives miserable." He succeeded. All were jailed, some for a year and a half, some for two.

Randy Semeniuk could go on and on. So can his colleague, Jill Manny. They see a lot of kids going through the system in the course of the year. How many? Randy Semeniuk: "Easily a thousand."

Jill Manny: "I was in young offenders court yesterday and there was a case involving an assault on these two kids, a young girl and a young boy, by three girls. And the amazing thing is, these girls are getting so violent. I see more and more young girls attacking not only girls, but boys. Vicious, vicious beatings. I don't know where it's coming from. You didn't used to see girls beating up other girls, or young little kids. They don't care. They carry weapons. They go in gangs. And gangs beat up on one person. One young kid.

"This case yesterday, these two kids were walking across the street. One was 12, the other 14. They'd just been to the store for an ice-cream drumstick and a pop and they're walking to their grandmother's house. A girl mentioned something about them walking on a red light and the kid turns and says 'no, it's yellow' and these three girls started attacking them, beating them up, pulling their hair, bang bang bang in the mouth, kicking them in the head. It's horrible." There were three attackers, then a fourth came in. All of them 15. And you see these girls, they're not that big. And then one girl gets up there (in court) and lies to save her friend. She gave a statement to the police saying this girl was involved, was in there kicking these kids, and then (on the stand) says 'I was intoxicated when I gave that statement to the police. I just drank a 40-ouncer.' She would have been dead if she'd drunk a 40-ouncer. She just got up there and lied."

What's going on in Jill Manny's head as she watches these performances, hears all these unpleasant stories, day after day? "First there's anger. There's sadness. There's some kind of sympathy. There's a whole range of feelings you go through when you deal with these kids. And there's disgust with the parents. I don't think these kids are born criminals. You just can't believe what some of these kids are capable of doing. They do some terrible things and you feel they have to pay."

Case in point:

"Here's a kid who's never been in trouble before. I was asked to consider him for Alternative Measures where they do some community service work and the charge is dropped. Now, this kid broke into a Co-Op store and he did the most awful property damage. This kid is 12. His lawyer, who's a very close friend of mine, was talking to me about him and wanted me to go out and see him. And I refused to go out and see him and I'll tell you why. This is a police report:

"'I attended and viewed the damage to the (Co-Op) building. Several doors were damaged. Grease was thrown around the floor and the walls. Fire extinguisher was emptied. Several brooms were lit on fire and thrown down to the basement floor. Ticket office where moisture testing is done on grains was forced open with a crow bar and was severely trashed. Grain tester was smashed on a bench. Can of black tar was opened and poured over papers which had been thrown on the floor. Phone was tampered with. Machine-starting switches on wall were tampered with. Partitions between silos were pushed to the ground.'

"Over $5,000 worth of damage was done to this place. And they want this kid to go to Alternative Measures! I said no. They wanted me to go and see him. 'Oh, he's so cute, Jill. He looks just like my eight-year-old. He's just a wee little kid.' I didn't want to go out and see that kid. I was so pissed off at the damage he did. I didn't want to melt and say 'Oh, all right, I'll put him in Alternative Measures.' And that's the problem I have. You end up feeling sorry for these kids and you think. 'Oh God, this poor little kid, look how cute he is, how can we do something . . .' and you've got this guy who's done all this terrible damage. He might look cute, and butter won't melt in his mouth now, but what was he doing in there?

"These kids have absolutely no concept of property value, no sense of morals whatsoever. They do not give a shit whether it's a person's home or a business they go in and they destroy. Some adults might go and break and enter a home and steal the VCR and jewellery and whatnot, but it's very rare they absolutely destroy the home, ransack, put paint on the walls, absolutely destroy the home. I mean, apart from the personal violation, you come home and your treasures are broken, all the things you've worked for all your life. A lot of adults won't do that. They go in, they get what they want and they get out.

"I blame the parents, mostly. You look at the parents and you say 'what hope is there for this kid.' You're angry, it's such a horrible thing this kid has done. And you think this guy should do six months, nine months, even though it's a first offense, you're so pissed off, because this person's home is destroyed. Or his business is destroyed. I see some of these kids and I just want to shake them. I see what this kid's done and I turn around and see this little kid, cute as can be, and you just want to yell 'Why did you do this? Why did you do this terrible thing?'"

What's worse, the kids are laughing. One of the girls in court for beating the two children outside the corner store was laughing on the stand as Jill grilled her. "Laughing! And I said, 'You think this is funny? Do you think this is funny?' And of course I'm not supposed to say that. 'Objection' from the defence. How are you supposed to feel sorry for these kids after they beat up little children, after they knife people. They do horrible things. And they're laughing. This was a big joke. You ask, 'What can we do to help this person?' And then you think, 'Help them?' Why should we bother helping these kids? They don't deserve it. They think it's a joke. They're not taking it seriously. They don't even care if they get up there and lie. Taking an oath means nothing to them. Absolutely nothing. Why should we taxpayers waste our money on these kids who do not give a shit? And then there are kids who are really disturbed, and kids who need help, who are sorry for what they've done. And so you say, okay, let's bend over backwards for these kids so they don't do something really serious later on. So there are all those feelings. Sometimes I feel sorry for them. And sometimes I could just bash them. It's so frustrating."

Judge Saul Nosanchuk: "I had one (trial) today where this young fellow was in tears. He was caught rifling through cars. His mother is a psychiatric patient, his father couldn't stand him and kicked him out of the house. He had no where to go, he was totally out on the street, and I said to him 'I think I'm going to have to sentence you to six months. And he said 'I hope so.' He was all alone. He was just tired. He was exhausted from trying to live on the street. He had nowhere to go, no one to turn to. He was 16."

8:13 a.m. ――――――――――――――――――

The kids sleep and spend their quiet time on the second floor, but they spend the rest of their day down here on the ground floor.

On the right is the rec room: a couple of sofas, a ping-pong table, and some chairs stacked against the wall. Everyone gets to use the rec room at least once a day. Directly across the hall is the honours lounge: sofas, stereo, TV, pool table, pop machine. As the name implies, you earn your way in. The better your behaviour, the more points you'll have. The more points you have, the more times you'll wind up in the lounge.

Just past the honours lounge on the same side of the hall is the dining room. There are four tables bolted to the floor. They have grey formica tops and four swivelling turquoise seats. There's a wall of windows looking out into the playpen. Between the asphalt yard and the building there are some garden boxes: greenery and flowers, red and pink.

Two of the dining room walls are painted white. Signs on the wall:

'Be Flexible
And You Won't Get Bent Out Of Shape'

'Don't Follow In Negative Footsteps'

'Take S-P-A-C-E
if problems are tight

The third wall, separating the dining room from the kitchen, is panelled. In this wall, there's a rectangular opening through which the cheerful kitchen boss, Veronica N., slides the plates and bowls of food. Veronica is leaning on her elbows, looking through the opening. "Good morning." She counts the heads then disappears for a moment before pushing through a tray with seven plastic glasses of orange juice. Mary takes the tray and goes table to table.

Helen S. is standing in one corner, window wall to her left. Larry is standing near the door. After Mary returns the tray, Larry starts calling out the names: "Fred, you can go up." Veronica serves up cereal.

When she started here, the year the jail opened, Veronica used to ask the staff what the kids had done to wind up in jail. "Some terrible things. Truly terrible things. And I'd think 'these kids? These cute little kids. Some of these boys, so handsome. The girls, so beautiful." Veronica shakes her head at the memory of it. "I don't ask anymore." She just serves the food and makes sure the kids get enough and she keeps the conversation on the light side. The kids clearly like her and joke with her. And confide in her, occasionally. One boy told her that when he gets out, he'd like to be a dancer. "He dreams of being a dancer." Dream on hold.

Maxine D. comes smiling through the door. She's a teacher, one of two here. She chats with Larry, but she's looking at the kids. She wants to see who's doing well and who's not, how many kids are at breakfast, how many in time-out rooms, so that she'll know what she'll be facing when the kids turn up for class. Larry fills her in, and she's on her way.

Seeing Maxine, the kids are now thinking of the homework Maxine and Marilyn L. had assigned yesterday. Some got it done, some had problems. John, he of the gelled hair, looks up at Larry. "I did four questions and they're all wrong. And I don't care." Larry

40

tells him he'd better care, and work at his schooling. "You don't want to be flipping burgers the rest of your life, do you?"

There's a table in the corner: toaster and plastic jars of jam, honey, and peanut butter. Larry is taking orders for toast. "Two for me Larry." "Me too, Larry." "Can I have four, Larry?" Larry pops the bread in, pushes the handles. "Two, two and four. How many's that?" "Six." "No, it's eight." "Is not."

The kids go up, one at a time, spread what they want on their toast and carry the plates back to their table.

Rick: "Can I clear, Helen?"

Helen nods. Rick passes by, shows her the plate, the bowl, the cup, the plastic knife, the plastic spoon. "Go ahead." She watches him push the dishes through the opening to Veronica.

John is the last to clear. Larry eyes the hair. "You're going to have to wash that out, John." "No I'm not." "You've got so much gel in there it's dripping," says Helen . "Shake your head and we'll all have a gel shower." One of the other kids laughs.

Helen pushes the talk button on her walkie-talkie. "We're coming up." "10-4." Larry walks backwards down the hall, keeping an eye on the kids, Helen brings up the rear. We single-file our way down the hall and up the ramp to the second floor. Helen unlocks the door. The other group is at the far end of the hall. As soon as the staff members in that group see the door opening at this end, they open the door at their end and lead the kids out and down the stairs. As soon as they're gone, Helen leads her group into the hall. The kids head for their rooms.

8:32 a.m. ———————————————————————————

Larry keeps an eye on the kids who go from their rooms to the bathroom and back: cleaning up, brushing their teeth, getting a book or a walkman. After breakfast, the kids have half an hour to read, or sit, or make phone calls. Then classes begin.

Helen pulls on a pair of rubber gloves and starts her environment check. She goes into the bedrooms of the kids who are downstairs having breakfast. She starts at the window, checks the curtains to make sure nothing is hidden in them. "We check for screws, paper clips, pencils, pens" — anything a kid could use as a weapon. She checks the radiator to make sure the screws are in place and pulls the comforter off the bed, making sure the zipper tabs on the pillow and mattress are still sewn shut. Then she feels in the drawer openings of the desk, and pulls at the table top to ensure it's secure. "We've had kids rip the top right off when they're in a rage." And not the biggest kids, either.

Larry, down the hall, is having a chat with John. "About that gel, John. I think you should wash your hair." John doesn't think so. "Well, it's your choice." But making the choice, John should think for a moment about the consequences. He should think about the time he's already spent in the time-out room. The answer is still no. Sort of. "I'll wash the back half. But not the front half." Larry points in the direction of the time-out room.

By quarter to nine, all the kids in Helen and Larry's group have brushed their teeth and gone to the john and are in their rooms. The other group comes up from breakfast and those kids take their turns in the bathrooms.

Larry checks his watch. He goes around the corner and pushes open the door of the time-out room. John is on his haunches in the far corner. It's time for a little heart to heart. Larry takes John through the steps, slowly: What was the problem here? What choice did you make? What were your other choices? Would any of those choices have been better than the choice you made? How would you deal with this problem the next time?

Oh, and by the way, about that gel, John . . .

Teacher Maxine D. is standing by the board, holding a piece of paper up for all to see. She points at the left side of the paper. What she'd like the kids to do is write the names of their friends on the left side of a piece of paper. As many names as come to mind. One below another.

We are in one of two classrooms which are on the lower floor of the jail, just around the corner from the dining room. There is a wall of windows looking onto the courtyard. You can see the blue high-clouds sky, you can see cars passing by in the street. The kids, facing Maxine, see none of these things, see only the sheet of paper she is holding up.

The room is about a quarter the size of a regular classroom. I'm sitting at Maxine's desk, back of the room. There's a phone on the desk, just in case. Between me and the door there's another desk. Helen S. sits, silent and watchful.

Sign on the wall

In Our Classroom, Everyone will:
1. Be treated with respect and consideration.
2. Remain seated.
3. Speak at appropriate times.
4. Wait patiently until teacher can help you.
5. Discussion will be positive.

Taped to the wall beside that poster is another:

Guidelines for Time-Outs:
1. Rude or silly behaviour.
2. Disrupting the class.
3. Noncompliance (not following directions).

4. Lack of respect
  (teasing or annoying peers or staff)
5. Swearing.
6. Physical threats or aggression.

"How many names are we supposed to write?" This is Rick, a new kid. "As many as you can."

Mary is writing, began writing as soon as Maxine had outlined the task. Now she pauses, tapping the blunt end of the pen against her chin, and says, almost in a whisper: "It's been so long since I've seen some of these people."

Five minutes, ten.

Norm counts the names on his list, lips moving. "Forty-seven." He looks up. "It could have been more."

Walt? Walt has written 37 names. Mary, 35.

"All right. Now." Maxine holds up her piece of paper and runs her finger down the right side. "Along the right side, I want you to write examples of the way some of these people have misused you. Two or three examples."

Mary wonders what she means by 'misused'? Maxine turns the question around. Rick thinks he has an example. But he isn't sure it's appropriate and he doesn't want to get in trouble. Maxine congratulates him for thinking before he speaks. "We're just getting to know each other, and you'll find out from the staff what's appropriate." She goes over to see what he's written. "If you'd said that in the dining room, or somewhere else, it might not have been appropriate." Because there, she'll later say, he could have simply been bragging. "But here, it's fine. It's a good example." She'd like Rick to tell it to the others. This one friend Rick is thinking of, "when I had drugs, he'd always be around. But if I didn't have no drugs, he'd go somewhere else."

Walt: "I had a friend who only used me to get to my girl-friend." Write it down.

They've got the hang of it now and all the heads are down, all the pens moving, fast. There is no shortage of examples, apparently. After another ten minutes, Maxine asks Mary if she's got an example she'd like to read to the group. She sure does.

One day, her boyfriend showed her a letter he'd received from one of Mary's girlfriends. The girl told Mary's boyfriend that Mary was a pretty girl, wouldn't have any trouble finding another boyfriend, so why didn't he dump Mary and 'then you and I can get together.' The boyfriend thought Mary would laugh. She still flexes the muscles of her jaw, just thinking about it.

Norm had a friend who always hung around, wanting rides from Norm's parents. But when Norm's parents couldn't drive, the friend was never around. Fred had a friend who was a really good friend when he needed a place to crash. When Fred couldn't let him stay overnight, the friend dropped him.

Excellent examples, one and all. And how did it feel, when these friends behaved this way?

"It all depends." Rick never liked doing drugs alone, so even if he knew his friends were hanging around for the dope, it didn't bother him much. Walt: "Yah, you don't care at the time." Rick: "But later you do." Much later, more than a year later, Mary still seethes at the thought of her girlfriend trying to cut in on her boyfriend. "I just felt uncontrollable anger. I freaked out totally. My boyfriend thought it was a joke. He was laughing. But I wasn't laughing. I got into a fight with her. It wasn't pretty. My friends were telling me to calm down. But I couldn't calm down. All I thought was 'she's not going to get away with this'. And she's supposed to be my friend. I couldn't understand it."

Curiously, Mary doesn't wonder, out loud, why her boyfriend would have shown her the letter in the first place.

Maxine likes what Mary has said: 'she's supposed to be my friend.' Mary: "I've got a lot of friends like that."

Which brings us to the next part of Maxine's lesson. The people we know can fit, generally speaking, into one of four categories: acquaintances, casual friends, close friends, intimate friends. Examples?

Acquaintances? George: "Someone you see at the mall." Yes, says Maxine. You'd recognize the face, but probably wouldn't know the person's phone number, might not even know the last name. Casual friends? The kids aren't sure. Maxine: "Let's say you're both on the football team, or the basketball team. You're friends on the team, but apart from that sport you probably don't have a lot in common, and after the season you don't keep in touch."

Close friend? Mary: "You see them all the time. Someone you could tell personal stuff to." Maxine: "Could you have a difference of opinion and still be friends?" Mary: "Sure." Maxine: "So you could have a difference of opinion with this friend, but the friend would still respect your opinion?" Mary: "Sure." Maxine: "Could you sit with this person and not talk for a few minutes and not be uncomfortable?" Mary thinks about this for a moment and then thinks, yes, you could do that.

Which gets Rick thinking: "When I was on the outside, I had a lot of friends. A whole bunch of us who would hang around together. We were all mutual friends. That's why I don't like it in here." Maxine: "That's why you'll have to work hard while you're in here and behave yourself when you get out. Then you can be with your friends."

Now, says Maxine, what if you made an all-star team. You know your friend knows about this. How would you feel if that person didn't call? Depends on what kind of friend the person was. Very good. "What if the person were an acquaintance? Would you feel hurt?" No, they wouldn't. "If the person were a casual friend?" Probably not. "A close friend?" Yes, they would.

All right. Now, let's talk about intimate friends. "And," says Maxine, "we're not talking about boy-girl stuff here." Smiles all round. What constitutes an intimate friend? Fred: "They care about you." Maxine: "Let's say something awful happened in your life. Maybe your mother died. Now, your friend has booked a holiday to Florida, has the tickets, and your mother has died. Would your friend give up the trip to be with you?" Acquaintances? No. Casual friends? No. Close friends? Maybe. Intimate friends? Yes. "Not me," says John. "I'd go to Florida."

Now, says Maxine, go back over the list of all the names you wrote in the first place and mark down beside each name whether that person is an acquaintance, a casual friend, a close friend or an intimate friend.

Walt: "That's a lot of acquaintances."

Maxine: "That's what I'd have predicted."

Norm: "For all of us?"

Maxine: "For all of you, and I'll tell you why." She spends the next few minutes explaining how, when you're young, you need to be surrounded by people all the time, or at least most of the time. This need is so great that young people don't care whether they're with acquaintances or friends, so long as they're not alone.

Rick:. "Ten of us, we're all close. We're kind of like a little family. One time, I was really depressed. Really depressed. And they all sat around and talked with me. I'd gone off by myself and they found me and they sat down and talked."

Which is, says Maxine, what friends are for. "You're lucky to have friends like that." And now she'd like them to go over their lists of people who misused them and see which category those people would fit into.

Acquaintances, mostly. Or casual friends.

Maxine: "Sometimes the problem is this: we get hurt by people we expect too much from." If you're expecting an acquaintance to act the way an intimate friend would act, you're setting yourself up for disappointment.

"To be continued, tomorrow. Pack up your things."

Helen checks all the cups to make sure all the pens, pencils, rulers and erasers made their way back in. Then she nods and the kids put their cups on the shelf.

Maxine says goodbye. They head out the door and down the hall.

What was the point of Maxine's lesson? "They're always saying what great friends they've got. Many of them have been in trouble with their so-called friends. So I'm going to pursue this a little further. Most of them have the concept now, and most of them ended up with a good number of acquaintances rather than friends. So that's a start. You have to be careful they don't go off on a tangent and blame their friends for the trouble they're in. We have one in particular who's still saying his friend did it, not him. So we'll look at how many of these people are true friends. Because one of the things we stress with these people is, if you're going to go back out maybe you need to take a look at your friendships and choose some different friends. And we're going to be doing some work on saying 'no.'"

How successful will she be reaching these kids? "Realistically? Not very. I can't remember where I saw it, but someone was saying that people's values are pretty well entrenched by the time they're two, three, four years of age. And when you figure we're not getting them until 12, at the earliest, well, by then?"

By then, these kids are living in a far different world than Maxine D. "Their life is so alien to us. It really is. We had a fellow here who did a workshop on criminal thinking. He used an example: if you left your wallet there and a kid stole it, the kid would say 'that's your fault, and the wallet's mine now.' It's always the victim's fault. They think differently, and empathy is a hard one for them. This kid last year, he'd been picked up while he was riding his bike and he wanted us to call the police, he wanted to make sure the bike was going to be there when he got out. Well, it turns out he'd stolen the bike. But it was his bike now.

"One of the staff here told a kid 'when you break into a house and steal the wedding rings and trash the photo albums, those things can't be replaced.' And this kid comes back months later and the first thing he said was 'I didn't steal the wedding ring. I left it there.' So, it sounds funny, but maybe there's progress there. At some level, anyway."

And she can point to some kids who've done fairly well after leaving. Generally speaking, the successful ones are those who've been in the jail the longest. "If we have them for a long time, six months or more. I had one kid who said when he came in 'I get Es in school' and I said, well you've never been in my class because no one gets Es. I had him almost three years and by the time he left he was doing algebra. And his self-esteem went up greatly.

"Many of these kids have been through horrible school experiences where they don't go to school or have repeated failures so they're very defensive, quite fearful, low achievers. So the first thing I want to do is make a connection with them, build up a relationship with them, get them to trust me. Trust that I'm not going to ask them to do anything they can't do, or embarrass them. This one kid, I think if he went to school at all they probably let him sit there and do nothing. We don't do that here. We expect them to work. So, you've got to get them to trust you. And you've got to learn what they can and can't do. It takes time, because a lot of it is behaviour, a lot of them are dead lazy and they want you to believe they can do nothing, because then that's easier for them."

Like many of the other jail staff, Maxine uses humour to her advantage. "Sometimes, I'm an idiot. If they're in a bad mood, I'll come in and say, 'I went to doggie school last night with Waldo (her new puppy) and my Waldo did not let me down. The other dog pooped in the ring, but not my Waldo.' I'll just be stupid, to get them going. If they don't want to do math, I'll tell them, 'Well, it's gotta be done. I am like Velcro when it comes to math.' So I try to use humour a lot. And I'm honest with them. I'll tell them 'I'm gonna win. I can win quickly, or we can make this awful. Your choice.' "

9:28 a.m.

Leave Maxine's classroom, turn left, go down the steps, down the hall and you'll walk right into an unused office. Bill is sitting at the desk, jumpy as a flea on a hot brick. Who wouldn't be? Any minute, now, his social worker is going to come and take him away.

Time's up.

After almost a year, he's about to be a free kid.

All morning, the staff have been dropping by to say farewell, to wish him the best. Bill doesn't quite seem to know how to deal with all the attention. For the most part, he looks down at the desk when someone is talking to him and looks up only when they've finished. Maybe he's embarrassed, or just confused.

At one point, with two staffers near the door, Bill and I are alone in the room. I ask him if he'd mind answering a couple of questions. No, he says, he wouldn't mind. I turn on the tape recorder, place it in front of him.

Q: "What's going on in your head right now?"

A: "Well, I'm a little anxious, I'm a little scared. I'm a little excited about this place I'm going to. Plus, I really don't want to leave this place, but I have to sometime. Like, this place seemed to sort of be my home. I grew attached to people. They helped me through bad times, and we had good times together."

Q: "When you say you're scared, what are you scared about?"

A: "About a new place and stuff, whether it's going to work out."

Q: "Must've been tough, these last few weeks, not knowing where you'd be going?"

A: "A few weeks ago, I didn't even know where I was going. I just found out (three days earlier)."

Q: "How do you feel?"

A: "The same thing I just told you. Anxious. But a little more than before because it's the day I'm leaving. And a little sad."

Two doors down, same side of the hall, the jail's director, William B., is in his office. He's been thinking a lot these last few days about Bill. "I'm repulsed by what Bill has done in his past, the way he thinks now, and the way he's victimized staff. We've laid several charges against Bill for his actions against staff and property here. This is a kid who'll bring out the redneck in anyone. 'Good riddance, see ya later,' is what you'd expect to say. But Bill's in many ways as much a victim as a victimizer. He's not had much of a chance in life. I guess what sets him apart is that he's found a way to strike a chord with all of us. I don't know what he's done, or whether we've done it, but he's found a way to relate to us and us back to him in a really meaningful way. Even in spite of all this other crap, all the victimizing he's done and still has the potential to do, I bleed for Bill, a fair bit. And this is unusual, coming from me. Usually I'm pretty clear about how I stand with these kids. So I feel contradiction with Bill, quite a bit. We've had kids here for three years before, and I've felt no compassion for them. They were clearly victimizers. But Bill is a kid without a place to live, a place to grow up, without an identifiable family. And I feel bad for him that way. When I say goodbye to him, it's going to be hard for me and maybe hard for him at some level, but certainly hard for me. And this is one kid I wish we could keep."

Why? "I think we'd help him grow up. I think we've started to make an impact on his values, on the way he sees life. And when he victimizes people here, he has to be accountable. I don't make any bones about that. But his aggression is usually triggered by him feeling hopeless and desperate and out of control. Whenever he does things you can almost directly connect it back to feelings generated from his real-life situation. We try not to say, 'Well, no wonder you're hitting us, or spitting on us, or whatever you're doing because you must be feeling so desperate' because he would just keep doing it. But in our hearts and our minds we know that's the case."

William B. doesn't think Bill is ready for freedom. "If we had him for another year, until he was 16, I think we could help him solidify his self-esteem, his sense of identity, his ability to be empathetic and caring about other people. He's started some really good relationships with the staff, with Sandra (the jail's social worker) and with the teachers. I think he just feels better about himself. Really it's a crime in reverse to have to discharge a kid like this who I think is going to be a threat to the community."

Bill is to be released to an open-custody group home. "He can run away any time he gets the hankering to do so. With less structure and less supervision he's more prone to feel vulnerable and out of control and I'm afraid he'll victimize people again out of his feelings of desperateness and loss of control. And that's a shame, really, for him. Because the more he victimizes others, the more he punishes himself emotionally and psychologically and certainly he punishes other people and that's not fair to other people.

"This is a kid who, under the old Juvenile Delinquents Act, could be kept until everyone felt good about releasing him. The judge could say, 'I want you to stay there for another year or six months.' With the Young Offenders Act it's fixed-term sentences for kids. You can't say, well, we'll let you out when we feel you're doing okay. When it's over, it's over, and that's too bad. It's expensive to keep kids in here, but here's a case where I think it would be worth it. I know, I'm sure of this, Bill is going to be back in trouble. We may see him back in here, because he's young enough, and that'll be hard. But I believe he's going to be victimizing people still because he's got all kinds of baggage that's following him around."

I tell William B. what Bill has just told me: his mixed feelings about leaving the jail. It comes as no surprise. "I don't think being locked up bothered Bill because he didn't need the freedom, he needed the people, the security, the supervision and the structure around him and I think that at some level he knew he needed it."

It must be frustrating, feeling you've got a kid like this within reach, and suddenly, he's out the door. "It is frustrating. And like I said, Bill is not typical. Bill is really a lost soul. A sad case."

There is ambivalence down the hall as well. Supervisor Frank M. is leaning against the wall outside the room where Bill is talking with a couple of staffers. Frank had Bill do what is called a self-inventory, a kind of summing up of his time in jail: what he thinks he's learned during his time here, how he feels he's improved. "His answers I found to be insightful. He's starting to see himself as a different person, someone who's changing and maturing." Bill sees the biggest change in his self-esteem. "He's able to recognize some good things about himself where he didn't see those things before. He's able to interact a lot better with people now, too. He's got better social skills and that's making him feel more comfortable."

Frank and Bill talked about the future. "Basically I said, 'hey, this is a new chapter in your life. You're moving on, and that's fine.' But it's a sad situation. What he needs, and he's identified this himself, is a sense of belonging. He hasn't gotten that from family and I think that's why he's a little excited about this place (he's going to) because it looks like they'll provide that for him. He needs to feel accepted, that he belongs." Personally, Frank M. finds it difficult to see Bill go. "I've worked with Bill here and I worked with him in another treatment facility where I used to work. So there's a little bit more investment for me. In some ways it makes it easier for me, because I see how far he's come. But he's a sad case. He's a bright kid, he's got a lot of potential, but he's got a lot of obstacles within himself. I'm concerned that he'll do something to jeopardize his future. I guess I'm really hoping that he'll be able to hold it together."

What are the chances Bill will stay out of trouble, and out of jail? "Twenty, thirty per cent. His history of victimizing is just too strong. It's such a pattern. We can be as hopeful as we like, but we have to be realistic." It can't be easy, knowing that and watching him go. "Not at all. We've been agonizing over this all week."

Sandra J. goes into the room and gives Bill a card, has a word with him, then leaves him with the other staffers. Her thoughts? "I'm hoping it's going to work for him. He's worked so hard in here and he's come so far, but I'm really afraid for him. I'm probably feeling over-protective. He's going to have a lot of responsibility all of a sudden when he just hasn't had any, and I wonder how he's going to handle it. We're pushing him out of the nest and we're not sure he's got the wings to fly."

Which explains her gift to Bill: A tiny gold-coloured angel to wear on his shirt. And this, on the card: 'Wear an angel on your shoulder to guide you through the days and nights, and brighten your life.'

Bill pins it to the left shoulder of his T-shirt.

Finally, at 10:18 a.m. the Children's Aid social worker comes down the hall. Bill is up on his feet and out in the hall. Goodbye goodbye goodbye. And, would it be all right to go up the hall and say goodbye to the kids in the classrooms? Yes, that would be fine. And so he jogs up the hall, up the stairs, stops at one door, then the next. A chorus of goodbyes echoes. Then Bill waves and comes back down the hall, makes a right, passes the dining room and William B.'s office, the rec room and the honours lounge, the search room and the hall that leads to the door that leads to the playpen.

Frank M. unlocks the steel door and we all walk up the ramp. Frank unlocks the next door and Bill is in the lobby.

On the table in the lobby there are several black plastic garbage bags, four with his name on them, and a white bag that holds his medications. Because he's grown more than five inches in height since coming in here, clothes in two of those bags don't fit. They will be sent home for relatives to try on, wear or discard.

On the floor is a pair of running shoes with laces. Bill kicks off his jail-issue slippers and puts on the runners, bends down and ties them up. "You still remember how to tie laces Bill?" He smiles. "A sure sign of freedom, eh?"

And there he is: runners laced up, Tigers jacket on, Tigers cap on. Staff member Susan A. gives him a big smile and a big hug. "Stay out of trouble. Make good choices." Bill flushes a little at all the attention, all the smiles. He wants to get out of here, on his way.

The Children's Aid social worker goes to the phone, calls Bill's mother to see whether he should drop off the bags of clothes now, or later. He returns after a moment: "Mom's on the phone. She wants to know if you want to say goodbye." This is the same Mom, I'm thinking, who won't have him back, who hasn't been to visit him in all the months he's been here, the same Mom who says he's given

55

her nothing but grief. Mom wants to say goodbye, as he leaves town and heads for a group home. You figure that one. As for Bill? "I'll be too emotional." But, clearly, the tug is more than he can resist. He looks from face to face, then out the window at the car and then at the social worker. "All right."

After a final round of hugs and handshakes and best wishes, Frank opens the inside door and then the next door and Bill steps out into the sunshine. The sun is pale in a high-cloud sky. The birds are chattering in the trees. There's a mild breeze. Bill's voice echoes from the jail's walls. "Free! Hey!"

A couple of minutes later Bill sticks his hand up through the sunroof and waves as the car moves toward the parking lot. He's still waving as the car turns onto the street.

Sandra J. stands in the lobby, looking at the parking lot. Her thoughts? "Terror. Fear for him. A lot of hope. But we're kind of hoping against logic. Logically, it's not going to work, he's not going to beat the odds. But it might work. He's sure got all the supports behind him. His social worker is going to hang in there. The place he's going to, it sounds like they're very willing to hang in there. You just hope it's enough."

10:50 a.m. ───────────────────────────

Snack-time is over. The kids return to class, one group going to Maxine D.'s to learn the secrets of friendship, the other going to Marilyn L.'s to tackle the mysteries of typing. The Olympia electric relics have been scrounged from various city high schools as those schools acquired computers. Keeping the typewriters operational is a challenge: "Just to get a typewriter repairman down here costs $40, and that's before he does anything." But today, the typewriters are working. So, too, are the kids: Bob, Sandy (a new girl), Curt, Stew, Elizabeth, Grant and Pat.

The day she entered the jail, Sandy announced to one and all that, though she had completed Grade 10, she could neither read nor write. (An exaggeration, as it turned out). And further, she hated school. She never liked school from the beginning and she wasn't about to change her opinion. "Well," Marilyn told her, "I think you'll like the school we have here."

There isn't a kid in the class who hasn't said the same thing. "They'll immediately tell you they hate school and they're not going to like it, in spite of themselves. So we let them know that our program is so interesting that they're going to want to come in every morning." Marilyn smiles. "Mostly, they're fearful." Mostly, they haven't spent much time in school and, as a result, they've done poorly when they have shown up so they just drop out. Most of them have been told all their lives that they're failures. "We try to give them a good positive experience. On the whole, their experiences have been negative and their self-worth is down the tubes. They're pretty down on themselves. They don't think they're worth very much. Even though some of them come in here with bravado, Mister Macho. Usually it's the guys who come here like that. But underneath, they're afraid."

What these kids have been through "would break your heart. We had one boy who, when young, was just left in a room, with food thrown in. When he came to us, he cowered in a corner and he just howled and howled and howled. The pain that kid was going through, you can't imagine. He just couldn't stand the thought of being locked up again." But no sooner does she say that than she says this: "I have to add that poor environments aren't an excuse for what they've done." But poor environments help Marilyn to emphasize just the opposite in her classroom, and to do what she can to build self-esteem. "We try to keep a positive atmosphere here all the time." Marilyn's cardinal rule: never challenge a kid beyond that kid's ability to succeed. As a kid succeeds in one area, gradually challenge a little more. But always let them succeed.

"Math is a good example, because with most of them, that's the subject they're most fearful of because they've missed so much school they've missed the basics. I just let them know that math isn't that threatening. I always start at a level where they can be successful and then when they succeed I say, 'gee, I thought you said you couldn't do this subject.' I give them a lot of positive encouragement so they'll continue. It's easier to start low than to start high. We try to build that self-esteem and let them know that it is possible to succeed. And some of them are amazed at what they can do."

That's the theory. Here's the practice:

Marilyn holds up a cardboard sheet upon which she's written the five rules of typing: 1) Good posture. 2) Feet flat on the floor, one slightly in front of the other. 3) Wrists up. 4) Fingers arched. 5) Eyes on the copy.

"Ready?" Set. Go.

"If your elbows are out at the side, that means you're too close to the keyboard. Move back a bit." Sandy, the new girl, shoves her chair back until she can barely reach the keyboard. She gives Marilyn a look. Challenging, you might call it. Marilyn smiles and says nothing. But she doesn't shift her eyes from Sandy. Ten seconds. Fifteen. The girl moves in, just slightly.

Tap, tap, tap.

The object here, eyes never leaving the copy which is propped to the left of each typewriter, is to type certain letters in repetition. KKKKKKK. LLLLLLL RRRRRRR TTTTTTT. And so on. "You're all doing very well, hitting the shift key." Not to mention the space bar. "Keep it up." And don't forget: "I'm not worried if you make mistakes. Mistakes don't matter in this exercise." What matters is that each of the students adheres to the Five Commandments of Typing. What are they again? Posture. Feet. Wrists. Fingers. Eyes. "Very good."

Marilyn makes the rounds of the room, careful not to linger behind the typers typing. Looking over their shoulders makes them nervous. But she will stop and lean down and whisper words of encouragement. "That's very good, Stew. Very good.' Stew smiles. Marilyn moves on. She catches Curt looking at the keyboard. "I had to," says Curt. "I forgot where the C was." "That's all right." A little pat on the shoulder.

Marilyn moves over near Bob and looks down at his sheet. "Having a good day?" "Not really." "Why is that?" "I don't know." "Well, you're having a good typing day." She sits down beside him and looks at the work Bob has done so far. "That's very good, very good."

"I'm not typing any more." Why not? He doesn't want to. Period. Marilyn says that's too bad, because he's been doing very well. Bob doesn't care, he's had it. "You don't have to type right now, if you don't want to. We can find a special time for you to type if you wish." When? After lunch hour, when the rest of the kids are out in the yard. That would be fine by Marilyn. It's really up to Bob. Why doesn't he just think about that for a minute?

"How's it going Elizabeth?" "Bad." "I don't believe it. I was watching you. You're doing fine."Elizabeth catches herself before she smiles.

Tap, tap, tap.

It's Bob who's doing the typing.

Piece of paper on Marilyn's desk:

C DHELLO MY NAME   IS ISLI CAN NOT TYPE VERY GOOD

                                                        well

WOWO   THIS   IDS   WOW   THSI IS FUN
FOOEY

59

WHY DO YOUNG OFFENDERS
DO THE THINGS THEY DO?

"Some of theses kids have a real anger problem," says the jail's director, William B. "They have very short fuses and a lot of anger boiling in them. And it's this anger that gets them in trouble with the law." Whence the anger? "You've got to understand that a lot of these kids have had horrible lives. I don't want to blame the family, because some parents are terrific, but there are often causes in the home." William B. also doesn't like blaming the family because he doesn't want the kids to be able to use their biographies as excuses for hurting people. As he says, more than once, there are a lot of people out there in the world who have been abused and mistreated by their parents and have determined never to turn anyone else into victims. Still: "Acting up is often a symptom of what's wrong in the family. We've got a lot of throw-away kids in here."

Sandra J., the jail's social worker, has an inmate list on the wall above her desk. She doesn't have to consult it to tell you this: of the 14 kids in the jail just now, 13 don't have any contact with their families. The fourteenth has a father who keeps in touch, but that kid won't have any contact with him.

Generally, says Sandra J., "there was not a good fit between these kids and their parents, for whatever reason. Maybe the parent doesn't have the capacity. I think most parents try to do the best they can. But for whatever reason, the fit isn't there. These are our most disturbed kids. If their needs aren't being met, if they're not being fed properly or cared for properly, if Mom isn't there when they're scared, then I think the child says 'all right, if nobody else is going to take care of me, then I'd better be able to take care of myself.' They're so egocentric. They tune out their own feelings. It's too tough to deal with the sadness and the loneliness they feel, so they replace it with anger. They beat people up, or they rape people. And if they're not tuned in to their own feelings, how can I teach them how other people feel? The people they beat up or rape?

"Anger is powerful. When they're out of control in anger, and I think they're rarely completely out of control, they're high on their own adrenaline. And they lack any kind of attachment to anyone else. 'So I beat him up. So what?' 'So the goof left his keys in his car. That's his problem.' A lot of these kids just don't feel bad for what they've done."

Then there are other kids who are a mystery to her. "You can't put your finger on what happened to them, and that makes you think that with at least some of them it's genetic. We've had one kid in here who I think lacked any capacity to feel. Maybe he was born with a limited capacity for empathy. In his case, his parents were distant and cold, so maybe the little bit of empathy he was born with wasn't nurtured. But you'll never know."

What people in the field do know is that a great number of hard-core young offenders are victims of abuse. Sandra J. says "about one-third of our kids are sexually abused. With girls, that's about average (in the general population). But one-third of our boys have been sexually abused, and that's about twice the national average."

Alec Marks is executive director of New Beginnings, which runs a pair of 10-bed open custody group homes for young offenders. About a quarter of his residents have come to him after doing their time in jails. After working with criminal kids for more than two decades, Alec Marks can tell you this: "A majority have been sexually abused at some point in their lives. And certainly, sexual abuse is one of the main causes of problems later in a person's life."

So, it's no surprise the kids are angry. But as the jail's social worker, Sandra J., says, "We have to be careful not to let them say 'I can't help it, I've been abused.' Even kids with horrible backgrounds, sexual abuse, physical abuse, emotional abuse, that's not an excuse. Some people go through all that and would never think of hurting another person. That's probably where genetics comes into it. But I don't know."

Those outside the jail have some pretty definite opinions about what happened to these kids. Dr. Robert Orr is a child psychologist and professor at the University of Windsor: "You can't make the judgment that somebody who's been abused will be delinquent. But almost without exception, delinquents have been abused. And delinquents, almost without exception, have delinquent fathers. It's very rare to find a serious juvenile delinquent who doesn't have a father who's also delinquent. You probably see it in your own kids, what incredible powerful models we are. I remember walking down the street when my kid was about five and I spit; three or four steps later she spit and she wasn't even aware of it, completely unconscious." Kids see, kids do.

"It's probably not until the kid hits the teens that they're really focused on the fact that this (their homelife) isn't the way it is everywhere, this isn't the way it has to be. Part of the unfortunate thing about being a child is that you believe that what is, is. So it's easier to accept things at the time. The pain begins to emerge at 11 or 12 when kids start to think about things other than immediacy. You can start to think about hypothetical things. What might be. You can start to think about better parents than the ones you've got. So there's a shift in almost all kids at around that time that makes some of this stuff (at home) suddenly intolerable. And that causes major problems."

What some of these kids have endured you don't want to imagine. They've been raped, they've been sodomized. They've been forced to perform every imaginable sexual act on others, including their brothers and sisters, mothers and fathers and, for pimping fees, complete strangers. They've been beaten when they've refused and they've been beaten when they've complied and they've been beaten for no particular reason they can think of. They've been thrown against the wall and they've been thrown down stairs and they've been thrown through windows and doors. They've been cut, burned, bruised. They've been locked in closets and locked out of the house. They've been humiliated and embarrassed. They've been 'taught a lesson' all their lives. They've been set out in the snow in their bare feet to be taught a lesson and they've been forced to sit at the table, no food on their plate, and watch the rest of the family eat to be taught another lesson. They say you should be careful what you pray for: your prayer might be answered. You should also, probably, be careful about the lessons you try to teach your children. The lesson you intend is not always the lesson they learn.

"I really believe," says the jail's director, William B., "that the first three years of your life are the most important in terms of whether you learn to really trust that it's a decent world and that people are basically kind and can be counted on or whether you, from day one, get so dissociated, so untrusting, that you go through the rest of your life like that." William B. has seen enough kids pass through the jail to know that: "you can often trace neglect back to when the kids were infants. If the kid didn't get fed for two days, so what? Or the kids got knocked around indiscriminately, so there was no sense of logic to when you got beaten up and when you didn't. You've heard about the backgrounds of these kids. Inevitably, it shocks the average person, it shocks their emotions and their sense of decency. With most of these kids, abuse and neglect happened day after day after day. It wasn't one horrendous event and then life went on normally."

Example: "Things like parents not being able to tolerate a kid crying, so they lock the kid in the closet for days with no light on. It can sometimes be less obviously disgusting physically and be more emotional. Demeaning them at every turn, teaching them that you never take responsibility for yourself and it's entirely the rest of the world and other people to blame if life goes wrong for you and you have a right to take it out on them and be angry. Day after day after day these kids have no recourse. For the first four or five years of their lives they're not exposed to anything except what their parents expose them to, so they grow up with that deeply entrenched, that that's what people are like and that's what life is like. I could get a lot more specific, but ..."

William B. leaves it at this: "To me, the best analogy is to the physical body. Kids in the third world who suffer malnutrition, they'll be crippled. It's that simple. And this is the same thing." Many of these kids have been starved emotionally, psychologically and spiritually and just like the kids half a world away, "you can't go back and undo it. That's what we have to keep telling our staff, our young staff especially, when they start to get over-involved. We tell them 'you cannot replace what they didn't get early in their lives.' And you see them getting so frustrated. They're giving the kid all this good stuff and the kid is not responding. Well, it's just too late. The receptors were killed. They can't take in what you're trying to give them. They are crippled kids."

"In a sense," says supervisor Patricia P., "it's not their fault that they wound up this way. You look at some of them and you think 'how atrocious.' He beat up an old lady, or he raped someone. And then you read their background and 'aha, this is understand-able.' Some of these kids have seen so much. And by the time they're 12 or 13 they've gone through more than some of us will ever go through. Which doesn't make their acts any less despicable, but at least you can understand how they got to be here. The big trick is understanding why they're the way they are, but holding them

64

accountable for their actions. So you say, 'Listen, we feel bad that you've gone through this, and that this has happened to you. Let's get you some help, some counselling. But you've got to stop what you're doing.' You can never excuse what they're doing. At the same time, you look at some of the parents and you think 'how dare you take a child, your own child, and damage him like that.' "

A good many of the most severely damaged children are beyond anyone's reach. "You see the staff work so hard," says William B., "and you know there isn't going to be one change made in that child." One child he's thinking of is 15. "It's like he's literally a burnt-out soul at his age already, and he's going to live how many years like this, doing damage to others." Sad enough. "But the part that haunts you is what was done to him for years and years and years." What was done to him William B. can't bring himself to describe. Worse than locking him in a closet for days at a time? Far worse than that, says William B.. Far, far worse. "And you just think, what are we going to do about this. As a society?" And, like Patricia P., he adds this: "How dare we do this to kids."

Cathy B. has worked as the jail's nurse for two and a half years. The first thing she said to me when we met: "I don't think many people know enough about young offenders. I don't think the government does either. I don't hear a lot of empathy being expressed for these kids." Although she disagrees with all the talk of stiffer penalties, she's quick to add her name to the list of people who won't excuse kids for their crimes. "But they're victims, too. People don't do what they've done unless something very traumatic has happened in their life. One event or more."

Child psychologist Robert Orr: "There's a wonderful writer named Alice Miller, a German, who writes an analysis of Adolph Hitler's life on the basis of his parenting, the cruel coldness of the Germans who essentially treat children as slaves, which is probably

65

what most of these kids have experienced. Most of them were probably used, simply chattels. You probably over-dote on your kids. They're a big part of your life. Well, these kids ain't a big part of anyone's life. They're there to get the beer and the parents don't give a shit what else they do or where they go. And sometimes they'll get beat up for being too slow with the beer, 'don't want that beer now,' and sometimes they'll get beat up for being too fast, 'told ya not to run.' "

No surprise these kids are angry or, as social worker Sandra J. would put it, "They're filled with rage." They are also lonely. Robert Orr: "What you'll find in these kids is that rarely will they have any adult in their life who listened to them as they were growing up. Kids can survive a great deal, even abuse, if they've got an adult in their life who says, 'I'm frightened to death of that person, too, and I know you're getting hurt and it hurts me too and we've gotta somehow survive this together, but I can't do anything to help you.' Kids need that. They need someone who acknowledges and validates the pain and the fact that it's happening to them, that it's coming from a sick person and it's that person, not the kid, who's sick. So you find kids coming out of horrific abuse who are fine. Well, not fine, but they do okay. But these kids, the kinds of kids you're looking at in the jail, kids who have demonstrated this overt rage and who have not controlled it or done something more socially acceptable, there's been no one in their lives. Mom was either not there or powerless or mom was the abuser and dad was the delinquent. So they're true victims."

Not all of the abuse is obvious. Child psychologist Janet Orchard: "With a lot of the kids we work with, there's maybe not hugely dramatic beatings happening." But some very important things are not happening. "Children grow up in situations where all the basic kinds of lessons that you should learn as you grow up don't happen. Those lessons are things like the ability to care about somebody else's feelings. You're not born being able to care whether or not you hurt somebody else's body or feelings. You have to learn that from watching your parents respect you and respect one another and respect themselves and care about how people are feeling inside their family and outside their family. I think a lot of times, the kids we work with have not been exposed to that. In fact, many times they're exposed to the exact opposite. They grow up in a situation where their experience has been that if you're bigger than or more powerful than somebody else, then you can do to that person what you would like to do or take from them what you want to take and it doesn't matter. I think a lot of these kids have been hurt and have been raised in an environment where it was basically okay to not care about somebody else's feelings."

Tom 'Bomber' Bromley works at the Regional Children's Centre in Windsor. He's a child-care worker in one of the centre's residential units for troubled adolescents. He's been working with kids for 21 years. "The kids who are getting in trouble with the law, one of the things I see is a lack of guidance. I think what's happening in our society is that both parents are working and they're working so hard on what they have to do to keep the family going that the kids get shuffled back. We forget about guiding them, and we get to the point where we're just providing. In the old days, you had guidance. You had families sitting around together, all kinds of talking. And I think adults and young people now, they're not communicating. I think we have to be available to agree to disagree. What I see is a lot of power struggles between kids and parents. 'I said do this.' 'I said do that.' These are the 90s. There have to be some changes. A lot of these kids are fairly mature. They need to be able to have some input, and if they don't, they rebel."

All manner of households. All manner of kids, too. Child psychologist Robert Orr: "You've got the difficult kid. Quick to rage, quick to anger, quick to jump to conclusions. They're very sensory oriented, respond to everything, and it's hard for them to act in a temperate way. If you've got a parent who's equally aggressive or assertive, then there's a tremendous amount of conflict and very little attachment in the relationship because they don't meld. It's like trying to grow shade plants in bright sunlight. Then there are the slow-to-warm kids who take a long time to get comfortable, to respond to an environment or situation. And so you need parents with lots of patience, tolerance and empathy. If you get a parent who wants it now and has those kinds of hard-core concrete values — 'you do this, you do that' — the kid isn't going to be in sync with them. I don't think that this kid is the type who's going to go into the kind of despair that you're talking about. And then you've got the placid kids.

"You're more likely to get rage out of this impulse-oriented, less impulse-control kind of kid. Kids who are quick to make a judgment about the way the world is, quick to react, and if you compound that with some kind of distorted cause and effect way of looking at the world . . ." Well, as Robert Orr says, you've got a problem. "Most kids have a pretty good sense of A causes B. If I do this in my world, then B will happen. If I study hard, I'll get good grades. If I'm a good kid, I'm going to get a lot more from my parents than if I'm a bad kid. So they get this 'if A, then B' kind of thing. But these kids over here, they have more trouble processing 'if A, then B.' They make impulsive judgments, they don't take time to reflect on what they're doing or what's happening out there. Also, if they're in a chaotic parenting environment where what you do has very little relationship with what your parents do, basically what happens is these kids lose touch with any kind of outside controls and it's all driven by their own schemes and structures and very little sense of the fact that society matters. They're just not that thoughtful. And they all have grand schemes."

Sometimes, quite literally, this isn't the kids' fault. And it's beyond the kids' ability to control or correct. Janet Orchard says some of them, not a majority, but "a significant percentage" have what is known as Attention Deficit Disorder. "Younger children, depending on how severe the disorder is and if it's associated with hyperactivity, can't focus, can't sit and attend in class, even the amount a Grade 1 child is expected to sit and attend. They're moving constantly. They are completely impulsive in their decision-making so that if they want something on the schoolground they'll run across the schoolground and take it from somebody else. Doesn't matter if that kid is bigger than them or not. If the thought crosses their mind that they want something or want to do something they'll take it or do it before they pause to think about it. Which seems like a simple thing to correct, but it's tremendously hard for people with this disorder to learn to stop and think. Very hard.

"Now, that sounds like it might not be such a big deal, but if you grow up that way and teachers don't recognize that as being what you're struggling with, you can look like a big pain in the ass in the classroom. And then it starts. You're bounced around from one classroom to another, from one special learning environment to another, parents become increasingly frustrated with you in the home because you won't pay attention. You seem to be able to pay attention if it's a fun thing, like a TV show, but if they want you to pay attention to help them do some cleaning, you won't do it, no matter how hard they punish you or how hard they try to set up incentive systems for you. So kids can end up, by the time they're 12 or 13, with everybody, all the adults in their lives, convinced that they're smart enough to do it, but they're lazy and only do what they want to do."

69

The problem is compounded by the fact that psychologists have only, in these past few years, begun to understand the disorder and to properly diagnose and treat children affected by it. "I'm not of the opinion that most of the kids we work with have that disorder," says child psychologist Janet Orchard "but there's a significant percentage of them who end up in trouble because of it."

It's a fairly simple progression, if you think about it. "You go through school for eight years with the impression of yourself as lazy and everybody treats you as though you're a lazy person who's not living up to your potential, who's a pain in the neck. You hit adolescence and all the stuff that happens in adolescence happens to you on top of what you've already got. Then you can end up developing an identity as a person who IS a pain in the neck and you can start taking pride in that and doing it well." And almost all the kids who have gone through this "are terribly, terribly angry. There's a real tendency with these kids, by the time they reach adolescence, to take on a real armament of 'I don't care' — the anger, the hostility associated with not being able to be successful, ever."

Angry kids. Angry kids who can't control their impulses — sounds like a recipe. And as if that isn't enough, a lot of these kids are abandoned by their parents.

There are lots of reasons parents pull out. Some are guilty and ashamed of what they've done to their children. Some don't want to be forced to admit what they've done, or to take responsibility for it. Some are just fed up after years of hassles and heartaches and late-night calls from the cops. Some don't care. Some never did care.

William B.: "So, the parents have pulled out and I don't always blame them. These are tough kids to live with." But when the family pulls out the kids are left in an emotional vacuum. Love leaves, anger enters. "I think most of the kids hurt like crazy when they realize they can't go home again."

In the mind of a child, things work like this. If the parents have pulled out, there must have been a reason. The reason is, the kid isn't worth loving. If the kid isn't worth loving, whose fault is that? For a lot of these kids, there's no question about it.

Sandra J.: "A small percentage of our kids have grown up, literally, in institutions and group homes and treatment centres. They're always out of control. And I think those are the ones where attachment to other people never happened. Right now we have three kids like that, raised in institutions. One, the mom just wasn't able to help. One, he has ADD (attention deficit disorder), along with his mom not being available. And the third one, we don't know. He's one of the most disturbed kids I've ever met. I don't know whether it's some kind of chemical or physiological disorder, or whether he's just a total sociopath. The family is very closed, so I can't get a handle on it. Nobody has been able to get to the family, so something is missing there."

"I don't think the general population begins to know," says William B., "that there is a group of children out there who have this criminal thinking." These aren't stupid kids, for the most part. In fact, some of them would achieve impressive scores on an IQ test. "But their thinking isn't clouded by any empathy or emotion, which for most of us it is. They are really much more like computers in the way they go at things. There isn't an emotional component to anything they do." Could these kids kill someone and feel nothing? "Yes," says William. They had a kid like that in the jail. He killed someone. "He didn't feel anything."

Kids who are abandoned don't often feel good about themselves. And if a kid thinks others think he's worthless, then often as not he'll act as though he's worthless. Bad kid, bad attitude, bad action. Or, as William B. says, "How you feel about yourself affects how you act."

71

Psychologist Robert Orr has a friend who works with delinquents in Detroit. "She says there are three things in the delinquents she deals with. The first is low self-esteem. The second is no sense of competence, no sense they can do things, outside of maybe hotwiring a car or stealing hubcaps. And, third, they have no sense of belonging. Now a lot of people think low self-esteem is the cause of all this shit. Low self-esteem is not the cause. It's all this shit which went into producing the low self-esteem that acts also to produce this deviant kind of behaviour."

"If you don't have that connection with your parents when you're young," says Sandra J., "then who do you learn how to be in the world from? We get our sense of self, in large part, from our relationship with our parents. If they meet our needs, then we feel worthwhile. If not, we feel worthless. It's from that relationship that we form our conscience. It goes back to the earliest years. When you're one or two and Mother says 'don't touch that' and we don't touch it, she smiles. So then we won't touch it so that she'll smile at us. Kids want approval. They want love and warmth and acceptance. They need that in order to develop. And if they don't get it, they can't develop. They might do what mom says, out of fear, so that mom won't hit them. But if that's the case then they don't internalize the social rules and values that make us able to live in the world. When we're growing up, we want to beat up our little brothers. Eventually, we don't beat them up because we've internalized mom's values, and we know it's wrong to hurt someone else." But if we act or don't act simply out of fear of being punished, then we'll wait until nobody's looking and whale the crap out of little brother and take his toy truck, knowing we won't get caught. "The more I work here, the more I value the importance of those first few years in the life of a child."

Question: if these kids are so badly damaged by age three, if they can shoot someone, or knife someone, and feel nothing at all, not the slightest trace of guilt or shame or remorse, what are we supposed to do? Write them off? Robert Orr thinks about the question. "You want an honest answer?" Yes. "Yah. Essentially." What a tragic waste of life. "Welcome to the world."

"One of the phrases I'm sure you've heard," says William B., "is 'throw-away kids.' I'm sure that offends a lot of people. It offended me before I got into this business. I used to think people hadn't tried hard enough, or found the answers. But that's what these kids are." And of these chilling kids he says, "There's no point in spending a lot of money hoping to rehabilitate them. And those are the kids I don't have any trouble saying should be in a locked setting for their own safety and the safety of society."

It certainly makes you think of the luck of the draw. Crown prosecutor Randy Semeniuk has seen so many hundreds of kids going through the courts, so many kids whose background stories are so similar, that he has to wonder: "Is it just a function of where you're born and who you're born to? I mean, if things had been different, maybe I'd have been a criminal as opposed to a prosecutor. Or is it that once the child is born, it's the environment from then on?" He doesn't know, but his hunch is, it's a combination of the two.

For instance: "This one young offender had a horrendous background. His mother would drop him off downtown and tell him 'make your own way back home.' He was five years old. So, what can you expect from somebody like that? By the time they're fifteen, they've got a different view of the world." Then again, you can get kids from relatively normal households doing terrible things. Such as some kids who invaded a home in Windsor, tied a woman up, terrorized her, robbed her, left her on the floor. Those kids "come not

73

from affluent backgrounds, but certainly upper middle class backgrounds and you think 'well, what's the reason for that?' Sometimes I think in today's society, kids just aren't learning values and therefore they don't put the same value on human life as other people do. I think if there is a lack of values it's one of two sources: the parents, or the teachers. That's where you learn your values when you're young. And I tend to think it's the parents who are not teaching these values.

"We see a lot of young offenders who are children giving birth to children. I did a case involving a gang in Windsor called The Hood that went around robbing houses. One of the members of the gang, who was dating the leader of the gang, was 14. She was pregnant. The leader was 30. He's in the penitentiary now. I mean, she's 14 and having a child. Now what parenting skills does she have? She doesn't know values herself. So how's she going to teach this child values?"

The past in whatever form — history of abuse, lack of values — comes back to haunt these kids. No question about it. But no question about this, either, in the mind of William B.: "A lot of them do a lot of things on purpose. They walk in with their eyes open. They plan it."

And who knows why? Alec Marks, of New Beginnings: "There are some young offenders who come from families where there doesn't seem to be much going wrong. There are good values in the home. The parents are trying really hard. The siblings are normal, the peer relationships are normal."

Sandra J.: "Some of our kids, they've been through counselling, they've been through all the community services and nothing has worked and the parents say 'I don't know what I've done wrong' and I have to tell them 'you haven't done anything wrong.'" The sad, weird fact is, as Sandra says, "Lots of kids just love the thrill and the excitement of crime. Especially when they're 13 and 14 and 15. With them, it's still too much fun to want to quit and they're the hardest ones to deal with. Once they get to be 16 and 17, they start to think 'I don't know if I want to live my life like this.' But the younger ones, it's hard to overcome the rush they get from getting away with it.

"One kid, he was very up front about it. 'I love gold, and I love nice clothes and I don't want to work at some minimum wage job to get them. I don't want to wash dishes.' And so he goes out and steals what he wants. And he says, 'I make more money than you do, and I'm not going to give it up. And ... hey ... that's a nice necklace, Sandra. Fourteen carat?'" Sandra J. smiles and shakes her head. "Sometimes it's a facade. But with some, you know they mean it.

"A lot of our kids are runners," she says. "And they've been on the run for a long time. They live with their friends, or in the summer they just sleep out in the park or in cars. A night here, a night there. They talk about it like it's an adventure. Never, 'Oh, it was awful.' They'll come back in here and they'll look like hell, dirty and drawn, but there's not one kid who ever said it was awful. It's either a high time for them or it's just simply better than the alternative." Which once was home.

"These kids will tell you there's a sense of excitement and danger in committing crimes. They find regular kids boring. A lot of our girls are like that. They like living on the edge." Why? Sandra J. thinks they've worked so hard to numb their feelings of pain and humiliation that they "numbed out their feelings as well and so they need really high excitement to feel anything at all. Boredom is a pretty consistent theme with these kids. They get bored really easily. If they were 'legal' they'd be skydiving and climbing mountains. But they're not, so generally to get that high they have to be doing something that's against the law. They need to feel they can get away with something. So it has to be a crime. These kids love being chased by the cops. They love the idea of being wanted." I ask Sandra J. to think about what she's just said. She smiles. Yes, there's that, too.

But there's another shade of meaning in all this running and chasing. "The person doing the running is the person in control of the situation. It gives them a chance to say 'I'm smarter than they are.' It proves they're smart. And they all want to be the best." Sandra J. will then point out to them that they are currently in jail, having lost the race and been caught. "And they'll say, 'yah, lucky for them, this time.' "

Why this overwhelming need to be the best, to be in control of the situation? Sandra J.: "If they're not the best, they're the worst. There's no middle ground with these kids. They don't accept that 'in between' is okay. They're very concrete thinkers. They don't see grey areas. With some of them, maybe Mom and Dad have taught them this. Maybe someone was always knocking them down, so now they've got to be on top. 'I've got to be the best or others will walk all over me.' And our society is so competitive, it's all around them: win, win, win. These kids have bought into that. The only problem is, these kids don't care about the rules. And they don't care who gets hurt."

These are the ones who puzzle Judge Saul Nosanchuk, "the cases where people just act up" for no apparent reason. "They just act out in cases where you'd never dream they would. Their parents are wringing their hands and wondering 'how'd this ever happen to us, that our children would do this kind of thing?' But that's perhaps the anger against the middle class family that comes up, a family where things just haven't jelled."

Whatever the path they took which spiralled down into the world of crime, the judge will say this of the kids who are paraded into his courtroom: "I feel a lot of empathy for them because they seem so lost and so unable to function and, in some ways, so out of control in their lives."

Sandra J. would agree. "Most of these kids are directionless. They don't have goals. Even if they have goals, they seem to lack the motivation and willingness to work toward the goal. Take the kid who loved gold. With him it's 'I want it, and I want it now' and he's doing anything to get it. Except work. 'Work at a job? Save money?' These kids have an inability to tolerate any frustration, any delay in having their wants and needs satisfied. 'I want it now, and I'll do anything I need to do to get it.' Maybe it comes from that feeling that nobody else is going to do it for them, so they'll have to do it themselves. They get physically anxious when they can't do what they want to do when they want to do it. They get agitated. They'll say 'I want to see my lawyer' and you tell them you've put in the call and that you're waiting to hear back from the lawyer's secretary. And they'll say 'I want to see my lawyer now. I have a right to see my lawyer. If you don't let me see my lawyer, I'm calling The Advocate.' They act quite omnipotent." Why? "Sometimes it's a cover for feeling vulnerable and insecure. It's like: 'the more scared I am, the more omnipotent I'll act.' " She pauses, and catches herself in a smile. "But then, of course, some kids truly believe they are omnipotent." A few. But most, as Sandra J. will tell you, "are just afraid of feeling afraid. They're afraid that would make them seem weak, and they already feel weak. They worry about what their friends would think if they ever found out they were afraid. As one of the kids told me, 'You can't be afraid on the street' and he's probably right. He said, 'Your world and my world are two different worlds.' Right again."

They're artful and wilful little dodgers living in a world far removed from ours. And angry little dodgers as well. Crown prosecutor Jill Manny, thinking of the kid who trashed the Co-Op building, says, "To do that kind of damage, that kid must be so angry. I'm not a psychologist, but I wonder 'what made this kid so angry?' What can he be so angry about, at 12 years of age, that he's going to destroy the place?"

Janet Orchard is a psychologist. She says, "Often the rage is born of terrible frustration because they don't fit in and they know they can't fit in. It's almost a haves and have-nots frustration some-times. They want things, the way we grow up wanting things in our culture."

Loving parents, maybe. Or a battle-free home zone. Or a mother who isn't dead drunk when you come home from school. Or a bed you won't have to share with some uncle, or stranger.

"And they can't have these things. And that makes them angry. I think a lot of the kids, especially the boys but also the girls, have grown up never knowing how to have any feeling other than rage. If you talk to these boys and ask them 'growing up in your fam-ily, how did you know if someone was sad or happy or loved you or cared about you?' they'll say 'I wouldn't have a clue. But I sure knew if somebody was mad.' And that's their experience of the world. It relates to the whole male thing, that there's no feeling except when you're mad. And that does a really good job of keeping you moving. If you give in to being sad, what can you do? But when you're mad, you act. And 'mad' allows you to fit in with your friends because they're all acting on the same anger. It has the effect of scaring other kids away who you're afraid of. It serves a lot of purposes. And often the parents are mad, too." It's a vicious circle, literally and figura-tively.

That circle cuts through the courtrooms of people like Judge Saul Nosanchuk. One recent day, he had two girls before him, charged with the vicious beating of a third. The accused were 15 years old. "They were both from dysfunctional homes. They didn't know where to go, they had so much time on their hands. This is a frequent hallmark of young offenders. They're directionless. They don't know where to turn, so they turn to substance abuse to fill in their emptiness, to do something about their feelings of insecurity.

They use drugs or alcohol and that gives them a temporary boost, they feel better about themselves, they feel big or they feel inflated in their own perception of things. But it's a losing situation, because they can't control their behaviour."

The judge is the first to admit he's no child psychologist. But he's been seeing kids parade through one courtroom or another for more than two decades. And he can tell you this: "The drugs fill an emptiness in these youngsters. If you have a youngster who's involved in dance, or in sports, any of these activities on a regular basis, if their time is filled and their family is functional, or reasonably functional, or not too dysfunctional, they're not as likely to end up in this kind of difficulty, although we have some of those too, some athletes. Even sports doesn't do it." The judge can tell you this as well: from his perspective, on the bench, he sees a direct correlation between the degree of dysfunction in a home and the degree of lawlessness in a child. "Absolutely. I see the children, if not the grandchildren, of people I defended years ago. Oh absolutely. It starts very early. They are rebellious and angry and hostile and they carry that through. That's the world they live in, that was the world they saw, that was the picture window of their home, that's how they looked at the world and so that's what they see. They see conniving and stealing as the way to do things. So, yes, a large percentage of these people come from dysfunctional homes where there's excessive alcoholism and drug abuse, where there's previous crime, and they don't know any different. Very sad. And I don't know how you turn those people around."

Crown prosecutor Jill Manny thinks perhaps the system may be contributing to, rather than helping solve, the problem. "Some kids really need help. And I'm very empathetic to those situations because some kids come from awful homes and you think 'this kid's never had a chance. What do you expect? Look at his family. Drugs. The welfare system, which seems to go on forever. What hope do these kids have?' But a lot of these kids, you give them probation, they think it's a joke. Probation is 'getting off' to them. Getting off like nothing happened. And then you watch them graduate to the adult system. And a lot of them do."

Staff Sgt. Mike Wilson has his theories: "These kids don't have a lot of respect for authority. When you and I used to go to school, they had corporal punishment. I'm not saying that I advocate corporal punishment to an extreme, but the problem today is that when we have a problem with kids, we don't have any 'or else' in school, or in the family."

Roger Montchamps spent the last four years of his police career in the department's youth bureau. He's noticed the same change Mike Wilson has seen. "We went from one end of the pendulum to the other, from the point where anything a parent did to a child in terms of discipline was okay and everyone just turned a blind eye, to the point where kids are now saying 'go ahead, touch me, I'll charge you.' And you hear of a few cases, usually in the United States but some in Canada, where parents have been charged and have just gone through hell. So parents are running scared and many will say 'well, I can't do anything to the kids anyways.'"

When he was growing up, Mike Wilson once went down to a construction site with some pals. They threw rocks at the partially constructed homes, rocks which went right through the tarpaper covering the wood. "A cop kicked me in the ass and told me to go home. And I can tell you, I never went anywhere near that construction site again, and I never threw rocks again. I'm not saying cops should go around beating kids up." But Wilson, cop and parent, thinks: "sometimes a swift kick in the ass doesn't do a lot of harm." Retired cop Roger Montchamps: "If your 12-year-old is ready to go out the door at night and you say no and he's still going, you can grab him by the arm and sit him down." If common sense doesn't tell you that, the Criminal Code, Section 43, does.

Mike Wilson and Roger Montchamps think too few people exercise discipline. "There's a thin line between respect and fear," says Wilson. "Today, a lot of these kids don't respect adults and they don't fear authority. In the schools, they'll tell the teachers to fuck off; the teachers tell the principal; then the kid'll tell the principal to fuck off and if the principal tries to throw him out, he'll threaten to lay charges. In the old days, you'd confront a kid and tell him to do what you wanted him to do and if he said 'and if I don't?' you'd grab him by the scruff of the neck and move him. Today, they say 'what're you gonna do if I don't?' and the teachers don't do anything. Which is crazy. Under Section 43 of the Criminal Code, it says teachers and people in authority may use reasonable force to effect discipline. But the teachers are afraid to use it. I was talking with some principals out at the teachers' college and I told them that and you know what one of them said? He said, 'We know that, but the board told us 'you touch a kid and you're fired.' "

"We've gotten so far away from the concept of discipline, enforcing discipline. You've gotta wonder. I'm not advocating harsh punishment for these kids but when a kid tells a teacher to fuck off, you can't take that. And we shouldn't be leaving teachers on their own." The way Mike Wilson sees it, the parents should be doing more. "It doesn't hurt to whack a kid on the ass if you can't talk him into doing what you want him to do. You can't always talk them into doing what you want. Sometimes you have to smarten them up. And I'm not talking about beating a kid. I'm talking about a whack on the ass. What we have here is a lack of respect for authority. The kids have no fear of authority and like I said, there's a thin line between fear and respect. If you don't have the one, you won't have the other."

Next door to the jail there's a convent. Kids doing time in one building, nuns doing life in another. Sister Grace is one of the nuns, Sister Gabrielle another. They've got a soft spot for the kids next door. Every Christmas they string lights and hang ornaments from a little pine tree which is just below their bedroom windows and just on the other side of the path from the jail's playpen.

When the sisters are out for their walks around the grounds, they'll wave and smile at the kids, say hello. And the kids will wave and smile and say hello back, calling them by their names. There isn't a day goes by the nuns don't think about, and pray for, the kids next door.

What do two nuns from one age think of the kids from another? Sister Grace often wonders, "Why did they fail? Was it because they didn't have enough love to begin with? One of the staff told us some of these kids leave the jail and go out and get in trouble, just so they can come back. They have nobody out there to care for them." Sister Gabrielle: "Some of them say they've never had it so good. Food on the table every day. Good clothes. They say 'I never had it like this at home.'" Sister Grace: "I would say it's mostly a lack of love and attention. Now, many parents do love their children and from the best of homes children can go wayward. But I think basically these kids want a different kind of attention than they got at home, a different kind of care. And, too, they get in with a gang that's not too good and the first thing you know they're caught in the middle." They get into the gangs, she thinks, because the gangs give them what they weren't getting at home. "They won't tell you that, they won't admit that, but basically there's a yearning in them to feel wanted, to feel accepted for what they are. My heart aches for these kids. I feel like taking them in my arms and hugging them." No surprise to Sister Gabrielle that these kids are as promiscuous as they are. "With sex, what they're really looking for is happiness and joy.

They have a hunger for happiness. They turn to sex because they feel lonely. It's pitiful."

There's no shortage of theories to explain why these kids are doing what they're doing. Take your pick. Mix and match. As Alec Marks of New Beginnings says: "There is no single answer, at least not one that I've come across, and I'd be very suspicious of anyone who claims to have the answer." Some of the kids who wind up in his group homes and in the jail suffer mental illnesses. No question about that. Where the illness springs from is anyone's guess. Maybe it's innate. Maybe it's been caused by the environment. Maybe it's a mix of the two. Then again: "We've relied on the stereotype that most offenders come from broken families, dysfunctional families; that very often they were identified as being the problem child in the family; that the family values may not be consistent with the family values we hope for in society in general, that (these families) view crime as being the norm." That may be a stereotype, but it's true. "Those offenders who do wind up in custody," says Marks, "a very large percentage of them do come from broken homes, dysfunction-al families. There's no denying it."

But whatever the cause, there's an almost universal result. As jail director William B. says of almost all the kids in his charge: "They have a lack of moral structure, a lack of concern for other peo-ple, and if you lack that, then it's quite easy to take your wallet, or stab you. I could never do those things. I would feel awful if I hurt you in any way. But these kids don't feel awful."

Judge Nosanchuk: "I just want them to get a sense of values that will enable them to live constructively, to occupy their time with the kinds of things they'll enjoy and which they can do well. I want to see them happy in their lives. All this misery. They cause misery. Their crime is such a source of misery for people. Their victims are so abused. I feel about these young people as if they were my own children, in a way. I want to put something right for them, try to make it better for them so they can be better people in the community, so they can be more caring about other people, so they can be decent citizens, so we can have a more peaceful community. Because, after all, they're destroying themselves and they're destroying other people." And, most puzzling, they just don't seem to care.

Why not?

Good question. It's not one William B. thinks he can answer. In fact, it's not one he thinks anyone can answer. "There's honestly just something wrong with some of these kids and I know there's supposed to be an answer, somebody's supposed to have researched this and come up with an explanation. I referred to one international expert on criminal thinking, and he says, 'stop trying to figure out what's wrong with some of these kids. There's just something wrong, and you'll never know what it is.' There's something, and he uses these words, not wired right. They literally think coldly, calculatingly, as if they don't have a soul like the rest of us. It's not there to be found. So they're the chilling ones, the ones who really are true criminals." These kids form a minority — about 20 per cent William B. thinks — of the kids who come to the jail. Which is probably a far greater proportion than exist in the population generally, since the jail tends to collect kids like this. And it's not that these truly criminal kids do crimes that are worse than other kids. "But there's little hope, you're kidding yourself," if you think you can change them and rehabilitate them. What's weird, here, is that these cold and calculating and emotionless kids "often are the kids who have parents who have tried. You trace it back, you ask the parents what the kid was like when he was two and they'll say, 'He was incredible to manage even then.' And it didn't matter whether the parents loved the kid or punished the kid, the kid didn't seem to care, there didn't seem to be the capacity to emotionally give a darn. There's something wrong, but I don't know what it is.'

84

Child Psychologist Robert Orr, of the University of Windsor: "Some of that may simply be genetic. They don't have that built-in empathy processor. I don't think you get an individual who lacks morality unless they've got a haywire gene. We don't talk about it much, because we can't prove it. But over at Child's Place (a treatment facility for pre-schoolers) they've got three-year-old or four-year-old kids who are showing the kinds of behaviour your kids are showing in adolescence. You look at those kids and say, hey, there's nothing we can do. Whatever we do, it ain't gonna work. The behaviour-disordered kids are a major anomaly in our discipline (psychology). I don't think we know what the hell to do with them. You may get a moderate amount of conformity inside your structured clinical setting, or even in jail, but put them back in that chaotic world where there's all that stimulation and chaos, they can't process it, they can't sort it out." They act impulsively and violently and without giving the merest fraction of a second's attention to the outcome of their actions: the people they are going to rape, rob, hurt or kill. It is, I tell him, a frightening thought. "Scares the shit out of me."

Equally scary: "More and more and more," says William B., "we're seeing these kids, real criminal-thinking kids." The proportion of these kids isn't going up "by leaps and bounds, but they're certainly coming to our attention more."

William B. seeks, mostly in vain, for some trace of compassion, some flicker of empathy, in the kids in his jail. "We try to find that in them, and we've been successful with some kids. But with some we haven't been, and probably never could be."

Scary thought, I tell him.

"Some of these are very scary kids."

Helen S. has dragged her chair into the hallway so she can hear and see what's going on while she's filling out her reports. Every day, noon and mid-afternoon, while the kids are in their rooms for quiet times, the staff put check marks and X's in the boxes beside the lines describing the kid's behaviour.

'Listening to instructions ( )' . . . and so on.

Beside each line there is a numerical value. Get the check marks, you get points. Get points, you get rewards.

Helen asks Larry how well Mary had been listening to staff members and following their instructions.

"She did all right."

Check.

Fred: "Hey Helen?"

"Yes, Fred."

"Did I have a good morning?"

"I don't know, Fred I haven't got around to your sheet yet."

Patricia P. is doing paper work in the supervisor's office when, suddenly, there's a voice on the walkie-talkie strapped to her belt: "Patricia, can you come down here for a minute?"

Patricia is up out of her chair and on the run.

Helen S. watches Patricia hustle down the hall, then turns back to Larry. She and Larry have been talking about a conversation John had with Norm on the subject of absent fathers. Norm wanted his dad to visit him, but he knew his mother wouldn't think much of that idea if she found out about it and he was afraid to broach the subject. John had been listening to all this, John who seems entirely absorbed by his own problems. Suddenly, John turned to Norm and said, 'My mom didn't want me to see my dad either. But you can see him if you want to.' The two of them talked about it for a few minutes.

Small revelations.

Speaking of John, he's on the couch in the lounge. He's been watching Helen filling out those forms. "Helen?" "Yes." "Is Bill gone?" "Yes, he's gone." "For good?" "I hope so." "Oh."

And thinking of Bill, Helen thinks there's one who really surprised her. "I always thought he was a little slow. But he had a math test and got perfect on it. Perfect!" Helen had been fooled by Bill's slow and plodding demeanor. "But he's just meticulous. He's a perfectionist." He just slowed himself down to a crawl so there'd never be a missed step, whether creating ceramic dinosaurs, perfect down to the little painted horns, or a math test, cost minus expenses equals profit.

The future?

Helen shrugs. "You never know."

1:15 p.m. ────────────────────────────────────

Welcome to Victim Awareness 101.

The object here is to get the kids thinking about their victims. Not an easy task for, as social worker Sandra J. will say, these kids live in a world where "it's me first, me second, me third, and you after that, maybe."

Sandra tries to get the kids to understand the power of thought. On the first page of today's flip chart she has written 'You are what you think.' Which Sandy isn't buying: "I think about death, but I'm not death." Granted, that's true. "But if you think about death all the time, how do you think that would affect the way you live?" Sandy shrugs. Beats her. "What I'm getting at, Sandy, is that if you think in a certain way, it will affect your behaviour." Grant gets the drift. Shoots a hand up. "Yes, Grant?" "What you're saying is, if we think about crime all the time, we'll commit a crime." That's what she's saying. But Sandy shakes her head. "If I think

87

about crime, I'm not crime." Grant: "It's a figure of speech, Sandy.' Bob: "Why are we arguing? Let's go on."

Going on, Sandra J. wants to know if the kids believe it's possible to act without thinking. They chew on the question for a minute or so. Majority rules: no, you can't act without thinking. "That's right. We're thinking all the time. Now, we may not be aware that we're thinking, but we are." And our thoughts are very powerful.

✝ Elizabeth has a question for Sandra J. "Are you afraid when you're working with us?" Sandra thinks about that. "Sometimes, I am." "So, how do you do your job, if you're afraid?" "I'm not always afraid. I don't think I'm even often afraid. But if I am afraid, it would affect the way I work. So if there was someone here I feared, I'd want to make sure I could still work with that person and so I might tell the staff about my fears and ask them to stay close to me. Then I could work with the person and not be concerned about my safety."

"I'd be paranoid if I was in here working with us," says Sandy. "I'd be worrying all the time. I mean, you're hearing some pretty funky stuff when we're in your office. I mean, if I was working here and someone was in here for murder, I'd freak. I'd say, 'Oh my God, I wanna be outta here.' "

"Sure," says Sandra J., "our thoughts can do that to us. They affect the way we interact with other people. Let's say (staff member) James T. was in my class and I knew James always criticized me, then I'd come in here thinking 'oh my gosh, James is going to be watching me every minute and he's going to be criticizing everything I say,' that would affect the way I feel and the way I do my job. That's what I was getting at: our thinking is so powerful it affects how we feel and how we act.

"And if the way we act is a problem, the behaviour isn't going to stop, or get changed, until we stop or change the thinking that's behind the action. 'I'm going to stop drinking, as soon as I feel more relaxed with people.' Well, that's not going to happen. If you want to stop doing crime, you have to work at becoming more confident in yourself and your abilities, your talents and strengths, more confident that you can live a legal life." Once you work on that confidence, and change your view of yourself, then you can stop breaking into people's houses and beating people up. But the thinking has to change, first. And the thinking can change. Or, as Sandra would put it: "We create ourselves."

Skeptical faces in front of her. "You're all at different stages right now. Some of you want to make changes, and some of you don't and some of you aren't sure. But if you're saying, 'I don't want to change,' then you won't. Your thinking can keep you stuck." If, on the other hand, there's a kid in the room who wants to change, then that kid is in the right place.

Which brings us to today's topic: Thinking errors. How to spot them. How to correct them.

Sandra talks for a couple of minutes about some psychiatrists who spent years studying criminals, analyzing their thinking. What they discovered was a similarity in the thinking patterns of pretty well all criminals. It's what's called in the trade 'criminal thinking' and criminal thinking can be broken down into certain categories.

For instance? Sandy would like to know. For instance, many criminals minimize what they've done, make excuses for what they've done, create rationalizations for what they've done or, when all else fails, deny they've done anything bad. If you want to spot that kind of thinking in yourself, you should look for certain key words: only, just, never, but.

"I only break into houses, I never hurt anyone. I just stole some cigarettes, nobody got hurt. I never do arson; robberies, yes, but never arson." "If you can start to hear yourself, and hear yourself using those words, you can catch yourself in the act of criminal thinking. Catching yourself is the first step in changing yourself."

Now, says Sandra, there are many forms of criminal thinking. Some have counted more than 50 variations. Today, she wants to deal with just a few. The first: "you get a real high controlling others." If you're into this kind of thinking, "everything has to go your way." And if you're thinking like this you almost always have a lack of empathy for others. The two go hand in hand. And they're very common thinking errors in young criminals.

Sandra asks Pat if he could give an example of the kinds of thinking she's just been talking about. Pat thinks back to something he said to staff member James T. earlier today: "I'm going for a 50 today, James. And then I gave him the look." Exactly, says Sandra. "You're being aggressive, and you're trying to be intimidating. And often, in this kind of thinking, you will try intimidation. You'll use anger, you'll try threats. It's totally win/lose. If you don't win, you lose. And generally, you say 'I'm going to win here, regardless of who I step on.' "

Elizabeth raises her hand. "Power isn't always bad." "No," says Sandra. "Power isn't always bad. If you use your power positively, it can be good. You can say 'I respect myself and I respect others' and you can try to exert your power in a way that doesn't hurt anyone. And that's not bad." The problem is, many people who desire power don't care much about how that power-grab will affect or hurt others.

How about a little role playing?

Bob and Curt volunteer. Bob moves to Curt's table and sits facing him. Here's the situation: Bob is going out with Curt's girlfriend; Curt doesn't like it and decides to call Bob on it.

Curt: "Bob, I hear you're seeing my woman. I'd appreciate it if you didn't do that. It makes me angry."

90

Very good, says Sandra.

"Yah," says Curt "But this don't happen in real life, Sandra. In real life, you'd just go up to him and 'bam.'"

Sandra begs to differ. In real life, lots of people sort out their differences without the 'bam.' In fact, the vast majority of people sort out their differences without ever hitting someone.

Curt gives Sandra an 'if-you-say-so' sort of shrug. Sandra suggests they try again. But this time, Bob is supposed to have some empathy for his friend Curt, and should try to take Curt's feelings into consideration.

Curt: "You been seeing my woman and I don't like it,Bob. I'm angry about it. And I'd appreciate it if you'd lay off."

Bob: "All right, Curt. I didn't know it was buggin' you. Tell you what I'll do. I'll kick her to the curb."

Bob!

Bob looks at Sandra. He's a little surprised at her reaction. "What?"

"That was an awful thing to say."

"In real life, that's how I'd be talkin'."

Sandra would like him to think about it for a moment. He thinks about it for a moment. "I know it's not very respectful to the girl. But I wasn't taking her side. I was taking his side. He's my friend." Which begs the question why he was moving in on his friend's girlfriend. But we'll leave that aside for the moment. Does Bob see any thinking errors here?

"Apart from the disrespect for the girl?"

Yes. Apart from that.

While he's thinking about it, Curt has this to say: "Normally it wouldn't have come down to talking it out, Sandra. We'd have been duking it out."

"I've come close to doing that," says staff James T.. Like Bob and Curt in their make-believe encounter, James says he once argued

91

with a friend about a girl they both liked. James and his pal figured their friendship was more important than the girl, so they said good-bye to the girl. And it wouldn't have happened if they hadn't talked. "You learn to talk things out. Especially the older you get."

"It's not always the guy's fault," says Sandy. Sometimes a girl will try to play one guy off another, just for the thrills. "She should have said 'I've got a boyfriend.'"

Bob begs to differ. When two guys are friends, they share things. And they should share girls as well. "What's mine is yours."

Which Sandy finds disgusting: "That's like saying your underwear is my underwear."

At which point Sandra J. has this to say: "The important thing is to talk with each other." And we have to listen to other people as well. "We have to see where they're coming from. And sometimes that's hard to do." An example: suppose a staff member gives you a time-out. You think staff is picking on you, and you're angry. "Sometimes it would help if you tried to put yourself in the staff's position, take a look at things from their perspective. Ask yourself: 'If I were staff, maybe I'd see it that way, too.' But that's very tough to do."

So, lack of empathy and trying to overpower people are two pretty common thinking errors. Another is false pride. Blank stares. "That's when 'everyone else is wrong. I'm never wrong.'" Often, she says, we act in certain ways to cover up a part of ourselves that we don't like. "We all have a shadow side that we're not proud of. But we have to look at that part of ourselves if we're going to grow. It takes maturity and it takes confidence to say 'I don't like this about myself.'" Unless we admit there are parts of ourselves we don't like, then we can't begin to change those aspects of ourselves. And....

And there goes the bell.

"Darn," says Sandra. She shakes her head and smiles. "Oh well. We'll pick it up next week."

What she'd like the kids to do, meanwhile, is to give some thought to what they've been talking about, try to identify those times when they're making the kinds of thinking errors they've been talking about.

Curt: "All three, that's me."

Kids from A Group are in the lounge. John is reclining on one sofa, Larry beside him in a chair, the rest of the kids on the far side of the room, sofas and chairs.

Time for a house meeting.

Once a week, each of the groups meets to talk about changes they'd like to see in the program. Staff member Larry R. is chairing the meeting. The kids know the guidelines. "It's not 'he did' 'she did.'" In other words, no whining, no moaning. Keep it positive.

First, there are loose ends from the last meeting.

Kids want pictures on their walls. Larry took the idea higher up the management chain. Higher up, they're still thinking about it. "The problem is, we have to have a way of checking behind the pictures, for security reasons. And it would mean putting them up and taking them down."

Walt: "What about masking tape?"

Masking tape isn't permitted. "We thought about toothpaste, but you'd have to toothpaste them back up every time you took them down." Larry says if anyone in the group can come up with a good idea for putting up pictures and letting staff inspect them, front and back, let staff know. Meanwhile, there may be a possibility of letting the kids have 'brag books' in which they can keep photographs of their families and pets, books which could be kept on the cart and viewed during task time or before bed.

Also from last week: the rooms are being painted. If you write on the walls, or scratch graffiti into the paint of your bed, the damage will be repaired and the money will come out of your own account. Rooms will be checked regularly.

Larry: "But if you have an accident, if you drop something and chip the paint, tell us what happened. You won't get into trouble for being honest with us."

John: "What about coffee?"

The subject was to have been raised at a management meeting the week before. "Patricia didn't have time to talk about it, but it hasn't been forgotten."

Also from last week: the rooms have been sprayed for bugs, so the earwigs, ants and spiders should be long gone. "If you see more bugs," says Larry, "let us know."

Norm: "I hate those earwigs. They bite."

Larry: "They don't bite, Norm."

"Yes they do."

"No they don't."

Norm: "They do so."

New items of business: from now on, the staff running the cart up and down the hall during quiet time will hand out the envelopes to the residents, and will put the envelopes back in the slots. "Some people have been accidentally putting their envelopes in the wrong slots. And we don't want you to get in trouble for letter passing."

Staff is considering separate task times: one hour for each group. That way one group could be making phone calls while the other kids are in their rooms. It would cut down the confusion around phone call times.

It's time to go around the room.

Mary: "When we're outside (in the play yard) people are looking at us out the windows."

Larry: "I don't have a problem with people looking out the window at someone. But if you're throwing someone a finger, or waving and trying to get their attention, that would get you a time-out. Something to think about."

And?

"Walt? Any issues?"

"No. Nothing."

"Rick?"

"No."

"Fred?"

"No."

"Norm?"

"Nothing to complain about."

"George?"

"What about floor hockey?"

Great idea. But you need sticks and sticks are obviously a security problem. However, Larry is trying to find some sort of plastic sticks that would be non-threatening to staff and still good for playing floor hockey on the asphalt. He'll get back to the group on it.

Norm: "What about more time in the rec room?"

"At least once a day, if you're Level 4 or above, you'll have a chance to go to the rec room," says Larry. "If you're at Level 5, you'll go twice a day. Solve your problem, Norm?"

"Uh-huhhhhhhhh."

"Now, get up to Level 4 so you can use it."

The eyes roll.

Patricia is back, eating her salad and poring over reports in binders on her desk.

What happened downstairs?

"Two time-outs." When a kid gets a time-out, a staffer has to be stationed outside the time-out room, or in the hall where the kid is sitting through his time-out. So, two time-outs at once means staff supervising Curt, Sandy and the rest of Group B were spread a little too thin for their own liking. Thus the call to Patricia, and her quick trip down the back stairwell to the lower floor.

"I could tell, by the strain in the voice (on the radio) that there was a little tension." That's about as obvious as it will get on the radio. Kids have ears. "If they know it's hit the fan down there, then as soon as one or two of us leave they think maybe it's a good time to get it in the fan up here too."

If there had been an emergency, if they'd needed back-up, staff would have switched channels on their radios so that kids couldn't overhear the call, and would have appealed to people elsewhere in the jail for help.

Later, when the kids have gone back to their rooms, Larry talks about their meeting: "We've had the problem where they've always got great ideas, come up with great ideas, or ideas they want to happen, but they expect us to go solve it for them. So we're saying 'that really sounds good, now, give us some suggestions on how to do it.' Turn it back to them to come up with a plan that's safe and secure and responsible, possibly something on the Level plan so it could be an incentive. If you really want this, then work on it. We're trying to be caring of their own needs, but also to make them responsible for meeting their own needs."

In all of this, there's a firm underpinning: "You're trying to rekindle their trust in adults. In their past, a lot of their basic needs haven't been met. That's where our philosophy starts. You want to take care of their basic needs: food, clothing, shelter. If those are taken care of, the kids can learn to trust adults. In their past, they've learned to mistrust and deal with things on their own instead of relying on adults to take care of them. We attend to their requests, regardless of what they are. Even if they're outrageous. At least we can come back to them and say, 'well, this isn't going to work because of...' You let them know 'well, I brought it up for you and it was discussed.'

"Some of their ideas are fantastic and you come back and say, 'That was a great idea. Now, how can we make it work?' We get them more involved, and they feel like they're working with you as a team. They don't feel as though their requests are going into a black hole, the way adults have traditionally dealt with them. 'Mom, can I do this?' 'Get outta my face.' You're trying to teach them that they're at an age when they have to be more responsible. So you get more involved in their decision-making: what they want, why they want it, how we can do it. They've got to learn how to be more responsible for their own behaviours.

"The brag books — they're just photo albums — were misused before. People were hiding things in them, so they were taken away. I'd like to see them back. But we're going to question them on how we can maintain the brag books, how they can be responsible with them, and what happens if they're not. Get them involved in that process instead of just saying, 'okay, here they are, if you abuse 'em you lose 'em.' We'll try to make them responsible. 'Okay, how can we monitor this? When do you guys want to have them? What happens if someone misuses them? Should everyone lose them, or should that one person be punished? Make it a group issue and turn the peer pressure back on them. One kid's thinking, 'okay, I can misuse this,' but when you turn it to the whole group, he hears the responses of his own peers: 'I want to have my own pictures, I don't want to be punished for something someone else does.' It's good for them to hear that. Maybe they'll think twice about misusing it."

2:00 p.m.

Helen S. walks backwards at the head of the line, Larry R. walks frontwards at the back of the line, as the kids of A Group single file their way down the ramp to the rec room. They've got some time to kill while B Group finishes up in the outdoor yard.

Larry: "They got out there a few minutes late, so they want to have an extra few minutes now. They really do cherish their outside time." He thinks about that for a second or two. "I guess I would too, if I spent as much time as they do in one of those little rooms." During the week, the kids are outdoors at least twice a day; on weekends, three times a day.

While we wait, Walt and Fred grab the ping pong bats and go at it, Walt singing all the while:

> "When you're smiling,
> keep on smiling
> and the whole world smiles with you."

That's it for the lyrics, and he breaks into giggles, the second time through.

The song has no effect on John, who sits in a chair by the door, waiting to go out.

"Oh, sorry. I stepped on your lip, John." Patricia makes as

98

though to move his pouting lower lip with the toe of her shoe. John smiles, despite himself.

Rick is reading his Guinness Book of World Records. "Hey. I didn't know this. Did you know they used LSD to do research on the common cold?"

Larry: "Cured the cold. But the guy didn't know where he was for three days."

Frances E.'s voice on the radio saying that the outside group is coming in. We'll give them a few minutes, so the groups won't be passing in the halls, and the playpen's all ours.

The kids line up by the door. It's the quickest lineup of the day, thus far, including lunch-time.

The routine: at the end of the corridor, just inside the door leading to the yard, there's a mud room with rough-cut shelves along one wall, shelves divided into cubicles, each one numbered. Each kid has a cubicle in which to put his sneakers and an outdoor hat or anything else he wants to wear outdoors. Slippers and sandals come off, sneakers on. Line up. Let's go.

Today's activity is badminton in teams of four, with one staff member joining three kids to even out one of the teams. The game isn't five minutes old when John cranks a bird through the fence. A minute later, he's on the park bench for a time-out, his back to the group. Now and then, he turns to look over his shoulder. By the end of the time-out, he's got his chin on the top plank of the back of the bench.

John is having drug problems. He's off Ritalin. Wonder drug. The doctor wants to see if John can get along without it. The doctor isn't here. The staff are. And they're not so sure he couldn't use Ritalin again. But orders are orders. And whether John is a little wired or not, the orders stand. For now. And John sits.

Seven people sit around the long table in the board room. They're here to talk about George, what to do with him, once he's released in a few weeks' time. It's what's known in the jail as a Plan Of Care meeting. From the jail are supervisor Frank M., Frances E., who has been George's primary worker, nurse Cathy B., teacher Marilyn L. and social worker Sandra J. Also here are probation officer Laurie G. and a social worker from the Children's Aid, Ken L.

Frances E. circulates a memo:

'George's contact with his parents has been a few phone calls to his father. He has had no visitors in the last four months, other than his social worker and his probation officer.

'George is waiting for word of his placement, which has not been finalized. George has formed several attachments to staff and at times he has seen us as family.

The staff wish George the very best and are hopeful he will succeed in life.'

Supervisor Frank M. asks the jail's social worker, Sandra J., to go through George's 'risk assessment.'

George attempted suicide once. Though he talked several times of killing himself, he has made no other attempts. He has been on a suicide caution ever since this lone attempt. "He has talked on a number of occasions about the hopelessness he feels. He's said that when he gets older, he feels he'll likely commit suicide."

Sexual assault? Yes.

Assaultive behaviour? Yes.

Violent behaviour? Yes.

Conviction for violent behaviour? Yes.

Use of weapons? Yes.

Fire setting? No.

Escape attempts? No.

Psychosis? No.

Third party threats? No.

While in custody, he has had some temporary releases into the community. His behaviour has been exemplary. He made no attempts to escape custody, though once when he returned to the jail he told staff he'd felt like running while he was on his release.

Based on what she's heard, Laurie G. says, "George is high risk in every area: family, peers, school, record, attitude. Overall, he's high risk."

Ken L.: "Has he been assaultive, while in custody?"

George has been in jail for nearly a year. During the first few months of his incarceration, he tended to be very violent, often having to be restrained. Frances E.: "George doesn't like to be touched. When staff had to restrain him, as soon as they put their hands on him, he became very violent." But that behaviour has changed, radically, for the better. Cathy B. says he's on a drug which helps control his moods. Frances: "If you tell him what he's doing is inappropriate, he's able to understand that and change."

Ken asks about George's need for drugs. Sandra says the psychiatrist has suggested George would benefit from anti-anxiety drugs. Ken wonders whether staff could ask a doctor to put him on the drugs. Apparently not. Parents do have say about the medical treatment of their children who are in custody. "If we could get him on the drugs before he leaves," Ken says, "then staff could monitor the dosage and keep the psychiatrist informed about the side effects so that by the time he left, George would be on the proper dose."

Laurie says, "We could make a recommendation that the court order him to visit a child psychiatrist after his release." If

George is still in town, he could see the psychiatrist he's been seeing all along. If he's out of town, his new psychiatrist could consult the local doctor.

Ken L. asks about George's mental state. Sandra: "He wants a girlfriend, and a family." He was having fantasies about leaving, going to live with a girlfriend, though he doesn't have one, or living on the street, though he's never done that. When he was at home, he didn't have a lot of freedom, so there's no way he could survive on the street.

Which brings us around to the future. The near future. Frank: "Any word, on a placement?"

No.

Sandra has made applications on George's behalf to a number of residential treatment centres. "They won't have any space until the spring of 1995." There's a possibility of an opening at a centre in Michigan and there are chances, however slim, of him being accepted elsewhere in Ontario. A committee is meeting next week and members of that committee, including Ken L., will raise George's case. As Ken says, George "desperately wants to be with caring people." And those caring people seem to be George's only hope for the future. As it is, George is able to integrate with his peers and gets along just fine for long periods of time at the jail. "Then he just blows. And that's with nurturing people right at his elbow. If he does that with nurturing, who knows what he'll do if he doesn't have it? It's possible he could make it, but we're afraid. Some kids, I could say 'no way.' But I couldn't say that with George."

Sandra: "He's made tremendous progress, but the support here has been incredible. He's had people around him all the time he's been here."

One of the possibilities for George is a highly structured centre near Toronto where George could get the kind of support he's been getting while in jail. But that centre accepts only a few youngsters a year. Ken L.:"Are you saying George should be one of those placements?" Without hesitating, Sandra nods. "Yes. When he's in his angry hopeless moods, he can be out of control. What frightens me is that he's still one of those full-of-rage kids. And when he's hurting, he wants to hurt others." He's told her that when he thinks of his parents he gets in a rage.

The people in the room have to admit George is not without reasons for his rage. He has been raised by his father, his mother having walked out on the family long ago. Now his father has been, to use the jargon, 'very resistant to him.' Translation: George's father doesn't want to see him anytime soon. Regardless of the reasons for George's mental state, Sandra says, "I'm afraid what he'll do" if he's not adequately supervised and if he doesn't have access to friendly adults whom he trusts.

Laurie: "If he was in here for another couple of months, I'm sure he'd do well, but he's not going to be in here and there isn't going to be staff at his elbow."

And they go around again. Frances: "He's been very positive lately. He's gained the respect of his peers. They often turn to him for help, with drawing for example."

Ken: "Does he confront them?"

No. Not even when provoked? No. Frances: "He's learned to control his reaction to provocation from his peers. Perhaps in part because he so desperately wants to be liked by his peers."

Which has always been one of his problems. Ken: "He's always wanted his peers to like him. He wanted to be noticed. When they didn't notice him, he got a weapon. 'You won't notice me? Well, notice me now.' And of course they did."

Laurie: "How's he doing in his classes?"

Marilyn L.: "If he likes the subject, he does well. And the opposite is true. But if he doesn't do well in something, or doesn't like it, then he won't do it. If a teacher has the time to help him, and show him that the subject isn't all that difficult and that he can master it, then he begins to do well and sees that it wasn't that difficult after all. Out in the real world, he'd have to have extra counselling. He'd have to have someone he could trust who he could go and talk to if he was having trouble."

Frank: "He needs more structure than most kids."

Ken: "Is there any variance with male or female staff?"

Frank: "No. He goes to male and female staff. As long as he feels he can trust them." He is struggling with his sexuality. He's hit puberty since coming into jail. "He's starting to notice girls."

Laurie: "He's got to go to a structured setting. He definitely needs it. Without it, he's out of control."

Ken: "He's very positive about that."

Laurie: "His expectation is that he's going to some kind of group setting."

"He's very anxious," says Sandra. "He has no idea what's going to happen to him when he's released." Ken: "And neither do we." Frank: "Given the anxiety he's feeling, he's shown an enormous amount of self-control in terms of controlling his behaviour. It's really incredible." Particularly if you remember, as Frank does, how George used to blow when under pressure.

Sandra: "If he could just cry about his family, I think it would help. If he could just get to that sadness that he feels." Ken: "Do you really think he's that sad? Not all kids are. Some kids couldn't be happier to leave home." Frank agrees with Sandra. He's sensed a sadness with George, particularly when he gets depressed. He's said, in that indirect way some kids use, "They didn't want me. Why do I want to go back there?"

Which brings us back to the problem at hand. Sandra: "He's going to need some kind of aftercare. If he's still in town, he should be able to have phone contact with some of the staff here. He needs an assigned worker (someone who would work with him on a consistent basis). He can form relationships. He's shown that here with Frances. Frances has gone through hell with him and she's shown him that she'll be there, no matter what." Frances: "I'd like to work with him, if I could." Marilyn: "And he's very attached to you Ken. You've stuck with him, too, through the tough times." Ken: "I want to be involved with him. I think it's important for kids to know that you're there for them, that you want to help them with their problems. It's important for them to know that somebody cares. I think that's important, and I want to fill that role."

Other needs? He needs to go to school. He needs eyeglasses.

They all agree another meeting is needed. They set a date. Frances gets up: "Should I bring him in?"

Frank nods.

We wait in silence for George to enter.

Sandra compliments him on the strides he's made in relationships with others while he's been in the jail. But she does notice that at times he still seems to be angry. She can understand why. "But I hope you can get beyond your anger and get on with your life. You've done wonderful work in the area of improving your social skills while you've been in here, George. For the next couple of weeks, we're all going to help you to get ready to leave here. And the staff are going to miss you a lot once you're gone."

Ken's turn. "Well, on the home front George, nothing much has changed. Dad is still working at the same company." And speaking of dad, "he's saying it's not good for you to come back home, George. He's saying, 'I can't cope with him'."

George studies the floor.

"I know he cares about you, George. But he has trouble showing it. You know that when you were at home, you weren't getting many positives. And I think at this time, you need more than he can give you. Maybe in the future, things will change. But Dad's agreed to put you in the care of the Children's Aid. Do you have any questions?"

George: "Not really."

Ken: "We'll be working on a place for you to go."

Laurie: "You're doing really well, George. And I'll be around to help you. I'll come back and we'll go over the conditions of your probation, just to remind you."

George looks up from the floor to Ken, who is sitting directly across from him: "I can't go home."

Ken: "That's right."

Laurie: "When I come back, we'll go over all the conditions for you. Okay? Do you have any questions?"

George: "Not really."

3:06 p.m.

Three posters on the wall. One features the picture of a mouse, the second the picture of a bear, the third a shark. Beside each of the pictures, Sandra J. has written the characteristics of three very different personalities: passive, assertive, aggressive.

The mouse is afraid to take risks, doesn't stand up for himself, hides his real feelings, lets others decide for him, and can't say no.

The shark attacks everybody, sees everything as a threat, has no respect for boundaries, invades the territory of others, uses force when it isn't needed, and doesn't plan his attacks. He's reactive and impulsive.

The bear, on the other hand, knows when to stand up for himself, knows when it's smart to back away, knows who is a real threat and who is a ridiculous enemy not worthy of his time or trou-

106

ble, is not afraid to take risks, knows when to stay out of dangerous territory, respects boundaries, and plans his attacks so there is a better chance of success.

"When you get angry," says Sandra J., "which one are you most like? What's your style? It may be that you're a little bit of all three, or maybe you're more of one than the other."

Elizabeth: "It depends on the situation. Sometimes I'm quiet and sometimes I'm waaaaaaaaaaahhhhhhh! And it depends on the person who you're angry with."

But overall, which would she be: mouse, bear or shark?

Elizabeth: "Bear, I think. I'm pretty assertive. I'll yell, sometimes, but I won't take it too far. And when I don't care about something, I'll just walk away."

Well, that's what Elizabeth thinks she's like. What do the others think she's like?

Curt: "I think she's more passive. She lets things go by."

Elizabeth: "If it's no big deal, I'll let it go by. But if it affects me, I'll get my words in."

Good point, says Sandra. And it illustrates something important: sometimes we judge people by their actions. But we can rarely know their motives. So, if Elizabeth lets something slide, one person might think she's being a wimp, when really she's just decided that the situation wasn't worth getting excited about. Looks like a mouse, but is really a bear. "So," says Sandra, "you choose your battles?" "I'm not easily annoyed, but when I'm annoyed, get off my toes."

Sandy, what about you?

Sandy says she's a mouse. Very passive. "I let everyone do things for me, and I don't care what happens to me. I let things go when I shouldn't." Never a shark? "I can yell and punch and kick," says Sandy. But only when she doesn't get her way or "if I can't get my point across."

107

And what do the others think? Stew thinks Sandy is aggressive, definitely a shark. "Especially in the morning," says Bob. "She can be evil in the morning." Elizabeth thinks Sandy is assertive. "Yah," says Grant, "but assertive has to do with respect."

Sandy would like to add this: "If it don't work, forget it. But if it's worth it, I'll get my big mouth in there. When I think things should be going my way and they're not, I'll get assertive." And she'd like everyone to know that she can get her feelings out. She and Elizabeth have become friends here in the jail and Sandy says she can talk to Elizabeth about her feelings. "But with adults, forget it."

The verdict?

The verdict, all around the room, is that Sandy is more a shark than a mouse or a bear.

"I am not!"

"You're being aggressive right there." Grant grins.

The point here? Well, most of us construct a picture of ourselves and believe it to be true. "We create ourselves, or we try to," says Sandra. But the person we think we are may not be the person the rest of the world sees. The rest of the world sees our actions, our behaviour, not our motives. And, sometimes, blinded by our image of ourselves we can't see our actions for what they are. "We're not very good observers of ourselves. We want to fit the image of ourselves that we think is perfect." But others don't see our internal image. They see only our actions. "We have to be aware of how we seem to other people." If we behave like sharks, then we'll be treated as sharks. And if we think we're mouse-like when in fact we're sharks, then it's impossible to change the shark-like behaviour that lands us in trouble, and in jail.

Which is all we have time for, today.

Next time? "We'll deal with criticism," says Sandra. "And we'll learn some techniques for dealing with aggression. And we'll talk about the importance of expressing our needs."

A few moments later, in her office across the hall, Sandra talks about today's lesson, and where it fits in her anger management course: "I'm trying to ultimately get them to clue in to what's going on before they explode. So far, they've learned to identify the physical signs their bodies give them." When the kids are reaching the boiling point they may feel their jaws getting tense, they may get a knot in their stomach or a tightness in their throat, their heads may start pounding. "And when they feel that, they know they're pretty close to blowing. It's pretty late in the chain, but they can still try to make a choice." The choice would be to do something other than attack someone or commit some other kind of crime.

"They've also learned that their thinking is going to influence the way they feel and the way they respond. We spent some time having them identify the kinds of aggressive thinking that escalates their behaviour." An in-house example: if they get a time-out, instead of sitting on the floor fuming about 'what a jerk the staff is' — which will only fuel the fires of anger and rage — they learn to change their thinking altogether. How do you stop that kind of thinking? "You have to recognize it, first. Then you push it out of the way, you put in another thought, a calming thought. And we role-play that. We create a situation where someone is very angry and one person would have aggressive thoughts and another would have calming thoughts. And then they have to practice doing it.

"So, really, it's getting them to see that they control their thoughts. Their anger doesn't control them. They're not their anger. Anger is an emotion that is neutral and can be very beneficial. But you control your feelings."

Sandra also teaches them to know which kinds of events or thoughts will serve as triggers for their anger and their violent behaviour. She tries to show them that it's not the trigger which causes the violent action, but their perception of the trigger. Example: someone may not like Sandra. " 'Here comes Sandra. I hate her. She makes me mad.' But another person likes Sandra, and when they see me coming down the hall they're very happy to see me and feel very calm. I don't change.' " Their reaction is based on the way they're thinking about her. "And it's trying to get them to understand that concept, that they're in charge of how they deal with situations and how they deal with their anger. Really, the goal is to teach them to manage their anger themselves, to be aware of what triggers them and how they think and how their body responds and how they can change that cycle.

"So, we've learned some tricks. When you feel yourself thinking angrily or when you feel the adrenaline coming on, what do you do? Simple things." Sandra has taught them to breathe deeply. She's taught them to think pleasant thoughts, imagine places where they'd rather be, people they'd rather be with. She's taught them to count backwards, to tell themselves to cool it, to calm down and, with the kids who are a bit more advanced, to think of the consequences of whatever action they might be contemplating.

On a somewhat higher plane, Sandra has taught the kids the value of speaking their minds. Almost always, angry outbursts and violent behaviour can be traced back to a communications breakdown: the kid has failed to tell someone what he wants or needs, or he's expressed his feelings but no one has listened or responded. "Then we start with the negative thinking: 'nobody understands me,' 'he's such a jerk' and then the body starts responding or reacting to that. Clear, respectful communication, being direct, is one way of dealing with aggression and changing that cycle. Most of our kids think they're very direct, but they're not. They're very aggressive or they're very passive. They don't know how to say 'I'm really sad' or 'I'm really ticked off' or 'I don't think I deserve this time-out.' They don't know how to do that. They'll sit and they'll pout and they'll stew about it and then they'll swear at the staff." And whenever possible, Sandra illustrates her point by having the kids play the roles. The beauty of role-playing is that the kids use their own language which is almost a foreign language. "I don't know their language. I talk to them in very adult, probably very therapeutic language." But when they're performing in these little mini-dramas, they revert to the language of the street. And then there's an 'oh, yah' moment where they get the point.

And where does Sandra J. go from here?

"Well, I'll be teaching them how to handle criticism." Because criticism isn't something many of them can handle. Most of these kids have been yelled at and insulted and emotionally assaulted and so aren't all that adept at handling anything which calls their already fragile self-esteem into question. "Most of them have never experienced anyone who has encouraged them to be assertive and they probably think I'm from another planet. I think it shakes some kids up, because then they'll start comparing what some people actually live like and they'll say 'well, that's not what it was like in my house.' But it lets them know that there are other ways of dealing with criticism (than exploding in anger and kicking the furniture). "And it also lets them know that criticism can be very helpful." Sometimes not. But if someone is being critical just to be mean, or is being critical in order to manipulate them, then Sandra will give them the tools to handle that kind of criticism without blowing up.

In short, she wants to turn them into bears. "And I have to warn them that being assertive doesn't mean that you're always going to get what you want. Some of them misinterpret it and think assertive means 'hey, you, listen to me.' And it doesn't always get them what they hope it'll get them. But at least it'll get them some self-respect, because they'll know that they're trying and they have some integrity and they're letting people know where they're coming from."

She pauses and thinks about what she's been saying. And then says this: "But probably in their world, who cares?"

3:12 p.m. ——————————————————————

The smiling Job Club kid comes down the hall, bucket in hand. In the bucket, soapy water. Two other kids, two other buckets. Recreation director Mike D. hands out three pairs of rubber gloves and assigns each of the kids a bathroom. The goal: clean the tiles and the grouting between the tiles, and earn some money. Minimum wage. "If the kids don't have money, they can't buy batteries for their walkman." A walkman without batteries is just about the worst thing that can happen to any kid. Worse by a factor of ten for a kid in jail. Plus, if they have money in their 'bank account,' they can buy things at the tuck shop. Money is power. And it's the only kind that matters at the tuck shop counter.

"Each of the kids, once they reach Level 4, is free to apply for a job. Once they apply, I'll sit down and interview them. I'll ask about prior work experience, why they want a job. I try and see what their rationale is for working, how enthusiastic they are. And then I start them working. It's just like any other job process.

"I see it as a good training ground for when the kids are older and they have to go on real job interviews and work under someone who's giving them direction. It helps them get used to a job in the real world, a real 9-to-5, 40-hour a week job.

"As far as outside jobs, the only real experience most of these kids have had is maybe some yard work, cutting lawns on the side, but no real jobs.

"We just started a couple of weeks ago, and so far it's very positive. I don't know whether they're enjoying the jobs I've got them doing but they're definitely motivated and they're doing a good job.

"I pick the jobs. Today it's bathrooms. Soon we're going to be repainting the lines for our basketball court because those have been covered up. They're losing their out-of-bounds lines. Then, cutting lawns, weeding the gardens and, hopefully if we can get the space in one of the yards, making a flower garden. I'll use the kids I have right now who are eligible to work one or two hours a week. We'll put in our hour between three and four. As other kids reach Level 4 and Level 5 and apply I'll hire them on as well and hopefully my work-force will grow to include everybody."

The kids know they'll get fired if they don't do the job, right? "Yes." And Mike is the terminator? "Yup, I'm the terminator."

The Terminator and I stop in the doorway of Bathroom #2. How's the worker doing?

"This is his first day and so far he seems pretty eager. He's working pretty hard. Glad to be working and making money. The kids have tuck every once in a while, so the money allows them to buy pop and chips. If they go on temporary releases, they can take the money to the mall. Or if they're going to see a movie then they're allowed to use it for that."

Pat: "It's really caked on there."

Mike: "Maybe I'll try to get some scrub brushes for you and you can use those."

Pat: "Okay."

3:30 p.m.

Sign on the wall:

Quiet Time

*1. When coming up for quiet time all residents
go directly to their rooms to start quiet time routines.*

I.E. <u>Do Not</u>

> *— Ask for something from your closet.*
> *— Ask to go to the washroom or
> brush teeth.*
> *— Ask for a phone call.*
> *— Stop and talk to staff.*

*All these needs will be attended to when the cart staff
comes to your room.*

Here comes the cart. Larry R. is driving. The cart looks like one of those aluminum affairs stewardesses push up and down the aisle of an airliner. On top, some pads of yellow lined paper, a box of crayons and pencils, a stack of envelopes. Below, fourteen slots and in each slot, things belonging to each of the kids: papers, books, tapes — things they are permitted to have in their rooms during quiet time.

Larry raps at Stew's door and then pulls the curtain back. "You want anything from the cart?" Yup. Stew wants some paper. "One sheet or two?" "Two." And a pencil. Plus, Stew wants to know what happened to the things that were in the slot from the last time he was in residence here. Which was last week. "Didn't last very long out there, did you?" Stew shakes his head. "A day." He was no sooner out than he was back, awaiting trial on a charge laid the day he got out. "I'll see if I can find them, Stew, but I think you took everything with you when you left."

114

Larry makes a notation of the things Stew has taken into his room. At the end of quiet time, he'll go door to door, gathering up the things the kids have received. The list has to match. Exactly. If so much as a piece of paper is unaccounted for, everything comes to a stop until it's found.

Stew goes back into his room. The door clicks shut. Larry carries on down the hall. Rap rap rap. "Want anything from the cart?"

No. But Fred wants to make a phone call.

Larry: "Right this minute?"

"Yah. Right this minute."

Larry: "Who do you have to call?"

"My girlfriend."

Larry: "Right this minute?"

"Yah. She told me right now, because she's going out. I'm allowed. I got permission. I just need someone to make the call."

The staff do the dialling, and they only dial the numbers which have been authorized by William B. The numbers are those of parents, guardians or others who are approved by the director. The staff dials, then waits out in the hall while the conversation goes on. The staff isn't supposed to eavesdrop on the conversation, but they have to make sure the kid doesn't quickly hang up on the first caller and dial someone he's not supposed to. Which has happened, kids being kids.

Larry: "Well, I'll tell you. I've got to finish doing this and then I'll come back and we'll take care of it. Okay?"

"Okay."

3:33 p.m. ────────────────────────────

Mike D. heads to the bathroom, at the far end of the hall, to see how Curt is doing. Curt is down to his T-shirt, his long-sleeved shirt hanging over the knob of the bathroom door. He's standing in his socks in the tub, scrubbing.

"Are your feet wet?"

"Yah. But it don't matter. I got more socks."

"I'm not worried about wet socks. I'm worried about you slipping. It's a safety matter."

Curt slides back and forth in the tub, smiling. "It's fine. I won't slip."

Mike: "How's it going?" Curt: "I'm done." Mike: "You're done? I can't believe you're done. You've got this whole bathroom to do. Is it coming off?" Curt: "It's hard. I don't got no fingernails." Mike: "Well, just try to scrub the cracks as best you can. I'll try to get some scrub brushes to get some of the tough stuff out." Curt: "Want me to do the tiles too?" Mike: "Try to get between the tiles as much as you can, but you have to scrub 'em down. It's looking good. You like this better than weeding the gardens?" Curt: "Yup." Mike: "Do you like it better than washing windows?" Curt laughs. "Yah," he says, "I like this."

3:48 p.m. ————————————————————

"Hey Frances." Bob is in the doorway of the room where he's spending quiet time. He's used his two pieces of yellow-lined paper to make two airplanes. One is long and thin, like a Concorde, the other is short and wide-winged, like some kind of stealth jet. He lets go with the Concorde. A direct hit. Bob giggles. Then he ducks. Frances is a pretty fair hand at flying paper planes too. Bob picks up his plane and darts back into the lounge. A second later, the plane flies out the door. Crash landing in the hall. From the lounge, more giggling. Then, a head out the door frame, a big-toothed smile.

Frances makes her way to the other end of the hall, checking windows as she goes. When she gets near the staff office at the far end, Fred comes out of the library room, where he's made the telephone call. "Hey, Frances, can I touch base with you?"

There are all kinds of phone calls. Happy calls. Business calls. Upsetting calls. Fred and Frances sit knee to knee and talk of troubles on the homefront. After a few minutes of inaudible conversation she says, "Well, it's worth a try, getting back together."

Curt is in the doorway of his bathroom, limp rag in a rubber-gloved hand. "Hey Larry, nice shoes." "Yah," says Larry, "you keep working and earn enough money and I'll take you downtown where you can buy a pair just like them. Real moon shoes. Catch this." Larry moonwalks down the hall, to prove his point. Curt leans against the doorframe, waiting for The Terminator to check out the tiles.

3:52 p.m.

Frances E. opens Grant's door. She leans against the doorframe and keeps the door at bay with an upturned toe. Grant is sitting on the stool at his desk. Frances is not pleased about something that's happened a while ago, and she means to tell him.

"You can't lie to people. And you can't be so manipulative. Do you know what I mean? Whatever's in your way, you destroy, and you just can't do that. You've got to learn to talk through your frustrations so you don't feel like destroying things, and hurting people. You think about that. All right?"

Grant looks at her and then looks down and nods his head. "Good."

Frances backs out of the doorway. The door clicks shut.

One of the Job Club workers is sitting down on the job, on the edge of the bathtub. Staffer Barb C., just coming on shift, stops at the bathroom doorway. "When's your trial?" The trial is next week. "If they don't remand you." "They better not. I just want to get it over with." "Well, good luck."

Mike appears in the doorway, checks the tiles. "Hey, looks good. You've done a good job."

Time to put away the rag, the bucket, and the rubber gloves. Rec time.

Lining up, Fred turns to have a word with me. He wants to know about the book, whether I'll be putting his name in it. I tell him that won't be possible. He asks if I could put his nickname in it. "Everyone knows me by that name." I tell him if he's that famous then I couldn't use the nickname either, because I'd be identifying him and breaking the law.

He thinks about this for a minute, chewing.

"Shoot me one of your cards. When I get outta here I'll come around and see you, tell what this place is really like."

Staffers Sid G. and Joe C. are keeping an eye on all this.

"You oughta sleep here one night, find out what it's like. Sandbag pillows, sandbag mattresses. I'm 16 and I feel like I'm 60. Crick in my back all the time. And the rash. See this?" He touches the side of his neck. "My whole back's like that. Got the rash. And these words: 'inappropriate behaviour' 'be responsible for your actions.' Man you hear them words so often you start talking to yourself and sayin' them words." He slaps the sides of his head with both hands. "It makes you crazy. The rooms make you crazy. Which means you're crazy 80 per cent of the time, because you're in there 80 per cent of the time. You oughta come in here and spend a day just like we do. Find out for yourself."

CURING CRIMINAL KIDS

It's hard to get William B.'s words out of your mind: "We've got a lot of throw-away kids in here." It should come as no surprise that, as William B. says, these kids "have a lot of anger boiling in them" and come equipped with "very short fuses." Light the fuse, stand back and watch. What happens next is pretty predictable. Always the weak one, always the victim, when a kid like this boils over, he'll likely take it out on the nearest handy target. Someone a little weaker, a little smaller, a little more defenceless than himself. An elderly lady with a purse, a kid with a candy bar, a clerk with a cash register full of money, a woman alone in a parking garage.

William B. understands the sequence. But the kids who turn up in his jail can check their excuses at the door. Criminal kids have to come to grips with whatever ails them, or hurts them, and they have to learn to change their ways. At a minimum, they must change their ways. Easy to say, tough to achieve.

"Traditional therapy, psycho-analytical or psycho-therapy, one-to-one counselling, just doesn't work with most of these kids," says William B. "They aren't terribly interested in examining themselves. Not many are terribly verbal, so they don't seem to benefit from traditional therapy." Another fundamental reason traditional therapy won't work is that it plays right into the hands of criminal kids. Traditional therapy posits that you behave the way you do because of the things which happened in your past. Sounds good to most of these kids. 'I was abused, therefore. . .' Classic criminal thinking. "They don't need any more excuses for their behaviour," says William B. "They already have a whole series of excuses and rationalizations. We try to help them understand the dynamics of their life. 'Yah, you were abused. I understand that. It's very painful and very hurtful and we can talk about that. But you can't use that as an excuse to hurt other people. You must stop abusing people. And we must talk about how to help you stop hurting other people.'"

The jail staff can reach some of these kids more easily than others. "They have a depth of character and you can tell that if you have them here long enough," says William B. "With them, it's usually a matter that they've made some bad friends and some bad decisions." As supervisor Penny B. says, "they're nice kids who made a mistake. Some of them have made very bad mistakes. But they have good qualities, and that's what the staff is working on." William B. says, "In many of these kids there's a decent core. It sounds surprising, I know. My dad, when I told him that, he shook his head and said 'William, if they were decent kids, you wouldn't have them in there.' But they are. A lot of them are acting up and it's in reaction to something that's happened in the family. Some of them have missed out on that healthy nurturing that they needed. With some of them, it's a matter of their environment. With some, they've just made bad decisions. With some, maybe it's innate."

If the staff can see that decent core in a kid, they can work with that kid. The key ingredient is the ability to develop relationships with other people. If the kid can do that then, at least at some level, he can empathize with another human being. If this is so, then it's likely he will be able to feel badly for what he has done to another human being. As William B. puts it, "we massage that guilt and get them thinking of life in a different way than they've ever thought about it before." Some hope, however pale.

Even with these malleable kids, change doesn't come easily. "Some of these kids can be very repulsive to deal with," says child psychologist Janet Orchard. "They're rude and hostile and rejecting of a lot of adults' overtures, so they alienate everybody. And they can alienate counsellors quite well."

Even if you get past the repulsive exterior, you'll have some tough psychological sledding ahead. Bear in mind a lot of these kids have raped women, they've murdered their parents, they've beaten up little kids; they've knifed people and put the boots to people, they've burned places down and blown places up. Remorse is neither a word nor an emotion they'd know anything about. In some cases, just the opposite. "Some of these kids have a way of explaining away their behaviour against other people in terms that satisfy them, that makes it seem as though it was okay to do what they did," says William B. "To me and you it may sound pretty bizarre and bent, but these kids have a way of explaining it that makes it right."

Example: Kid does a B&E. In and out, nobody cut, shot or tied up. The kid can't, for the life of him, see why everyone's getting their shirt in a knot. "So, you try to help him fill in the blanks." William B. talked about the little child who lived in that house. "She can't sleep at night, now, because she's afraid someone's going to come in and steal her." A connection between action and consequence came as news to this kid. "He listened and he finally said 'I didn't think of that'." Most of them don't, and don't want to. "You talk to some of these kids and they'll tell you 'nobody was victimized. There was nobody home. And besides, they're insured. They'll get all their stuff back'. And that makes perfect sense to them and it's hard to argue with. So, we choose to argue, to challenge them on their thinking."

Every time a kid is convicted, the judge ensures a victim impact statement is read into the record. The victims state, in their own words, how the crime affected them. William B.: "A lot of these kids don't read or hear the victim impact statements. So Sandra (the jail's social worker) will get the statement and read it to them. Those are the kinds of things we do to get them thinking about what they've done because they're so good at explaining it away. It's quite scary how little empathy they have for other people. That's a striking feature of many of the kids who come through here. Most of us would never want to hurt anybody. But these kids who come through here could care two hoots."

A little outrage never hurts. Jail supervisor Frank M. never lets go the outrage he feels over the crimes these kids have committed: "We had a child in here who was charged with a very violent assault and rape and I remember thinking, 'How am I going to deal with this kid?' because it was such an outrageous crime. I had a very tough time with it. The only thing that saved me was seeing the face." Frank went to the floor first thing in the morning, watched the kid as he went through the morning routines, forced himself to deal with the person, the human being, rather than with just the details of the crime. "You don't lose your sense of outrage over the crime. You have to keep it alive, but keep it in check, too. You have to be able to call that up when you need it, especially when these kids say 'there's nothing wrong with what I did'. We see it as our responsibility to call up a little bit of that outrage and speak for the victim when we're working with these kids. We have to challenge what they're thinking and challenge their values, almost from the victim's point of view."

The arguing and the challenging happen in a number of ways and toward some very specific ends. Bear in mind, this is a jail, not a treatment centre. But the staff know this may be a last chance, or a next to last chance, to reach some of these kids before they go on to a life of adult crime. No one has been able to reach these kids yet, but no one else has had them as such a captive audience, either. So there's an opportunity here, and there's an urgency.

The goal? Supervisor Frank M. says, "We believe very strongly in the concept of self-mastery. That is the goal with these kids, to bring them to the point where they can start to make good decisions by themselves. Our goal is not simply to control their behaviour. That's just the start. This is a very controlled and structured environment. Kids who have all kinds of very severe acting-out behaviours and very anti-authoritarian attitudes have a real struggle with

122

that. But in most cases we get to the point where they at least know 'okay, these are the rules, these are the limits, I'm going to stick with it'. But that's just the start. Most people think, 'hey, you've done a good job with this kid because the behaviours have stopped and now he's listening to what the staff is saying.' But that's only external control. What we're really working toward is internal control. And so we have a process where we take that external control and get them to internalise it."

Psychologist Janet Orchard works with troubled teenagers and with young offenders. "We try not only to teach them to care about how other people are affected by their behaviour, but to teach them how to think about the consequences of their actions. If you do this, what's going to happen? To you, and to other people? These kids don't do a lot of that. Delinquent kids just tend to think 'I wanna do it, so I'm gonna do it.' And in combination with not being terribly caring about other people's feelings, it gets them into a lot of hot water. So we do a lot of working trying to get them to stop and think. And ideally you try to teach them to stop and think and care about how their behaviour affects other people and why it's wrong. Minimally what you hope to do is to get them to stop and think 'okay, if I do this, I'll be in jail again. That's not nice for me, so I won't do it.' "

So, there's the goal. There's the theory.

How to achieve the goal? "There's no cure-all, no panacea for dealing with offenders." Alec Marks has been dealing with offenders, adults and kids, for more than 20 years. What he's come to understand, and what he and his staff practice at two group homes for young offenders, is "offenders need specialized treatment plans developed to match their needs. That's not something we in corrections have done well down through the years. For much of this century, until the last little while, we've been searching for cure-alls.

Sometimes we think it's longer prison terms, sometimes we think it's more rehabilitation programs, but we're finally beginning to realise that we need to match the treatment with the young offender's needs.

"Some programs work better than others. We know that, at least in group-home settings, programs that rely on the principles of behaviour modification show some success." Do this, you'll get this reward. Don't do it, and you'll earn this consequence. And so on. "Programs that rely on inter-personal relationships and just on that, where staff develop good relationships with clients, have not been as successful. A good rapport with the offender is meaningful, but it's not enough in itself."

What will work? "Programs that develop new thinking or allow the offender to change his or her thinking. Very often, the negative behaviours, breaking the law, are the result of inappropriate thinking or values that aren't fitting in with the rest of society. Very often these people are very selfish, they're unable to delay gratification, so they're operating at a pretty low level in their thinking. They're into pain and pleasure. Minimize pain, seek pleasure no matter what that means to the people around them and often that can be very destructive, just thinking about oneself and not worrying about others. They're probably going to end up breaking the law and hurting people. And they're not really going to care."

The goal, according to Alec Marks "is not to make the offender change his thinking, because you can't force someone to change. What you can do is set it up where they're put in an atmosphere where they can change. There has to be some will, some desire on the part of the offender, to change."

And this, as you can imagine, isn't always easy. "Most offenders are quite happy in the routine they're in. If you're at the pain and pleasure level, then you're seeking instant gratification and you don't care about the long-term effects of your actions. You're quite satisfied with that and it's just bad luck you got caught. 'I ripped off 32 houses and got caught once. Well, that's the cost of doing business.' So," says Alec Marks, "we want to put them in an environment where that type of thinking is challenged."

In practice, in the jail as well as in open-custody group homes like the ones run by Alec Marks, some of the arguing and challenging goes on in organized group therapy sessions, some of them mandatory, some of them not. The sex offenders are forced to take part in counselling programs run by psychologists. The jail's social worker, Sandra J., runs in-house group sessions dealing with victim awareness and anger management. But the vast majority of challenging and arguing goes on, day to day, in the classrooms, in the halls and in the lounges at the jail. As Sandra J. says, if anyone is going to make a difference with these kids, it's going to be the staff who deal with them, day in and day out.

Before they can make a difference, the staff has to make a connection. Something of a challenge since most of these kids have never met an adult they could trust. Would you pick a jail guard as your first friend? Well, some of these kids do. Which is nice. But the people who work in the jail aren't interested in becoming pals to the kids. They're interested in working with them, challenging them, changing them, helping them to make their own changes. And all of that rests on the premise the kids will trust them, and listen. Where to begin?

One of the first people kids meet when they enter the jail is nurse Cathy B., who does a medical assessment of every new arrival. "I find out about their lifestyle. If they smoke, if they drink, if they do drugs. I find out about their sexual activity — and they're very sexually active — and whether they've tried suicide and their family history. They'll tell me a lot. They're very honest. I ask about their medical history. I ask if they have a family doctor. Most of them say 'huh?' I ask about their dental care, their vision care." She gets mostly short answers to a lot of those questions. Very few have had medical care of any kind so, where necessary, Cathy will connect them with the medical services they need.

And the answers to all the other questions? "Most of the kids do drugs. I don't know the stats, but it's very high. They're very sexually active. A lot of them have eating disorders. Most of them started smoking at 10 or 11. Attempted suicide is very high, mostly slit wrists. A lot of them shun it off: 'I just took a few pills' but then you ask how many and it turns out it was quite a few. But they're usually with somebody when they try it and it really doesn't seem like a serious suicide attempt. They want to be found. They want the attention, and they want someone to help them. I think they're really wanting help."

Elsewhere in the community where the jail is located there's a centre whose staff treats kids who have attempted suicide. Cathy sees a big difference between the kids in that centre and the kids in the jail. The kids in the centre want to die. "But these kids (in the jail) don't want to die. They want to live. They want to be healthy and they want to stay healthy."

Over the course of their stay, Cathy will give them a crash course in the basics: sexuality, birth control, sexually transmitted diseases, drug and alcohol dependence, relationships, stress management, self-esteem, body image, cancer (almost all of them are worried about getting cancer, "but they say they won't quit smoking."). When the kids leave, Cathy gives them condoms, tells them where they can get tested for HIV, and hopes for the best.

A lot of the kids are surprised, first day in jail, that anyone would care. Especially a stranger. Especially a stranger who works in a jail.

"I think the first thing is, the staff are respectful of the kids," says supervisor Penny B. From that foundation the staff can start to build relationships. Like everyone else at the jail, Penny B. never forgets the crimes the kids have committed, but the crimes are not front and centre in her mind. "I think it would be difficult to work with the kids if that was the first thing on your mind. We're trying to get to know them. We try to focus on their positives; we can find something positive in every kid, and we focus on that. We have a kid who had a horrendous background, doesn't get along with his peers, is full of behavioural problems and yet he picks up on things quickly, he learns. So we tell him how smart he is and how fast he learns. And that makes him feel good. Then he begins, over time, to trust us because we're not focusing on his negatives. Probably all his life he's heard what a bad kid he is, he was treated like a bad person and so he sees himself as a bad person. We have a youngster who can't handle a compliment, can't handle it. Probably never got one in his life. So we just look for any positive we can find."

"Sometimes," says psychologist Janet Orchard, "you can build a relationship and you've got the kid kind of thinking you like him." For a lot of these kids, this is a first. It's also a little suspicious. "A lot of these kids, nobody has ever liked them, so why would you like them? If you can point out to the kid that you see things in him that are good and interesting and appealing and worth finding out about, sometimes that can hook a kid into thinking 'I'll give it a run here and see if the other things you're saying are worth listening to as well.' "

"Kids a lot of times will say 'you hate me' or 'you don't like me because I did that,' " says supervisor Frank M. His standard response? " 'No, it's not that I don't like you. I do like you. But I really don't like what you did.' So we separate it for them. A lot of these kids have horrible self-esteem and they link what they're doing

with who they are. They've been called 'bad boy,' they've been verbally abused and emotionally abused and so we have to separate it
for them. When you form a relationship with the child, you see the
good things about them as well as the act they committed. One of
the things we have to do is separate the child from the behaviour,
without ever forgetting that behaviour."

So, show respect. And, as staffer Larry R. says, demand it in
return. In order to earn that respect, you've got to be firm, you've
got to be fair, and you've got to be consistent. "Initially, when they
come in, they're very testing. You ask them not to do something and
they'll do it. You ask them again not to do it and they'll do it again.
Or they'll have an inappropriate conversation, almost borderline,
just testing to see what they can get away with. Hopefully, by establishing the guidelines, you'll slow them down. You make very clear
expectations and you follow through and you make them make the
choices."

The key is to be consistent in your demands, consistent in
your praise of those who make good choices, and consistent in making kids face the music when they make lousy choices. And you have
to be fair. Pull this off, you've got the beginning of a relationship.
"Hopefully," says Larry R., "if they can establish a relationship with
some of the adults around them they'll start building up a little bit
of trust. I don't know whether these kids will ever totally one hundred percent trust anybody, really. But until you establish some level
of trust, the control doesn't come down." And if the kids want to
control the situation, they aren't going to get very far in changing
their behaviour, or their attitudes and beliefs.

These kids have very good reasons for not trusting adults.
The adults who weren't beating them, or sexually molesting them
or humiliating them were probably just not paying attention. For
some of these kids, food is not something you expect to find in a

fridge, or on a table. Clean clothes aren't something they've become accustomed to find in their bureau drawers. A lot of them have spent many a night on a park bench or on the back seat of a parked car.

"We know these kids aren't going to develop trust until their needs are met. So," says supervisor Frank M., "we put a great deal of energy into making sure they're being nurtured. We make sure they get all the food and clothes they need. We make sure they're warm and comfortable, even when they've earned consequences (for their actions). There's a big effort to make them comfortable. They could be exhibiting some terrible behaviour, but our first response is to make sure they're safe; we protect them, and that shocks them. But what we're doing is sending out a recurring message: you're going to have your needs met. And what happens over a period of time is they come to trust their environment." This is something new and different for a lot of these kids.

If the kids aren't in an environment they can trust, they'll simply revert to their old ways: doing what they've been doing to survive out in a criminal world. Establish the trust, you can start to teach them how to live in the world the rest of us live in and make decisions which don't turn people into victims.

"You're creating a nurturing environment, which really confuses a lot of them," says Frank M. "That really comes in under their radar. Even the kids who are looking for power struggles, they don't even realize what we're doing until all of a sudden they're starting to develop trust in us because all their needs are being met.

"One of the basic needs of these kids is the need to feel safe, especially the kids with a history of horrendous abuse. A lot of our security procedures are geared for the safety of everyone. We make a point of telling the kids it's not just for the safety of the staff. It's for their safety as well. That's why we have one kid in a room." If one kid loses control, starts yelling and swearing, refuses to toe the line, all the other kids get sent to their rooms. "A lot of times they'll complain: 'I didn't even do anything, and I've gotta go to my room'. But we let them know it's just to keep them safe, that if something does happen, they're not in any danger. And they know they're not going to be victimized by the other kids. Some of them have come from settings where the staff have turned their back and somebody has victimized them. So they need to know, and after a while they get to feel, that that's not going to happen to them here. And that makes them feel safe."

Here's a funny story: you take a kid from a maximum security jail on a temporary release. The kid's earned the privilege because he's been working hard on his behaviour and he's been making good decisions and the staff feel he can be trusted to go out. To the mall, maybe, with a staff member at his side. "The first time out of the building, they get very anxious because that sense of safety and security isn't there any more. Very strange. And at that stage, it's the staff who are anchoring them. They've got a relationship."

This is not something that is going to happen if a kid comes in for two weeks, or a month. But if the kid is here long enough, six months, a year, you can start to undo what took 12 or 15 years to create.

"If a youngster's experience was that adults aren't to be trusted because they hurt you, then we'll attack that," says the jail's director, William B. "We'll say, 'all right, why don't you trust adults?' and the kid will say 'because they hurt me' and then you can say 'have I hurt you?' and he'll say 'no' and then you can say, 'well, I'm an adult and I haven't hurt you and I won't hurt you and you can trust me, so maybe you can trust other adults, too.' With some of them, it works."

The object, as Frank M. has said, is twofold: put a stop to the kids' anti-social behaviour and teach them how to control their own behaviour. "It involves testing it, removing the restrictions along the way to see how they handle making these decisions on their own. I won't say 'do this or you're going to get a time-out'. That's a threat. What we do is explain the cause-and-effect consequences. We say to them: 'You need to make a choice. This will happen if you do this. And this will happen if you do that.' And of course, we're choosing the options. But it's a very fundamental step in letting them know they've got some control in the scenario. They're going to be making the choice. And then we broaden that out as it goes along. The staff add in more options, and they'll stand back and let the kids make the wrong choice. Getting internal control is a very gradual process. It takes failures along the way and you need support in place to help you deal with those failures. The lower functioning kids need a lot more support and a longer period of time before they can start to internalize. Even then, some of them can only go so far.

"We're not just regimenting what the kids have to do. If the kids have complaints we listen, and then deal with them. It's much easier to lock them up and leave them. Much easier to 'do what I say' type of thing. But we stress role modelling and democratic decision making, problem solving. It's a process. And a lot of it has to do with the thinking process.

"So," says Frank, "a lot of our energy goes into repetitive processes that get the kids used to making decisions. Our basic think aloud system has four steps: what's the problem; what can I do to solve the problem; what's the best choice; how'd I do? Very simplistic. But through repetition they get a sense of the fact that things don't just happen, that they can actually think about what they're going to do next rather than act impulsively."

Isn't this taking place a little late in the day? After all, this is the kind of thing most kids learn when they're, what, two or three?

"These are kids who didn't get limits and rules at the early stages of their development. They never learned how to deal with those things and move on, so they've been dealing with it their whole lives. We have to deal with that before they can start to gain some control (over their actions). They have to learn to control themselves enough so they can fit within social norms or limits, limits that have to do with respect of others. And they have to learn there are limits in life and they're going to have to deal with that. These kids don't know how to adapt to them because they didn't learn that when they should have. Normally kids start learning about limits when they reach the terrible twos. That's when kids usually learn the meaning of the word 'no.' That's when they're going to be testing the limits. It's a very critical period in child development because if you're too controlling with them then, they don't develop any initiative, they don't learn to explore, they're very withdrawn, and so become kids who don't want to take any risks. They become passive. They're not assertive enough." And if they don't have any limits imposed on them, then they wind up, like these kids, doing whatever comes into their minds. Laws or no laws.

"It's a very delicate part of their development," says Frank M. "And some of these kids have such horrendous backgrounds that not only did that not happen properly, but all kinds of other terrible stuff happened." So the staff has to retrace the steps back to that stage when these kids were two or three. "That's where they're still at, developmentally. Physically, they're adolescents and we're dealing with adolescent things, so they're dealing with all these stages of development at the same time. It's very confusing for them."

How best to work with these kids? Child psychologist Janet Orchard says, "you have to be able to find the positives and to make progress where you can, try to penetrate that hostility and see through that, see that somebody might want to get better and do better. Some people are better at doing this than others, at getting through to these kids. Some people are charismatic enough as counsellors to be able to have a personal presence and power to hook kids. That's one way to do it." There are as many other ways as there are child-care workers.

Watch Larry R. work with the kids and you find yourself smiling at the ease with which he works the kids to his advantage. One of the first things you notice is that the kids are often smiling, or laughing, at his jokes and his witty one-liners. And they're doing what he wants them to do.

"I'm non-threatening, that's the big thing. These kids all have trust issues, most of them have issues with authority figures. Other significant adults have been threatening to them." Or worse. "So, they don't trust people and when you don't trust people, you take care of yourself. In some ways, it's almost a natural thing. If you and I are feeling apprehensive, we'll take control of the situation ourselves, almost to protect ourselves. Some of these kids never had anybody to look out for them, so they'll take care of themselves. When they come into a place like this, they want to hang on to that control." So, putting them in a jail puts them nose to nose with the issues that already are driving them crazy. And they're not apt to be very happy, or very willing to be co-operative. It is, as Larry R. puts it, "a natural clash." Given that, the staff have to be pretty savvy. And they have to work hard at showing and gaining respect, establishing relationships with kids who don't much like them, and getting those kids to change.

If Larry's non-threatening, if he's joking and joshing with the kids, then he's less likely to get into power struggles with them. You'll never hear him say 'or else.' He lets the kids give themselves their own 'or else' scenarios. He just lays out the choices. Expectations, choices, consequences. Pretty simple. And Larry R.

says it all with a smile. "The humour, that's just me. And it really breaks the tension. I think I can joke around with the kids because my line is very clear. If you're going to break the rules, I'll hold you accountable. I used to think it was a disadvantage to be such a small guy (he stands about 5' 6"). But I'm not a threat to them physically and I'm not a threat the way I interact with them, and I think that helps."

"The staff have fun with the kids," says supervisor Penny B.. "They get out there and play basketball or whatever activity we're offering. There's always staff that will participate with them. They're almost on a buddy level and I've actually heard kids say 'I'm really going to miss the staff here, because you're more like a friend.' You know yourself, you want to please your friends and I think a lot of times the behaviours change because they want to please us. So it may start out that they're doing us a favour and then it works well for them and they keep that behaviour. Just the routines we have here help. I've had kids tell me that they went home on the weekend on TRs (temporary releases) and they were brushing their teeth after having something to eat in the evening which they never did before and the parents say, 'What are you doing?, you never did that before.' Just those little things, we condition them. And hopefully, they'll continue when they leave here." And when the positives don't work, and the kids have to be put in the time-out room to cool off, the staff never says 'you're a bad person' or 'you're stupid.' "We make sure it's what they've done that has resulted in consequences, not who they are. It's the act we don't like. And we're very, very patient with them. They can swear at us and tell us where to go and we'll say 'Fine, when you're ready to talk, we're here' and we let them work it out. Usually they calm themselves down, then we talk."

The staff certainly succeed in the first part of their objective. The kids are quiet, polite and pleasant, at least most of the time. But that's the easy part. In the jail, they're controlled. They're on a Level system and if they want any privileges, they have to work their way up that Level system. Some kids, even within that system, continue to be difficult, but the majority get into it: 'Well, I may as well make an easy stay of it.' Over time, being made to co-operate can lead a kid to the point where he feels like co-operating. At least you can hope it'll happen.

Larry R. thinks the jail itself is the reason some of the kids respond the way they do. "We have a lot of repeat offenders coming through here, a lot of returns. It's the best place they've had in their life. Three squares a day and nobody's gonna hit 'em. They have all the responsible adults they can talk to and after a period of time, the trust does grow. Very few will say 'I wanna stay' but it's on a lot of their minds. Look at the number who come back, and the number who start to have problems right before their release dates. They feel apprehensive about going back home because it's a chaotic place to be, or they're going out on the street or to a foster home and they don't want to go and they'll start acting up and what they're really saying is, 'Hey, I don't want to leave, help me out here.' "

Listen, again, to what Larry has just said: 'It's the best place they've had in their life'. 'I don't want to leave'. Larry smiles when the words are played back for him. And he smiles when I say that it's an horrific thing to suggest, that being in a maximum security jail is better than being free. "Yah. But you've been around here, now. You see that the kids look fairly happy, no matter how much we're parading them down the hallway. You've heard how much I natter at them and yet they seem genuinely happy. What's that say?"

What it says to Larry R. is that being in jail helps these kids and that even they, at some level, understand that. "It's a combination of a lot of things. It's the security. They know where they stand. We have very clear expectations. They know 'if I do this, I'll get this.'

Whereas at home if they don't show up for supper one day, they don't get supper or maybe they'll get a backhand across the head and the next time they're late, maybe supper's saved for them and they never know what to expect. It's all chaos. Here, everything is very clear. They can make their choices. The choices are more limited in here than out there, but ultimately the kids have to make the final decision. And I tell them, 'It's your call. I set the boundaries but within the boundaries you've got some decisions to make. You have a couple of minutes to make the decision.' The key is to stand back and let them make it. The minute you get in their face, they react. And that's what they want half the time." That's what they're used to. And that's what they like doing. If they can make an adult angry, they've succeeded in gaining control over that adult. "A lot of them are very good at finding your buttons and pushing them. It's part of that control thing. Power. Once they get your emotions involved then they're starting to succeed in gaining control over you." Which is the way they've learned, from an early age, to operate.

"Some of them are great con artists. That's how they've survived for years. If you stop and think about it, what makes a 13-year-old boy such a good con artist? Why does he have to be a con artist? How did he get to be so obnoxious? Well, things must have happened in his past. At some point there've been significant problems within the family that have had an effect on him: physical abuse, sexual abuse, emotional abuse which is extremely powerful. We see a lot of separated families, step-families, and all the issues that come into play there. It's a common thing. That's what I mean by dysfunctional families: lack of role models, lack of boundaries, no structure in the household. I mean, you tell me: what's a 13-year-old doing downtown at two in the morning?"

No surprise these kids wind up fearing the adults who have done these things to them. "And then it's natural to generalize that fear to all adults, teachers, police officers, social workers, everybody. So the people who want to help them can't help them because they don't trust adults in general and that, in turn, makes the peer group all that much more important to them." Which is why they're downtown at two in the morning.

So, Larry and his colleagues have their work cut out for them breaking through that wall of fear and mistrust. "Surprisingly, a lot of them do really well in here because of this structured environment. And I think they can see that. 'I'm doing this in here. I was doing that out there.' They realize their behaviour really stinks. I think after a while they do see the difference and they do see what this place does for them."

Psychologist Janet Orchard says you'll generally have greater success treating kids who come from families "where the parents have been more together, where there wasn't a long family history of criminal behaviour, where you could tell that the parents had tried their level best to support society's view of what's right and wrong, but were just having difficulties with the kid. At least you know the parents are going to keep trying."

Small victories. Some of the time. But they are not always easily won. Nor are they pleasant to watch. "The kids don't like to be held accountable for the things they've done," says William B. "And when we try to make them accountable for their actions, that's usually a trigger for violent behaviour. Often they get so angry it's beyond their ability to control it. And we just have to move them into a room where they have a time-out and cool off."

Sometimes, as William B. says, the staff can get the kids beyond their anger. "When we were kids and got angry, our mothers used to tell us to count to 10, right? By the time you counted to ten, you'd cooled down. Most of us learned that when we were very young. But these kids don't know how to do that. So we try to help them develop new ways of thinking, like counting to 10, which will help them control their anger. And if you're persistent, it will help. We try to help them resolve conflicts. We have a SNAP plan. Stop Now And Plan. What's the problem? What are my options in dealing with this problem? How well did I choose from among those options? How should I make a choice next time? So, you help them practice this kind of thing and if they're successful you reward them with points and when they accumulate so many points, they earn privileges. Maybe a pool game with a favourite staff, or a pizza night, or a trip to the mall, visit to a park (if they're eligible for temporary leaves). But they've got to earn these privileges, because they are privileges. This isn't the Holiday Inn."

"Some of these kids are really super kids," says staffer Larry R. "If you really look at someone, you can normally find some good in that person. When you provide an environment that's safe and secure, that's when their controls come down. That's when a 12-year-old starts to act like a 12-year-old, that's when you start seeing the kid in them. Some of these kids had to grow up pretty fast. But if they're here long enough, the barriers start coming down, and they become kids."

Supervisor Patricia P. is always taken aback when she walks into the kids' lounges on a Saturday morning and finds them silent and absorbed in front of the tube, watching Bugs Bunny. "Bugs Bunny! And you realize they're still little kids. Kids in big bodies, sometimes, which makes them dangerous. But they're still kids. And they often do things that younger kids would be doing: watching Sesame Street, or working on a puzzle. It's like they're trying to reclaim a part of their lives that they lost."

"Obviously," says Larry R., "they have stress and problems, they don't cope that well, they get aggressive and that always jolts you back. We do have some serious incidents here. You never forget that, for your own safety and the safety of the other kids. But some of these kids are really neat. Some of them."

Some of them are anything but. William B.: "With some of them, let's face it, the damage is permanent. There are those who leave here who we don't reach and maybe can't reach and who we know we'll read about in the paper once they're adults. You don't like to admit it, but you just do the best you can and then they leave."

Psychologist Janet Orchard: "It can be very discouraging. It's very hard to teach someone moral beliefs when they've reached 14 or 15 or 16 years of age with a value system that allows them to do what they want to do when they want to do it. You don't have much power in their lives anyway. We have to struggle with this, with how much influence we can have on someone's values. When the family tacitly supports delinquent activities, it's ridiculous to bring a child in (for treatment) even with the family, once or twice a week." They're going back into the same kind of environment you're saying they shouldn't be perpetuating."

How good a job is society doing, treating criminal kids and changing their view of the world?

"Probably pretty lousy," says Orchard. "The kids are really difficult to try to deal with by that point. So the percentage of success, in terms of reducing repeat delinquencies, is going to be small. We have to give ourselves a break and figure that even if we prevent that in a small percentage of the kids, then we've done a good job.

"We're starting to know the things that work. For example, setting up programs to deal with criminal thinking is a good idea. Because just modifying kids' behaviour isn't going to make any difference if they continue to believe the criminal things that are getting them into trouble. So we do know some stuff that's good. It's very, very hard to penetrate into the kids' outlook on the world.

Until you take them completely out of their environment and away from the social contacts that foster that (criminal) outlook, you have a hard time making any difference. In terms of coming in for outpatient treatment, for a lot of kids who are really criminal in their outlook, it's very unlikely to make a particle of difference. I think you need to have that kind of around-the-clock controlled impact on them to make a difference."

Even if you have that round-the-clock impact, getting to these kids isn't easy. And the ones who most need the help are often the most difficult to reach. "I'd say most of our kids have been emotionally abused," says the jail's social worker, Sandra J. "And they're usually very closed. Some of them will come in and tell you horror stories about what's happened to them, but the ones who start talking right away generally exaggerate. They may want you to feel sorry for them and they usually want to get something from you. But the ones with serious problems won't say anything until I've worked with them for a couple of months. With some, the closer they are to discharge the more they'll talk. You get the sense they feel if they don't get it off their chest now, they'll never be able to. Either that, or they feel it's safe to talk because they're about to leave and there's no way we can get too close."

Sandra J. says the kids who have been sexually assaulted tend to deal with that in patterned ways: "The girls are more likely to act out against themselves, the boys are more likely to act it out against others. We had one girl, she was a cutter. I asked her why she cut herself. 'I do it for fun.' I asked her, 'What's it do for you, when you cut yourself?' And she said she was feeling anxious. She didn't use that word, she said something like 'I was feeling shaky and then I cut myself and then I felt better.' I think maybe she was sexually abused. Often, they haven't talked about it with anyone. It takes a lot of courage to talk about it. It may be that they don't have the words for it. Or they may feel isolated. Especially the boys. It's so threatening to their sense of manliness. Even the physical abuse. It's like they're saying 'Am I going to wimp out and talk about this?' They get flooded with fear of their own feelings." And they're afraid of showing any signs of the weakness they feel, as a result of having been victimized. So rather than talk about it, and admit their fears, they'll tough it out. "They're very good at splitting that (experience of abuse) off from themselves. 'I forgot about that and I don't want to remember it.' They probably don't even know why they're cutting themselves or hurting themselves or acting out sexually.

"This one boy, the third time he came back, the day before he left, he finally talked about the sexual abuse he'd endured. This was a kid who always wanted the best." And Sandra had finally figured it out: "Why did he always want the best of everything? Probably because he felt like scum."

If the kids are this hurt and have buried their pain this deeply, it takes a long time for staff to get them to burrow down and deal with it. How long before you can start making some serious changes in the way such a child thinks? Janet Orchard: "I think you need to have the kids for a year before you start to see any difference, and you also have to have tremendous involvement with the family." It's not always possible. "Lots of times, by the time kids reach that age, families are very discouraged. They've been dealing with a lot of mayhem and they get really burned out, fed up, and disgusted." Other families won't get involved because it would bring them face to face with the abuse they've inflicted on their children. "So it's hard to effect any major change there."

Sometimes, as Alec Marks says, you have to be content with relatively minor victories. The executive director of New Beginnings group homes says, "The usual measure we use to see if we're successful is the recidivism rate, to see whether the person will get in trouble with the law again. That's not always the best measure. Let's say you have an offender who's been beating people up. Let's say he goes through a program, he's done his sentence, he leaves. Six months later, he ends up shoplifting and gets convicted. If you're looking at recidivism, that person has reoffended and by basic measures, he would have failed." But it doesn't take into account the fact that he didn't beat someone up. Nor does it look at the fact that he went six months without committing any crime. It may not look like success, but if the kid was beating people up every week before he went to jail, it's a huge success. "You have to look at more than what meets the eye," says Alec Marks. "You have to look at whether the person is committing less serious offences, or is committing offences less often."

Though the goal is to stop these kids from doing crime again, "realistically, we're trying to lower the recidivism rate, lower the frequency of contact with the police and the criminal justice system. That sounds like a pessimistic approach, but it's true."

You get them when the court sends them to you and you do the best you can to help the ones you can. "Our philosophy," says Alec Marks, "is that we don't give up on anyone. But we have this tiny group over here who show a lack of remorse, who lack any type of conscience. And this may be a group that no matter what we do we're always going to have some type of problem with them and, I hate to even say it, but in that group there's a percentage we're not going to be able to do a hell of a lot for. That's one of the sad, sad things about working in this field."

The jail's director, William B., agrees there are kids beyond the reach of his staff. "It's the ones who are iffy that we try to reach. They're the ones we can help, and change." How many victories? "It's hard to know because there's no follow-up." Once they're out the door, and William B. will have some further thoughts on this matter, they're beyond the staff's reach and sway. "But to do this work, you have to be hopeful. I've been here six years and I can tell you, it would be hard to come to work in the morning if we felt we weren't helping some of these kids in some fashion."

4:32 p.m. ─────────────────────────────

The lounge: in one corner, a four-handed card game is going on. Stew, Grant, Pat and Sandy are slapping down the cards, one after the other in a rapid-fire game of '13.' Elizabeth is off to the side, watching. In the other corner, Curt and Bob are playing a two-handed game in which you win if you get six pairs of cards.

Could be a scene from a summer camp, somewhere, or a private school. It's hard to reconcile these laughing kids with the crimes they've committed: crimes which had to be serious enough to earn them time behind locked doors. I say so to staffer Penny B. She answers, "A lot of these kids are nice. And some of the nicest kids have committed the worst crimes. A lot of them say they just got in with the wrong crowd. And these kids, the ones who've done the worst crimes, are the ones who do the best here. It's true. Sometimes, you look at them and you think all they need is a little parenting."

Curt is giving Bob the squinty eye. He's pretty sure Bob is cheating, but not sure enough to say anything more than "how come you get such good hands all the time?". A little later, his suspicions will be confirmed: Bob has some cards under his right foot.

Bob: "Put those cards aside."

Curt: "Sounds like a scam."

Bob laughs and shakes his head. "No. Go ahead. Just put them aside."

Curt: "Give me the cards. I'll do the shuffling."

143

Bob: "You lost and you're doing thirteen push-ups."

Curt: "We didn't agree on thirteen push-ups."

Staffer Joe C.: "You guys are supposed to agree on the rules before you start the game." He smiles.

Bob: "Do your push-ups."

Curt: "You didn't say anything about push-ups when we started."

Bob: "Hit the rug buddy."

Curt is spared by the dinner bell.

Penny B.: "Clean up. Then we'll go down for dinner."

Curt: "I just want to shuffle next game."

The kids put the cards down and head for the door.

Bob: "Penny, you should've seen what I ate at lunch."

Curt: "He had two servings, and the second one was bigger than the first. How much do you weigh, anyway?"

Bob: "A hundred and eighteen. How much do you weigh?"

Curt: "A hundred and four."

Bob: "I remember when I weighed a hundred and four."

Curt: "Back in the old days, eh?"

Penny B.: "Wash your hands, then we'll head down."

Sandy: "I already washed my hands."

Penny B.: "When."

Sandy: "A while ago."

Penny B.: "Think of all the hands that have touched those cards, and where all those hands have been. Think of all those little germs."

Sandy thinks maybe she'll wash her hands after all.

5 p.m. ——————————————————

The kids from B Group line up in the carpeted hall, single file against the wall. Staffer Penny, at the head of the line, starts walking backwards. Staffer Joe C. brings up the rear. Sandy, the newcomer, reaches up and touches the ceiling panels. Joe calls her name and when Sandy turns to look at him, Joe shakes his head. "Don't do that, please." Sandy looks a little puzzled, and surprised. Another rule she didn't know about.

Down the ramp and into the dining hall. We've arrived a couple of minutes sooner than Veronica expected, apparently. She and her co-worker are in the middle of a discussion at the table nearest the door. "And I was winning too." Veronica laughs and heads for the kitchen.

Bob takes a table by himself. Curt, Stew and Grant are at one table, Sandy, Elizabeth and Pat at the one beside it. Penny B. stands beside them, her back to the wall. Joe C. sits on the table near the window in the kitchen wall. Stew wonders out loud what's for supper. Veronica leans down on the counter, looking through the opening in the wall. "Roast beef on buns, potatoes and carrots." Stew isn't impressed, and says so. There's a ripple of comments around the room.

Penny B.: "I think you guys were all told today, no complaining."

Joe C. looks at Curt who is looking at him. "Go on up."

Curt doesn't need to be told twice. He's up and heading for the opening in the kitchen wall. "Meat?" "Yes please." "Potatoes?" "A little bit." "Carrots?" "Sure. Please." And when he takes the plate from Veronica, he smiles and thanks her.

Bob goes next. Then Sandy, then Pat. "Carrots, and some potatoes." "No meat?" Pat shakes his head. Stew: "Can I please have an extra bun?" Grant's turn. "Everything?" "Yes please." "That's what I like to hear." Veronica spoons another couple of potatoes onto the plate. Elizabeth, who is next and last in line, asks for a plate of carrots. "Just carrots?" "Just carrots." You want 'em, you get 'em.

Joe C. is talking, as he eats, about a trip he and his fiancée made to Niagara Falls. The kids are all ears. "We went on a boat right to the edge of the falls." Bob: "Why didn't you go under the falls?" "You can't. You'd sink." Bob thinks about it, for a couple of seconds. "Oh, yah." He grins. "And then we got our picture taken. We got all dressed up like cowboys. One of those black and white photographs that looks really old." "The sepia ones?" wonders Curt. "Yah," says Joe, "that's the word. Sepia." Grant says you can get those pictures taken out at the mall.

Stew: "Hey Veronica, can I get some mayonnaise?" "Sure." "What's for dessert?" "Your favourite." Veronica, who is leaning on the counter so she can see out through the kitchen window, says that when she went to Niagara Falls she had a picture taken in one of the tourist joints, a picture that made it look like she was about to go over the falls in a barrel. She dollops out some mayonnaise for Stew.

Joe looks at Grant's plate. Grant eats his food one item at a time. Carrots are all gone. He's working on the potatoes. "You're like me, Grant? Have to eat all the accessories first?" Grant smiles and nods, mouth full of food. Then: "Depends how hungry I am. If I'm going to McDonald's and I'm real hungry, I'll eat the Big Mac first.

Bob: "If I go out with my mom, Big Macs are her favourite." Bob looks at Joe, who's having a little fine-motor trouble. "Food attacking you, Joe?" Joe, wiping his shirt, smiles and says "yah." Joe's not alone. Getting roast beef with gravy in a bun from the plate to the mouth can be tricky. Curt.: "Can I have a couple of extra napkins, please? I'm having a difficult time." Joe nods. Curt goes to the counter to get some.

The kids at the other table are talking with Penny about their favourite food. Taco Bell and Big Macs are running neck and neck. Then Pat says something I can't quite hear, except for the words "since I had my freedom." He's speaking softly, and looking down at his plate. And the other conversation is picking up. Grant is still thinking about those pictures Joe and Veronica had taken in Niagara

Falls. "I had some relatives who had one of them pictures taken. It was really good. It made them look really old, eh?" Bob: "Can I have some more milk, please?" Grant: "The only way you could tell the picture wasn't old was, my uncle, he was wearing running shoes. They didn't have running shoes back in them days."

The dining room window faces the playpen. The kids in A Group are playing basketball. Three of them are in view. Rick and Fred are playing one-on-one. George is over by the fence, firing a basketball against the mesh with grim determination.

One by one the kids in the dining room ask permission to take their plates to the kitchen window. One by one, they're given the okay. Sandy the newcomer, is about to carry hers with the plastic cutlery still on it. "Put the knife and fork in there," says Penny, pointing to a cup in the centre of the table. "Oh." Another rule.

Dessert is chocolate pudding in styrofoam cups. One per customer. Bob: "Can I get some more milk, please?" Veronica, looking out through the window: "Like that pudding?" Bob: "Yah. It was awesome." "That's good. I'm glad you're eating. You didn't eat too much at lunch." "I was mad. I can't eat too much when I'm mad." Joe grabs a banana from the bowl of fruit on the table by the kitchen window. Peels the banana, then spoons some chocolate pudding onto it.

Outside, George is still firing the basketball against the fence.

"Hey. That's not fair." Sandy spots Joe's banana split. Sandy turns to Penny: "You said I couldn't do that." Penny looks at Joe's dessert. Joe looks up, grinning: "I didn't know that. Was there a reason, Penny?" Penny smiles: "I'll tell you later." Sandy is still eyeing Joe's chocolate-slathered banana: "You should give him a time-out, Penny." Curt: "We're going to tell your fiancée you're a bad influence on us, Joe."

Elizabeth is sitting across from Joe. She's giving him the fluttering-eyelash treatment. "Before I leave here, I'm going to give you a makeover." Joe: "You are, are you?" Elizabeth: "Yah. Hair, face, the works." Curt: "Pluck his eyebrows, like the women do?" Elizabeth: "Maybe." Curt: "I dunno why they do that. Pluck out all their eyebrows except for a couple of hairs, and then pencil new ones on. Penny, why do they do that?" Penny doesn't know. But she would like everyone to notice that her eyebrows are her own. Elizabeth: "You have really nice eyebrows, Penny." Grant: "Mine grow almost together. So I got someone to pluck out the hairs in the middle. It really hurt."

Dessert is done. Grant gets table-wiping duty. Penny presses the talk button on her walkie-talkie. "Penny to Sid. We're all finished. We're heading upstairs for clean-up. We'll call when we're ready to come out." "Sid to Penny. 10-4."

Delayed reaction: the kids are talking about the nutritional value of Stew's extra dollop of mayonnaise.

5:14 p.m.

The sun is lazing toward the horizon. Some high clouds drift west south west. This afternoon's activity: shooting hoops.

All the members of A Group are hanging around the hoop. All except George. George is down at the far end of the yard, keeping his distance. A sign of things to come.

The group has been unsettled all day. The omens were there, almost as soon as the kids came out of their rooms: sarcastic shots they fired at each other, the way they rolled their eyes, the demands they made ('I need to make a phone call,' 'when will we get our mail?') almost as soon as they came out in the hall, the way they strutted, the way they slouched. As Larry R. says, "You can pretty well tell first thing in the morning whether they're going to like you that day or not. Being demanding is one of the big things. A kid wakes up demanding, starts complaining, that's a pretty good indi-

148

cation." What you don't always know is what gets the chemistry bubbling. It could be there's some issue percolating just beneath the surface of the group itself, kids rubbing each other the wrong way, getting on each other's nerves. Or it could be one kid is having a tough time in his or her head, and is getting everyone else going.

Easier to find out if there's a problem in the group: the kids will snap at each other, and the issue will come to the surface. But if a kid is having a tough time, personally, then it's not so easy to get to the source. "You need to somehow get underneath that, but they don't like to talk about that a lot of times. So you've got to find ways of finding out what really is wrong."

Sometimes, it's pretty simple. "Sometimes," Larry says, "a kid is going to wake up and decide 'today, I'm going to be a jerk.' It's a matter of taking him aside and saying 'we're not going to put up with it.' A kid like that, he's been given clear-cut guidelines. If he acts up in the group, or is a negative influence on the group, he can be kept away from the group all day. This is a therapeutic approach, and if he's going to interrupt other people's treatment then he's going to be taken aside. It's a matter of nipping it in the bud."

Today? Who knows what got things going? But the signs aren't any more encouraging by the time the kids go out into the yard.

One sure sign: George is like a canary in a coal mine. Watch him, and you can pretty well tell what's about to happen. He's got the most sensitive antennae of any kid in the jail. He can sense, sometimes before the staff can sense it, that the group is coming unglued. He gets antsy. If there's one thing he can't stand, it's chaos. Given his background, which is about as chaotic as they come, this is no surprise.

Ever since the kids came out in the yard, he's been keeping as far from the others as he can get, trying not to make eye contact with

149

any of them, glancing at them now and then, turning to fire his bas-ketball against the mesh.

Barb C. has been watching George as he warily watches the group. She's been looking back and forth, from George to the group and back to George like a net judge at a tennis match. Time to make her move. She heads down to the end of the yard to have a chat with George.

Staffer Sid G. takes his cue. As soon as Frances heads toward George, Sid walks over and starts to chat with Norm and John. They've separated themselves from the group, too, and are standing with their back to the fence near the basketball hoop.

Walt and Mary are over near the picnic table. Rick and Fred are down by the hoop.

Rick and Fred are talking to each other. Hard to catch any-thing more than the occasional word, but the laughter which follows whatever they're saying has an edge. Hard and sharp. Walt and Mary seem to be picking up on whatever it is that's going on.

Staffer Sid has backed up to the perimeter fences so he can see all the kids, and Barb, at a glance. Whatever it is he sees, he does-n't like. He pushes the button on his walkie-talkie and a minute later staffer Dan E. pushes the mudroom door open, scans the yard, and goes over to stand near Norm and John. Sid is keeping his eye on Rick.

Rick has the basketball. He's also got an attitude, always seeming to smirk, always ready with a cutting comment. He's also got a temper. Not a great combination. He makes a move toward the hoop, but instead of shooting the ball, he wheels, suddenly, and fakes a move in Walt's direction, as though he's about to fire the ball at Walt's face. Walt's hands go up in a reflex action.

Staffer Sid is on the move: "Rick, take a time-out."

"Why?"

"You know why. Go over on the bench."

"I wasn't doin' nothin'."

"Go to the bench."

"Everybody else was doin' the same thing. Why pick on me?"

Sid G. stands his ground, bides his time.

Rick turns on his heel, heads for the bench which is down a few steps near the mud-room door. As he passes the dining room windows, he hammers a pane with the side of his fist. Not a smart thing to do, and also not a good sign. He's sitting down but he's also heating up. Fred has noticed and now he's making comments at the far end of the yard which we can't hear, but which Barb can. "Fred, take a time out. Over on that bench." She indicates a bench at the far side of the yard. Fred huffs and puffs, but he goes to the bench. Trouble times two. Sid moves in to be closer to the other kids and Dan stays right where he is, so that they are both between Fred and Rick.

Sid's seen enough to convince him a little more help might soon be in order. He presses the call button on his walkie-talkie, but keeps an eye on Rick, who's sulking on the bench. "Sid to Larry. Can you come out into the yard?" Better safe than sorry. Sid squats down so he's on eye-level with Rick, who is glowering on the bench. "You've got a time-out, and I want you to go inside to the time-out room. If you don't, there will be consequences. I want you to make a good decision, and you've got two minutes to make it."

Larry props the mud-room door open with his foot, takes a quick look around the yard, then focuses on Rick and Sid. Sid leaves Rick to mull things over, then brings Larry up to speed on the situation. Larry glances at the yard again. Rick is on the move, jumping up from the bench and turning to face the two staff. He's smirking, jutting his chin. "You want aggressive behaviour? Here's aggressive behaviour." He jumps up and kicks at the dining room window.

Kicks it again. Punches the window twice and, fists still clenched, goes toward Larry and Sid. He makes a quick move toward Sid who has his back to the wall, nowhere to go. Rick laughs: "Whaddya think I'm gonna do?" Then, quick as that, he turns and goes into the mudroom. Sid escorts him to the time-out room around the corner.

Fred hasn't missed a second of any of this. He's standing up on the bench at the far side of the yard. He's laughing, and turning around on the bench, arms outstretched. He's not saying anything, and he doesn't have to. "Sit down, Fred." Barb doesn't have to say it twice. Fred sits down with a thump, turns and flashes her a sneering grin.

Larry still has the mud-room door propped open. "I think we'd better move them in." He presses the talk button. "Larry to Penny. We're going to send you some residents. See them into their rooms." "Which way are they coming?" "Up the stairs."

"George. Come here."

"Did I do anything wrong?"

"No," says Larry. "You didn't do anything wrong. You're not being punished. I just want to make sure you're safe. All right?" "All right." Larry leads George through the mud-room and down the hall, opens the door leading to the stairwell. "Penny, you there?" "I'm here." "One coming up." Larry waits until he hears Penny talking to George. He goes back to the yard and motions for Walt, John and Mary to head inside, follows them down the hall, unlocks the door. "Three more coming up. See them into their rooms." Walt: "We in trouble, Larry?" "No, you're not in trouble. We just want to calm things down." "Good," says Walt. "I don't want to lose any points. I want to get a 50 today." "Keep working on it. You haven't lost any points here." Larry waits until he hears the door shut at the top of the stairs. He goes back to the yard, escorts Norm in, then goes back out. One to go. And Fred can be just as volatile and unpredictable as

152

Rick. "Fred, let's go." Fred gets up off the bench and swaggers across the yard. All show.

By the time the kids have been shown to their rooms, the jail's director is in the upstairs hall, along with more back-up staff. William B. heard all he needed to hear on the two-way radio in his office. Anytime anyone calls for back-up, William B. gets himself into the middle of things. He wants to know, first, how things unravelled. He wants to know, also, if everything was done that should have been done. He wants to be involved as the staff determine what consequences the kids will face for the things they've done. And he wants to know, lastly, if there's anything to be learned from this incident to help staff deal with the next one.

So, for the next fifteen minutes, with the kids safely in their rooms and Rick in the time-out room, the staff deconstruct the incident in the yard.

Sid G.: "When you're here, you learn to watch everything. You start seeing or hearing things, when people are whispering, you catch a word. You learn to scan and listen." When he saw Rick fake a throw at Walt, he didn't have to think twice about what he was going to do. "That's intimidating behaviour, for one, whether it's joking or not. You just don't do it here. You realize with young offenders that it could lead to something, especially if someone gets mad. We're always trying to stop things before they get started. It may seem like we go overboard, but you're better off being cautious instead of letting things go."

There was another factor: "A couple of days earlier Rick had done the same thing to another resident." And when Rick got a time-out for that, he kicked the basketball clear over the fence. "So I know the temper's there" and he also knew that if Walt had taken the fake the wrong way, there could have been big trouble, in a hurry. Rick's a manipulative kid, and he doesn't accept responsibility for anything he's done, including the crime which landed him in jail. "He tries to deflect everything. You saw it yourself: saying that he hadn't done anything wrong and that other people were doing the same thing he was doing."

Another factor: Rick is to be released in a few days and he doesn't much care what the staff say or do. He isn't about to co-operate or follow the rules.

And this: Rick admires Fred who is a charismatic kid, a leader in the group. And Fred is as manipulative as he is charismatic. Fred was goading Rick on from the far end of the yard and Rick doesn't need much goading at the best of times. And Fred, like Rick, is about to be released. Fred is smarter than Rick. "He's hoping to get out early, so he isn't really going to do anything stupid. We've already given him the message. He got seven extra days because he destroyed some stuff. He doesn't want that again." But he wouldn't mind steering Rick into trouble, just for the fun of it.

All of this was dancing in Sid's head as he watched things unfold in those few minutes. Reacting to blowups in the yard "is almost like playing baseball. When the ball's hit to you, you've got to know what to do with it. Same thing here. You learn about the kids, you learn what their tendencies are, you know what their situation is."

Sid G. knows that Fred was pulling all the strings in the yard, especially Rick's string. "With a kid like Fred, you know there are situations where he's going to go off. But you also know his limits. They may not be good limits, but we know his limits. Say you needed to restrain him, which would be a last-ditch thing, you know he's not going to go nuts on staff. He might take a swing at one, but that's his limit and you know what it is."

Rick is a little harder to read. "I didn't know exactly what he was going to do next." He'd already punched the window on his way to the bench. If a window, why not one of the other kids? Or one of the staff? "So I called for back-up." Even though there were three staffers in the yard. "Normally, we only have two out there, but we had three and, with you there were four, and it seems like an enormous amount of people." But suddenly, it didn't. "Yah. And you realize with different issues going on it can become pretty serious. And that's why in each situation it's important to try to isolate things, get everything safe as quick as possible. To call for back-up is just an extra precaution. We always take precautions so it doesn't become anything bigger. And as you saw, we needed the extra staff to take care of other things while we were taking care of Rick, who went further as it turned out."

Plus, when back-up arrives, it sends a message to the rest of the group that it's time to calm down. "In that situation, we require of the kids that they become angels. We won't put up with anything. We want to keep everything safe. If there's any principle we go back to, it's that. To keep everything safe, for both residents and staff, and that over-rides everything else."

With Larry R. in the doorway, backing him up, Sid went back to Rick to lay the cards on the table. A couple of objectives: he wanted to see what kind of shape Rick was in, and assess the danger the kid posed to the other kids and the staff. And he wanted to give Rick his choices.

Rick was still pretty hot, and still not admitting he'd done anything wrong. He was feeling unjustly dealt with. "What they try to do is deflect everything you've said to them. They don't own up to it. Every young offender who comes in here says 'I didn't do it'. They're so good at trying to con people that you've got to work at keeping them on the issue. You say, 'You can try to get away from it all you want, but this is what you did'. He started into 'I don't care' and then he tried to keep going even though he knew I had him. So I went through his options. I told him, 'If you don't go inside, you're looking at us moving the group, which becomes a bigger deal (with more consequences).' I told him there's no need to create a bigger issue. But through it all, you need to make him realize it's his decision, not something we're doing to him. The rules are set up. He's the one who decides what his consequences are going to be. If he decides to start damaging goods, he's the one who's going to pay for it and if need be we will use our back-up plan." The back-up plan for extremely violent kids is to call the police who will transport the kid to the young offenders' unit at the county jail. "Whatever way we have to deal with it, it's his decision what he's going to do."

Rick's response? "You're going to have to carry me in." Sid's response? "I don't think that's an option you want to get into and we don't want to get into that so we'll give you a couple of minutes to think about it. We just need you to make a good decision here."

Wishful thinking, as it turned out. There was a split second after Rick had kicked the window and was coming toward him with his fists clenched when Sid G. didn't know what Rick was about to do, which was the split second that Sid sensed his back was to the wall. "What I'm doing is looking at different situations. I can almost feel the wall behind me, and I'm looking for his hands. If he comes for me, I've got his hands. And it wasn't so bad because I had Larry right there. But you're thinking through all the scenarios and you always want to be a step ahead so you know where things are going. Just like playing chess."

And just like that, the chess game was over.

For the moment.

Staffer Barb C.'s first concern was to get a fix on George. He's a volatile kid and when he blows he can be extremely violent. But the staff have this on their side: George has finally started to try to improve. It's a struggle for him, and he needs a lot of help to stay out of trouble. Even from a distance, Barb could tell George was "fighting with himself: 'am I going to get into it, or am I going to stay positive?' That's what he was struggling with." And that's why Barb went down the yard and had a chat with him. "His body language was kind of aggressive, he was picking things up and whipping them, he was clearly agitated and I told him if he had things he wanted to talk about he should talk about them and I reinforced with him that I trusted him to make good decisions."

Those decisions are especially tough for George to make. "One, it's a peer thing. He very much wants to have relationships with his peers, whether negative or positive. He never really had any relationships. He thinks he has to move with them. Because of his treatment, his reasoning skills have improved and he knows it's wrong. So he's in conflict. And it makes him real nervous because he doesn't know which way to move. George is extremely intelligent. He knows right from wrong. And he knows what he's at risk of losing and I think that's what he was feeling. I think his confidence was working for him."

Once she felt confident about George, she turned her attention to Mary because "she was a little nervous and it wouldn't be unlike her to join in" if things got wild. "I was also aware that Fred was trying to work the group and take the lead and that Mary was keyed into that. So I walked over to Mary and told her that I was aware of where her thinking may be. I was reinforcing with her that I believed strongly she would conduct herself in an appropriate way and stay out of it and she told me she would.

"My concern then was Fred, because he was trying to get Rick's attention and he was also trying to get the group worked up, putting on a display for them. I had the sense there for about two minutes that they may all have run toward Rick to support him and I felt at that point it was a very dangerous situation."

157

If it had happened, she's pretty sure Fred would have been in the thick of things. "He was trying to get them to do everything and then he would have been seen as the guy who fell in behind." But he would have been there. And Mary? "She may have gotten into it. She's a follower." George? "I think he would've gotten into it too. It was a struggle for him. I think that's why he removed himself so far away from the group. I think he was frightened." Walt and John? "I think with them it was a wait and see thing. I wasn't as concerned about them as I was about Mary and George."

Given the number of staff, what were her concerns about safety? "I was confident that I had stabilized two, and I felt that with all our experience we'd have been able to control things. But for about two minutes, I was anxious myself." The wild card was Rick. Clearly, he was putting on a show for the kids, and for the visitor. He was also trying to impress Fred. But he was also refusing to do anything Sid G. was telling him to do. "He wasn't going to go inside, wasn't going to do anything that we said. He was threatening toward the staff and he was dangerous at that point."

The key, according to Barb, was the staff remained calm. Especially Sid G., when Rick rushed him, fists clenched. If Sid G. had over-reacted, grabbed Rick, and taken him down, there's a very good chance all the kids would have rushed them. And all hell would have broken out. "But because he responded in a calm way, he showed Rick he wasn't intimidated by him. And by staying calm, it kept the rest of the group calm. I think that's one of the keys right there, staff staying calm." As jail director William B. says, "It shows you how tenuous is the grip we have on the group." Barb: "And they all seem to move together. It's like they become of one mind." And that one mind almost always harbours dark thoughts about the staff. Even the "good kids," the ones the staff think they can trust, can be overwhelmed.

158

The most interesting part of it all for Barb was watching Fred once he was in his room. "The norm for him is to escalate," to get progressively more angry until he goes right over the edge. "But he didn't. I think he was thinking about an early release and he didn't want to jeopardize that. And he was thinking about that."

Smart boy.

"Yah. He is. Definitely a street kid."

Larry R.'s first reaction, when he opened the door, was to see where everyone was. He knew before he opened the door that someone was acting up. And he knew the group had been unsettled all day, and he knew that could spell trouble.

Once he saw where Barb and Dan had positioned themselves, he quickly scanned the yard again to see where the kids were and what shape they were in. And then he focused on Rick.

"Rick wanted to argue. We know he's an aggressive boy. And he's smart enough to know he'd earned consequences for punching the window the first time. He wanted to argue and he was choosing not to move. So after a short period of time I went over to help Sid. We gave him our expectations, that he had a couple of minutes to move in or we'd have to move the entire group in and he'd be held accountable for that, too. His response was 'I don't care'. And I told him, 'That's your choice' and Sid and I walked away. And, what, about ten seconds later he got up and started acting up."

Why clear the yard after the main troublemaker was cooling his heels in a time-out room? "I was feeling uneasy. And when you're feeling uneasy, you know there's something wrong. The first choice, normally, would be to ask Fred to move. He's the one having the issue, and he's the one who should be making the decision. But since Rick was in the time-out room downstairs, we had no place to put Fred. So we decided to move the group in."

Why move George in first?

Barb: "George can be extremely dangerous if he acts out. We've had a lot of experience where George has been quite violent. So Larry's decision was to bring him in first."

Larry: "He thought he was being punished. I told him he wasn't. They know that when there are serious incidents, they go to their bedrooms. It's for their safety. He acknowledged that. He said, 'Someone's gonna blow' and I said 'I don't think you want to be around when that happens' and he said 'no' and he scooted out of there pretty quickly. Being safe is a key thing with most of these kids, whether they show it or not.

"After bringing George in I got on the phone to the secretary and we got some more staff." While those staffers supervised the kids, Larry, Sid, Barb and Dan met with the supervisors and with William B. and decided what consequences Rick and Fred should face. "We tend not to make decisions on the spur of the moment. When you're emotional, you tend to make mistakes. So it gave us an opportunity to settle down and talk it over with William and that's when we came up with the consequences." Barb dealt with Fred who was pretty tame and Larry dealt with Rick, who was anything but. (Rick would spend the last few days of his jail term in a separate part of the jail, out of the group and out of harm's way.)

"Interesting day," says Barb.

Right. And it's a long way to bedtime.

5:38 p.m.

Two choices for the kids in B Group: cards or ping pong. Grant and Pat grab the paddles. Stew takes a chair by the wall, watching and waiting his turn. Staff member Penny B. stands beside him.

Curt: "Hey, Joe, I read in that Guinness Book about some guy who grew a third set of teeth. A complete set. That's awesome, eh?"

Grant has done something I missed. Or said something. But Penny didn't miss it, and didn't like it. "You're getting a little disrespectful, Grant. We can put the paddles away if this is becoming an issue." Curt asks Joe if he'd turn on the radio in the room across the hall, the honours lounge (pool table, piano, radio and TV). Joe thinks about it for a few seconds and figures, why not? "Which station?" Several requests, but majority rules: hard rock. Pat, paddle in hand, does a little dancing. Grant doesn't miss his opportunity: he slams the ball past Pat and against the wall. End of the game. Next up: Joe and Stew.

Elizabeth and Sandy are playing sidewalk euchre. Four cards face-down, four face-up on top of them and three extra cards in the hand not to be looked at. Pick trump from the ones you can see. It's daredevil time. You won't know until you play the top cards whether you've got any trump hidden, or in your hand.

Grant and Pat are playing two-handed something or other. Curt and Bob are at another table: "Are you nuts, discarding that?" Bob laughs and discards another. Whatever it was, the ruse works. A moment later, Bob sweeps up the cards, a winner again. Curt is puzzled: "He had to do it some way where he could get all the cards I needed. Are you cheating?" Elizabeth gives Penny the eyelash treatment: "You don't like cheating, do you, Penny ?" "No. I don't like cheating." Elizabeth laughs a phoney laugh, and a brittle one.

The Red Hot Chili Peppers serenade us all, from a distance. Stew holds the ball in one hand, paddle in the other, about to serve. "Eight for me, four for you." "No," says Joe, "Eight five." "Oh, lost track." Stew cranks one, which would have given him another point, if the ball hadn't hit the edge of the table and split apart. He tries bouncing the broken ball. Broken balls won't bounce. Penny checks the cupboard. The cupboard is bare. "No more ping pong balls. The other group must've used them all up."

Time to pack up, anyway, and head out to the play yard.

Elizabeth looks at Joe, who's taken a chair by the door. "Deep thoughts, Joe?" Joe shakes his head. Elizabeth: "You look like you've been crying. Have you been crying, Joe?" Joe looks at her, expressionless. "Your eyes look all red and puffy, like you've been crying. Are you upset about something?"

Mike D., the recreation man, comes in through the far door. Stew goes to greet him, makes a move for the sunglasses which hang by a cord against his chest. "Can I see them?" "No." "Aw, Mike..." "No." Mike puts a hand against the glasses, and gives Stew the eye. "Stew, I said no. And you're in my personal space." Stew backs off.

Stew: "Can we play football?" No sooner does he ask than there's a flurry of requests: volleyball, basketball, baseball.

Curt: "Can't we just have free time?"

"No."

"But it'd make your job so much easier if you just gave us free time. You wouldn't have to do anything. Just watch us." "How'd that look on my assessment? What'd you have them do Monday, Mike? Free time. What'd you have them do Tuesday, Mike? Free time."

"But this is our second time (in the yard) today. We had a game the first time, so if we had free time this time it'd all work out prime and pretty."

Joe: "Let's cool it with the complaining." Basketball. Baseball. Volleyball. Majority rules. Joe looks at Curt who makes a frowning gesture, raises his eyebrows, holds out his hands, palms up. "No comment. None at all." He smiles at Joe. "There's a fine line between begging and pestering, Joe."

"Line up."

In the mud-room, the kids take off their slippers and put on their runners, the ones they hate, the ones with the Velcro strips. "Why can't we have ones with laces? You guys are watching us. It's not as though we can do anything with the laces." Joe, his back to the door which leads to the yard, says he's heard just about enough complaining for one day. "We talked about this earlier." Silence. Then he backs through the door and out we go.

Baseball it is. Asphalt infield. Asphalt outfield. Eighteen-foot fences all around the park. Mike has Sandy and Stew put out the bases: bright orange cone markers. Then he gives Grant the bat: a foam kid's bat about a foot and a half long. Mike will do the pitching. From the looks of things, he's pitched before. He suckers Grant on a curveball, then flashes a fastball past him so quickly that Grant is just swinging the bat when the ball is hitting the fence behind him. But Grant has played before, too. He launches the next pitch against the far fence. Home run.

Three adults come up the walk by the tall fence. The woman calls out to Bob: "It's 6 o'clock." "I know. I've got to wait for staff to come." A few minutes later, supervisor Frank M. comes out into the yard and signals for Bob to follow him in for his visit.

Mike is at bat. Pat fires a fastball in under his chin. Mike drops the bat and makes as though to charge the mound. Next pitch, he hits a hard grounder to left field and makes it safely to first. "Pat, you're up."

Penny sits on a picnic table, watching the action. I ask her about the comment Pat made at supper, the one I only partly overheard. "I asked Grant what food he would like when he got out of here. A lot of kids would just rattle things off. Which is legitimate, because they miss it. 'Oh, I'd like Taco Bell.' And sometimes you can get a good conversation going by talking about things like that. But when I asked Pat he said 'well, it's been so long since I've had my freedom that I don't really remember.' Which on one hand I can understand. On the other hand he probably didn't have the ability to eat out or where ever he wanted when he was at home. That would be what I would assume. If he earns a 50 and gets to have a McDonald's here, that's something special for him. To have food on the table every day, I would assume that's something pretty special for him too." Sad comment. "Yah."

Two out. Grant's on third, waiting to be driven home though with Elizabeth at bat, this seems unlikely. On the far side of the fence, two nuns come into view, carrying a garbage pail between them. Elizabeth fouls the next pitch high and over the fence. The kids look at the ball, and then at the nuns. But the nuns are heading the other way. All eyes are on Mike. "Got another ball?" "Yup. But the next one who hits a ball over the fence, or onto the roof, does twenty laps, and the game will be over. Stew hits a pitch to the far fence and heads for first, holding up his baggy pants with one hand, hanging onto his hat with the other. Safe at second. Grant scores and comes back to bat and takes a pitch in the shoulder. "It hit me. I'm taking my base." Elizabeth is up again. Lines one fair, skipping down the asphalt to the fence. The crowd goes wild. Elizabeth goes to first. Stew scores, then goes into the field. Curt at the bat. He pops up the first pitch and Stew scuttles in for the catch. Nice catch, two hand-ed. "You're out. Eat that. Hey, Sister." The nuns stop, outside the fence. "Could you throw us our ball back. Please?"

One of the nuns spots the ball, picks it up, takes a look up at the top of the fence, fires the ball. It goes straight up, straight down. She tries again. Same result. Now she's laughing. So's the other nun. So are the kids. On the third try, the ball arcs over the fence. The kids laugh and cheer and thank her and go back to their game.

Sandy, in the outfield, is watching the nuns, not the game ball, which bounces off the asphalt a few feet to her left and skips past her. She hustles to grab it, fires it to third. Not in time. Elizabeth is safe. Pat at the bat. He pops one up. Stew fields the ball, then tags Elizabeth out as she tries to hustle back to third base. Double play. The side's retired. Grant comes to bat. "Looks like laps to me," says Stew, watching the ball land on the roof. "Laps? That was an accident." "Those are the rules." The nuns return, three of them this time, lugging a rolled-up carpet. Curt watches them, intently. They place the rug on the grass, beside the garbage tin they'd taken out earlier. When they return, Curt waves at them, a little-boy wave. They wave back.

Game over. Mike asks Stew to pick up the bases and Grant to bring the bat. The team adjourns to the picnic table to chew over details of the game. About those laps, Grant. "I'm not doin' no laps." "Twenty laps, by my count." Funny way of counting. One lap, by Mike's count, is three times around the yard. "Sixty laps?" Mike nods and smirks. Grant is saved by the nuns, who return with an old mattress. The kids all watch as the mattress gets deposited beside the carpet and the garbage tin. The nuns head back to their convent. Curiosity gets the better of Grant. "What do they do in there, anyway?" "They pray," says Penny. "Pray for what?" "Pray for you, among others." Grant says his grandmother wouldn't be too happy if she found out someone was praying for him. A nun. A Catholic nun, especially.

(Penny, later: "The nuns are out every once in a while. It's not like they stay over there and don't do anything. They're quite friendly and the kids are very curious about them. The kids don't think the Sisters have a life, outside praying all the time. They can't grasp the humanity of the nuns. The Sisters pray for everybody in this facility every day. It gives them hope they're helping us in the way they can. The Sisters also do the mending for us. I tell the kids the nuns are trying to be helpful in a way they know. But they do have a life too. And the kids have a hard time understanding that." Do the kids understand the concept of praying? "I'm sure some of them have had some religious training. Others, I'm sure it scares them. They aren't religious at all, have no desire to get into that. And that's okay, we don't push that on them. But they don't have to be rude or inappropriate. They should consider how others feel. If they don't want to be part of it, that's fine.")

Curt waggles his fingers at the last of the nuns. The nun smiles and waves back.

Grant is still thinking about those laps, and he still doesn't know whether Mike has been joking. But just in case there's any doubt, Grant would like Mike and everyone else to know he could run 60 laps if he wanted to, which he doesn't. Or 70. Or more. He's used to that. Before he came in here, he did 10 laps of the school track every day of the week.

Penny is watching, and listening, intently. She's also looking at the faces which are turned toward Grant. What does she make of the story? As she will later say, "A lot of the kids have stories like that. They want to feel superior to the others. He tries to assert himself, and feel like he's a somebody, like he's noticed, and brag in front of the other kids. On the other hand, he could be making the whole thing up, just wishing. And you never know. Because a lot of the kids who come in here, like Grant, they lie. Look you right in the face and lie. You have to feel it out. What was he leading to, where was he going next: was he going to be the superstar? You never know how far to go with their stories."

Stew wants to know if they could get one of the Rocky films on tape. No. Why not? Inappropriate, too violent. "What about Child's Play?" No. "Jeez. We can never watch the good ones."

"When you get out of here, you can watch whatever you want," says staff member Joe C. "Yah," says Stew, "like Jason Goes To Hell. That's a great movie." Grant: "Especially the part where the guy picks up the heart. I loved that." Penny: "Guys. Guys. Enough."

Penny, later: "You try, it's hard, but you try to have a nice casual conversation with them, you want them to feel relaxed and comfortable talking with you, but at the same time you have to make sure they're not getting out of hand and inappropriate. Their thinking is very, very mixed up. Some of it's criminal thinking, some of it's sexually inappropriate, some of it's vividly explicit. They tend to get off on their tangents and when they go, they just go. So here we're sitting around having what we think is a normal conversation, when suddenly one of the kids mentions (the movie) Jason From Hell or whatever and our conversation about movies suddenly turns into someone's fascination with someone biting someone's heart. The kids get a thrill out of that. And everyone joins in. They have to focus on the inappropriate and the disgusting, the wild side of it. And that's what they do with a lot of things in their lives, too. They distort it a little bit. So what was a very normal conversation about movies that they like or dislike turns into something where we have to say, 'No, let's stop this conversation.' "

And these sudden turns, in conversation, in mood, in behaviour, all take place in a matter of minutes. "Yah. And the hard part is, when they first come in here I'm sure they think 'Oh, we can't talk about anything.' They think we're so strict, so structured. We are. But we try to explore different avenues and get a normal conversation going and bang it goes into something inappropriate and morbid. That's what a lot of their thoughts are a lot of the time. It's difficult to have a conversation because it always develops into an inappropriate conversation and we have to shut it off."

167

DEALING WITH KIDS WHO COMMIT CRIMES

1. THE YOUNG OFFENDERS ACT

There is no shortage of kids getting themselves in trouble with the law. In 1993, police in my city were involved with young offenders on more than 3,300 occasions. And yet they laid only 1,200 charges. The vast majority of these kids did something dumb and fairly minor. "Believe it or not," says Staff Sgt. Mike Wilson, "we try to keep these kids out of court." First offense, minor crime, the cops will call the parents in for a chat. They'll sit down with the kid, talk about what happened. They have two objectives: give the kid a scare, and give the parents a wake-up call. As Wilson said, "Eighty per cent of these kids we'll never see again. They're good kids who did something dumb and, like kids doing dumb things, they got caught and they were scared shitless and their parents had a talk with them or maybe cuffed them and told them to smarten up."

"This one kid did a B&E," says Crown prosecutor Jill Manny. "He was arrested (in a nearby township) and his dad came down and he was really pissed off. The police officer, with the father's approval, decided to teach this kid a lesson. So they put him in a cell for maybe fifteen minutes, something like that. Gave him a little taste of it. Let him know: 'This is serious, and this is what's going to happen to you if you do this again'. The police did this with the father's approval, he wanted to scare his own kid. The kid had given a statement, confessing everything he did. Well, when they got to court, the judge was appalled that this police officer had done this. He thought it was terrible, absolutely terrible, that they should do this to this kid. Terrorize him, I think he said. Terrorize! Well, it wasn't terrorizing. They shook him up is what they did. We're sometimes overprotective of these kids. If they come from a decent family, and they're sufficiently scared about what they've got themselves into, they're not going to do it again."

"Despite what you read in the media," says Wilson, "we do everything possible to help these kids. It's not unusual for us to warn a kid three or four times before we finally charge him." Even then, most of those charged will get just what they needed: a further scare, maybe some community service hours, or some time on probation. And it'll be the last time most of these kids will ever stand in the prisoner's dock. It's not uncommon for parents to thank the cops. "The parents will say they're glad we're involved because the kid's out of control and they don't know what to do with him, so we can help direct them to some help."

However. Sometimes the cops will call the kid's home, tell the parents what happened, ask them to bring the kid down for a chat and "they'll tell you 'He didn't do it and there's no fucking way I'm bringing him down there' and they'll hang up." Remember the name, you'll see him again. "Twenty per cent of the kids, we'll see again. And ten per cent we'll see a lot of. They're our hard-core chronic offenders."

It's these kids, really, we talk about when we talk about kids and crime, kids in the jail. These are the ones who make the morning headlines and the evening news. These are the kids who get us wondering, 'What's wrong with kids today?' and, 'Boy, they ought to do something about that Young Offenders Act.'

The Young Offenders Act certainly isn't perfect, but you won't find many people — cops, Crowns, judges, youth workers — who would prefer to bring back the Juvenile Delinquents Act.

"The Juvenile Delinquents Act came out in the early part of the century," and at the time, says Alec Marks, "it was a very progressive piece of legislation and it did very well without many major revisions for much of the century and it was very effective".

On the down side, at least to modern eyes, the Juvenile Delinquents Act reflected the times in which it was born. "It was very paternalistic. It said, 'These are misguided, misdirected children who are in need of care, in need of direction and we have to do anything we need to do in order to put them back on track.'" And as Alec Marks said, people at the time felt they could do just that. People in the corrections system, in the courts and in police departments were given whatever power they felt necessary to put those children back on the tracks.

Then times, and theories, changed. "The Young Offenders Act, even though it came into effect in the mid-80s, had been in the works for 15 or 20 years. It came at a time when there was different thinking about how we should deal with young people who commit crimes. There was a growing emphasis on offender responsibility for his or her behaviour." No longer was it to be society's business to change the way kids behaved. Now it was to be the children who saw the need for change, and changed their own behaviour. How realistic was that hope? Alec Marks: "When the Young Offenders Act was being developed, there was a growing body of literature that was suggesting that for offenders to be changed, they need to willingly participate in a treatment program. So it was up to society to make those programs available and it was up to the offender to take part in those programs."

People working in the field may like The Act, or most of The Act, but that's not to say they wouldn't love to tinker with it if they could.

What Judge Saul Nosanchuk likes about The Act is that it guarantees young people a fair hearing. "They have a right to a lawyer, they have a right to an adjournment, they have a right to a fair trial, they have a right not to be searched without reasonable cause, they have a right to be free of arbitrary detention. It's a very fair system for the accused. They can't be found guilty unless their guilt is proved beyond a reasonable doubt. So I think it's a system that gives the accused person a real opportunity to have their day in court. I hope the court provides a good forum. I like to think of it almost as a temple of justice where you can get your hearing, a place where nobody's going to jump on you before you say a word, or knock you around or bully you. Everyone's going to hear what they're accused of, they'll be given a chance to be heard, and they'll have help all the way through."

The judge also likes the structure which The Act has imposed upon the proceedings in the courtroom. Under the Juvenile Delinquents Act things were, well, "much more informal." Part of the new structure demands, for instance, that parents attend when their kids are in court. "I think that's helpful, because parents can give you a sense of what's going on in the family." And they also give you a sense of what's not working in the family. "You have every different permutation and combination: you've got parents who are totally blind to the situation, who want to do everything they can to get the young person out of there and they'll say almost anything they can to do that, to try not to admit their responsibility. And you have, at the other end of the spectrum, parents who even charge their children with offenses and want them to be put into custody, want them to be punished. But then in the middle, most frequently, you have good caring parents who realize their children have gone astray and are very concerned and want to do everything possible to see that they're rehabilitated."

The judge gets a read on the family, first and foremost, and that helps him determine how best to deal with the child in his courtroom. "I want to hear from the parents, call them up, get some input. Because after all, it's the home that really should be the primary place where the children get their sense of security from, their goals, their values. Frequently, it's a wake-up call for some parents to get moving, to change their approach."

Just as important, he wants to hear from the accused. "I want to listen to them, because many of them haven't been listened to all their lives. I always ask, 'Is there anything you'd like to say?' And many of them say 'I really think I've had enough of this, I'm tired of it, I don't want to do it any more, I really want to change my ways.' Now, is this the line they've been thinking about for this boob up on the bench? It could be that they think, 'Say this before this judge and he really eats it up.' Could be. But I do feel that many of them are frustrated, they are fed up. It's very debilitating not to be able to control your own anger, rein yourself in. You don't know what's going to happen to yourself in certain situations. That's a very difficult way to live. Because of that, other people are going to be angry with you, and then it's a vicious circle. You're living in a morass of anger. That's got to be tough. So they do say it. Now mind you, they're a captive audience and I know that. But I still love to hear it."

The judge admits The Act has its downside. "I think the Young Offenders Act has brought a legalization into the field, and this is to overcome what was felt to be a rather paternalistic and perhaps not a just court." Under the Juvenile Delinquents Act, the fairness of the hearing often depended on the person sitting on the bench. "Was he some benign former social worker or was he some hard-nosed ex-prosecutor who was the judge?" Those informal paternalistic days are over.

"There's much more emphasis now on legal rights. Everybody's entitled to a lawyer and people frequently will be guided by what a lawyer says. They may be inclined to come in and plead guilty, take responsibility for their actions, but the lawyer's advice is not to do that. Many times lawyers get in the picture and the case drags on for six or seven months and then the kid pleads guilty any-

172

way. So you wonder whether that's really helping the situation. I do understand that everyone wants to have their rights protected, but there's a certain amount of focus by young people on their legal rights and the game aspect of it. It's another game, you see. Don't admit what you did. Try to see if you can get out of it. And one has to ask himself whether that's ultimately going to be beneficial. I'm concerned about the game playing. I think it's desirable that people accept responsibility for what they've done.

"On the other hand," the judge says, "people have a right to a trial and they have a right to have a lawyer advise them as to what they're doing. But some of the most impressive people I've seen are the ones who come in with their parents, the first time the case is up, and they say, 'Well, this is what I did and I'm going to take responsibility for it. I'm prepared to do community work, I'm prepared to do whatever you want me to do. I'm prepared to take my penalty.' Those are the ones you feel the greatest hope for. Because the families are there, the kids are there, 'that's what I did.' Whereas if they come in and want a remand, two remands, three remands, the lawyer gets in there. 'How do you plead?' 'Not guilty.' The case goes over six months, ultimately they plead guilty and one has to wonder what their perception of the system is. They're angling to squeeze out of it the best way they can. They take their legal advice and the legal advice is to wait it out, see what happens, see if the witnesses show up, see how it plays out. And I don't think that, in the long run, is healthy for the rehabilitation of the accused. So I'd like to see things move more quickly, to impose some time limits. I'd like to see cases move through the system with dispatch. I'm not sure that's something that can be legislated, but I think these things shouldn't drag on and on for these kids."

Staff Sgt. Mike Wilson likes the Young Offenders Act, but he'd rewrite part of it so that it covered kids aged 10 to 15, inclusive.

Kids 16 and older would go to adult court. Judges in adult court already have the ability to divert first-time offenders into community service, open-custody and other kinds of non-confinement punishments. So kids who wound up in adult court wouldn't automatically wind up in The Big House. But if a kid committed the kinds of heinous crimes some kids do commit, then he could get the kind of sentence Mike Wilson thinks is appropriate. "Right now, a kid could rape 100 women and get three years."

Crown Prosecutor Randy Semeniuk: "The cops are frustrated. A lot of them think they're wasting their time with young offenders. They see individuals who get out of custody and break into houses. It seems to them that nothing's being done. They have a great sense of frustration, which I share with them."

"On the occasions when I see offenses committed when the young person is out on bail, that causes me concern," says Judge Doug Phillips. "My sense is I see it too often. So I may want to tighten up on those provisions (in The Act)."

Tom Bromley has been working with troubled teenagers for more than 20 years. "I believe the Young Offenders Act has to be looked at because one of the things being said on the street is 'I got kissed by the judge.' They're out before the cops get done writing (the report of the crime). You've heard that. Respect for the law is gone. Look at all this joyriding. What's a kid get for stealing a car? Nothing. There's no fear. They stand up in front of the judge and say 'I'm a young offender.' Now I don't believe every guy ought to wind up in the lockup, but we need to set some guidelines. Serious crimes result in this. And if you do adult crimes, you do adult times. No matter what the crime is, you've got to pay a price. And the sooner they pay it, hopefully the sooner they'll learn and get out and be productive citizens."

Part of the frustration with the system stems from the fact that judges don't have to 'kiss' the kids. The Young Offenders Act allows them to impose stiff penalties. "Some do, some don't," says Crown Prosecutor Randy Semeniuk. "Some judges treat young offenders more harshly. Some treat them more as children, some treat them more as criminals. So the sentences are all over the map and that's the problem. There is no certainty. And young offenders know that. They know the first time they get in trouble, nothing's going to happen. I mean, the young offender who was charged with tying up the elderly lady, she even said to the cops 'we're just kids. Nobody will do anything to us. We'll be out. Just wait and see.' If they perceive nothing's going to happen to them, and nothing really does happen to them, then there's no deterrent to the Young Offenders Act."

The Act may allow judges to impose stiff penalties. But as Semeniuk says, it also states that "the last resort should be that they're in custody. So that means they should get bail. So they're outta there. And what's the message they get? Well, 'I got outta custody. I got caught, but maybe the next time I won't get caught.' So they get caught again. Maybe this time they might be kept in custody, but it comes time for sentencing, they're not going to get much. You have open custody, which a lot of people take to be a joke. And you have closed custody which I'm sure some of the young offenders think is a joke as well."

Semeniuk figures it's time the laughter stopped. "If someone commits a robbery for the first time, goes into a house, ties up an elderly woman and robs her, give them a year in closed custody. If an adult committed the same offense, he'd be looking at going to the penitentiary for two or three years." So tougher sentences are needed. And more uniformity in sentencing. "I'd like to see some minimum sentences for young offenders. If you commit a robbery, there should be a minimum sentence of six months closed custody, no getting around it unless there are some exceptional cir-

175

cumstances. You get that time. I think if there was more certainty in the sentencing, the Act itself might have more teeth." Or be seen to have teeth.

Crown Prosecutor Jill Manny would lower the age for criminal responsibility to seven or eight (from 12) "because some adults are using young kids, younger than 12, to break into homes so they will not be criminally responsible. And some of these kids are out of control, seriously disturbed and a danger to the public. I would certainly have life imprisonment for murder, the same way it is in England. And I would also have an extension of the sentence for aggravated assault in which people are shot or stabbed so the perpetrator knows this is not a game any more."

A life sentence. For kids? Manny has this to say: "Life is not life anymore. We know that. Even for first-degree murder, you're supposed to get 25 years with no parole but that's not true. Fifteen years, you're eligible for parole. Life is not life, like it is in the U.S. You can't give consecutive sentences like you can in the U.S., you know, hundreds of years to make sure you never get out. There should be a life sentence for murder and let's see how the person is responding (to treatment). You can always review it."

"I'll tell you foursquare that I don't have any reservations about the idea that dispositions for the most serious offenses — murder — have to be changed," says Judge Doug Phillips. "Parliament is moving in that direction, and that's great."

But Judge Phillips will quickly add this: "It's really simple to say, let's just change The Act and make sentences much longer. And, sure, there are those cases where I say to myself 'I can see far more of a problem here and my instincts say let's impose a very heavy sentence, let's put this child in a very structured facility' but am I really trying to fix a problem that isn't within my jurisdiction? I'm supposed to be providing a disposition for an offense, here, not correcting the whole of this youngster's background and behaviour." That's exactly what many people in the community think he, and other judges, should be doing. And he knows that. "I certainly don't stop listening when people complain. I think it's important that judges listen and read the newspapers and listen to the radio, hear the debate, have some appreciation for what's going on out there, keep in tune with it."

But what he hears, increasingly, are calls for the criminal justice system to be doing things it's not designed to do. "I think there's a thought in the community that the answer is time (for the offender), the more time the better, and let's hope that doing time will be enough to make sure the person behind the bars doesn't do it again. I don't think that's what happens. Packing someone off to a facility, that might help provide some (counselling) resources, but it isn't the cure-all. There are a lot of other problems that got this youngster to this place and we're only dealing with part of the problem. I agree that the community looks to the criminal justice system not only to punish the offender and protect the community, they look to the criminal justice system to fix the ills and that's not what our purpose is.

"The problem is that the young person hasn't got good parenting, a strong family." Very often, the kids don't have any parents in the picture at all. "Forget about blame," says Judge Phillips, "forget about who's at fault, the reality is that when these young people need a parent figure, there's nobody there. Well, we better address who will be there to serve in that role when we release the kid back out into the street because if that isn't done then my gut reaction is to think it's more than likely that youngster will be visiting court again. And the revolving door is right there. But that's not the court's job. It's something the lawmakers should think about and something that our resource people have to think about, something that we as members of this community have to think about. We all have a stake in this. And people who choose to parent have a role and a responsibility. It goes right back to that."

So, though society cries for the judge to fix the kid, the judge is looking at the sentencing from quite a different perspective. "I don't discount that there are some arguments that say sentences are too light, that maybe the emphasis on rehabilitation is simply too great," says Judge Phillips. "I listen. I figure, not only do I have a responsibility to the young person in terms of rehabilitation, I take very seriously my responsibility to the community. Every day I go into that courtroom, I look at a balancing of interests: the need to protect the community in which I live against the interest of the young person, the seriousness of the offense, the wishes and views of the victim and the deterrence factor, which I think is uppermost in the minds of those who complain most bitterly about the system. I'm taking into account all those features and I hope and think that at the end of it, when I impose a disposition, I can say that it's the right disposition under these circumstances and I can explain why."

Life sentences for kids? Judge Saul Nosanchuk: "Each case has to be dealt with on its own merits. In very difficult cases, where there've been heinous crimes, I can see people saying 'Well, you know, I don't care if he's 16. If he's committed a vicious murder, he should be dealt with in adult court, because of the punishment.' On the whole, I'd have to say it's probably pretty dangerous to put young offenders, 16-year-olds, in penitentiary with seasoned hard-nosed criminals. I remember one case I had, when I was practicing as a lawyer, a guy shot two people on the east side. He was found guilty, he was sent to the penitentiary at the age of 16. I know for a fact he was abused by some of the people there and he came out and not more than two months afterward he blew two people away on the street. He was in such a fragile state. So I think there's that argument to be made that to send a person of 16 or 15 to a penitentiary is, in the long run, going to destroy that person. They're going to get out, you know, eventually. So unless it's first-degree murder, I have a concern about 16-year-olds going to penitentiary."

Better, thinks the judge, to send such kids to places like the jail. "If they could keep him there for a period of years, the chances of making some inroads are far, far better than in a penitentiary. A place like Kingston, they're double-bunking the prisoners. It's rough. You put a 16-year-old in there and you can just about guarantee that person is done. If you want to reclaim a life, if you believe you should reclaim a life if possible, I don't think that's the place to send them. But then there's the argument: 'Well, they killed someone in a cold-blooded way, why shouldn't they be treated like a cold-blooded killer is treated?' But it's not an equal situation. You're putting a 16-year-old in there with hard-nosed killers. It's very humane, I think, not to do that." The judge ponders, for a moment, and then says: "But I know that's not going to satisfy some people."

As for Randy Semeniuk's argument that sentences are all over the place, Judge Nosanchuk has this to say: "I don't think one can safely generalize and say 'judges are too soft' or 'judges are too hard.' Giving a sentence is a matter of doing what's just and there's no easy formula for that. Sometimes it involves incarceration, sometimes not. We deal with cases one by one. Every case has its own biography, its own personnel, its own history. We try, judges try, to give each case a proper hearing and to do what appears workable after hearing all the representations. Sometimes it's top heavy from the accused: we frequently hear from the accused's family, the probation service, the youth's lawyer. But I always also want to hear from the victim. I always call the victim in: 'Now, what do you want to say about this? I've found this person guilty. Would you like to make a comment? Would you like an order that this person stay away from you? Did you suffer a loss? Are you out any money? How have you suffered?' And I try to make things right for the victim.

"There was one swarming incident outside a local high school, one person was swarmed by a whole group of people. I heard from a teacher who said he'd never seen anything so vicious. And I sentenced the person to six months in secure custody just like that. Now I've been appealed on some sentences as being too tough. I don't think I've ever been appealed as being too lenient. But I don't know that there's an easy answer to that question. I think what we've got to bear in mind is that we want to prevent this from happening again. We want to get a message across that this is wrong. We want to get the person to change their lifestyle, to change their pattern of living. In my view, if you can get them to do some work in the community, if you can get them involved in activities of some kind, if you can get them into some program where they can do something useful for the community, to me that's helpful. On the other hand, some of them need to be placed in a structured environment. It just depends. If you've got a family already there and the family's willing to put the effort in, why should the state pick up the slack for this person? Let the state be there for those where the family has failed."

But as the judge admits, "It's a tough call, because we often hear the cry for tougher sentences and I think you call 'em as you see 'em. In some cases, the crime cries out for a harsh sentence, but you can't forget that this person is going to come back some time." Send a kid to prison, you may be creating, rather than solving, a problem. "I like to tap into the soft part of a person, and everyone has a part like that. I defended people for eighteen years, and I can tell you there's no individual without that. Even a murderer, there's a decent part to him. Most people, anyway. There's a vulnerable spot. So some people can be reached. And if you can reach someone and turn them around, especially a kid, you have to."

Roger Montchamps spent the last four years of his police career working in the youth bureau. And he spent a lot of his time trying to turn kids around. "I've had kids come in at 16. First time they've ever stolen, or shoplifted, or whatever. The report says they've been good kids, helped out around the home and everything and I'd tell these kids 'I have three options. I can warn you. I can send you to a diversion program, or I can charge you.' Some of them will say 'I've learned my lesson' and from talking to them and their parents you can usually tell. And I say, 'I'll give you a warning. Think about this as a reward for being good for 16 years. As a police officer and as the police department, we're saying 'good job.' There's a lot of pressure out there and this is the first time you've stolen and you've been handling yourself the right way.' " Roger would tell them to consider the value of a good reputation and to think about that reputation before doing something dumb again. And it worked. He can show you the numbers. "Eighty per cent of the kids we dealt with once. I talked to Judge Nosanchuk about this and he said 'any system that gets an 80 per cent success rate has got to be applauded.' "

Crown Prosecutor Jill Manny says, "I think it's important for young offenders to get breaks. If they deserve a break, give them a break because then they'll think 'they're giving me a break, and I'm really going to try, I'm going to try to get a grip on my life, I'm really going to do something with my life.' If you don't give people breaks when they deserve them, then they build up resentment. 'Well, what the hell, I'm not going to get any breaks, nobody's going to listen to my story, so why should I make the effort.' So psychologically, at least in my mind, it's important to give people a break if they're sincere."

181

And she thinks that for the majority of the kids who get in trouble, jail is the last place they should wind up. "I'm a great believer in community service. I think it's important for these kids to give something back to the community. Go and do some chores for elderly people. There are all kinds of people who need help. The elderly. The disabled. Fix things for them around the house, if they can be trusted not to steal from them. Do all kinds of things to give something back. You know that when you give something, you get ten times back. You really do. You feel good about yourself. You see that you're doing something positive. And they do get community service. I don't know how many come back into court, obviously a number do, but I think if you give them hundreds of hours of community service to do, that can be a lot more beneficial than giving them 10 days in jail."

Barry Clark thinks far too many kids wind up in court. He's executive director of the John Howard Society, a group which works with former prisoners. "Since the Young Offenders Act was implemented, we've had a doubling of police charges, a doubling of young people institutionalized, and in some areas — particularly 16- and 17-year-olds — a dramatic increase in the length of time young people are spending in custody. This is a tremendous cost both financially and socially. And it's hardly a deterrent. A study done by the Ontario Ministry of Correctional Services indicated recidivism rates are approximately 70 percent." Fourteen percent of the released convicts didn't waste much time getting back to crime: they were arrested the day they were released from jail. "They were simply not deterred from crime, and they said they weren't. And why were they going to return to crime? Because, one, nothing had changed in their lives and, two, they had learned better ways to commit crime and, three, because it was an exciting way of life. Those aren't addressed, those are exacerbated, in institutions."

Clark thinks the current campaign to have kids jailed for long periods of time is "a red herring created by conservative politicians and rednecks in the media." If politicians cave into these demands, Clark fears we'll see here what people are seeing in the United States where more than a million citizens are in jail. "If you lock enough people up, society begins to reflect institutional norms. And this has occurred in the United States." In jail, in-your-face violence is part of day-to-day life. "And this has spilled over into the cities so that the cities come to reflect the prisons."

Clark would have us leave that path and try another: an entirely new form of Alternative Measures. Most kids wouldn't wind up in court at all. With the exception of those arrested for the most serious crimes, youngsters who come into contact with the law would be detoured into a community-based program. "The police could refer them to the program, no charges would be laid. The program would involve an apology, restitution, personal service, community service. It could involve attending a program of life skills, and others which deal with education, sports, crafts, tutoring, family therapy." The whole approach would consider the child's actions as symptoms of personal problems, rather than problems in and of themselves. And the programs would be voluntary.

Voluntary programs might work for a lot of kids. Perhaps the majority of kids. But there's a minority of kids — maybe 10 percent of all those who come in contact with the cops — who need something whether they want it or not. "That's the 10 percent that has to be recycled," says former youth bureau cop Roger Montchamps. "They have to be taken out of that environment they're in, away from their parents, their school and their friends. And not a year after they get into trouble. It has to be much quicker than that, otherwise it just goes on and on and on."

Roger Montchamps knows, from experience. He can tell you about all kinds of kids, boys and girls, who've been arrested — sometimes for violent crimes — and who've gone on to commit other, sometimes violent, crimes while waiting to appear in court on the first charge. "Most of them have so much peer pressure, no respect for any authority, and no sense of worth." And none of that is going to change as long as they're living at home, or living on the street, or living with their criminal pals.

These kids have got to go. "My idea of recycling is, if you could ever get the money, instead of building a new prison, build a farming community, a commune, where these kids could go for one to six months." There'd be a very high ratio of staff to residents: one for every four. And no one would get a free ride. "You either have to grow something or take care of an animal, you have a certain chore that you have to do so that the whole community can operate. Some of these communes have really taught people a lot of things about dealing with one another."

In Roger's commune, each kid would be judged by his peers and the staff on the performance of his duties. All the kids would have to take part in regular school classes, in life skills programs, and in therapeutic programs. They would be offered training in trades and general skills. "After your first month, you're evaluated. Have you learned anything? Have you changed? Are you starting to get a sense of values? Do you understand what you're doing?" If the other residents and staff felt the kid was doing well, and ought to be allowed to leave, they'd approve a release. The kid's lawyer could request that his client appear in court after a month, or at regular intervals. The staff would then provide the judge with copies of the kid's reports and the judge could decide if the kid had made enough progress to warrant release.

"You have to have something where a kid can grow, and get some self-esteem. And that's the big thing about working with an animal or doing chores, or growing things, or whatever. They'd get some independence, some self-esteem. And they'd begin to under-stand that you get back what you give. And they'd be praised for what they did right.

"A lot of these kids have ideas of what they want to be and they're always knocked down. 'Oh, you'll never be that.' 'You can never do that.' Their parents will tell them 'if you don't go to school and get an education, you'll never do that.' But it's all negative. It's not saying to the kid 'well, you can be this, but this is what you'll have to do and it's your choice.' It's all how you put it to them."

"The programs that tend to work best," says Clark, "are those that work voluntarily and those that work at an early, informal, more collaborative, community-based level. The more formal, the more reactionary. The more delayed the program is, the less effective it will be. And coincidentally, the more dangerous it will be. We can hard-ly say that we have to lock people up because things are out of con-trol and nothing else works. We haven't funded alternative measures programs appropriately enough to make any kind of decision." Given what Barry Clark thinks is a failure of the criminal justice system, he doesn't see why society wouldn't at least try something else.

The public impulse, these days, at least in some quarters, is not quite so forgiving. In fact, as Clark notes, it's quite the opposite. Judge Saul Nosanchuk, for one, thinks this cry for the lash, literally or figuratively, is short-sighted. "These kids have lost something. What is it? Lashing out, they're displacing anger they don't know how to channel against their parents. I mean, kids who can speak up to their parents, tell them off, feel they can get it off their chest and have parents who can accept that for what it is, that's a healthy sit-uation. A kid has to be able to get that out and a parent has to be able to take it. But these kids, they get bottled up, they want to kill, sometimes literally, and they end up hurting not their parents, but some other kid or someone else. It's pent-up fury, I think, in many cases. They're filled with rage. But who's the rage against? The rage is obviously against the people who are closest to them, or should be, and who have let them down or who they feel have let them down. Maybe the people didn't even let them down, they just feel let down. Or maybe they've just gotten off the track. I mean, you have some fine families of good people whose kids are in trouble. You don't know, sometimes, what went wrong. Sometimes it's just something in the kid that snaps. I like to let them know that what they did was wrong, let them see the victim, point out to them what happened, and hopefully something will sink in.

"From my point of view, I have to provide a place of caring, firmness and fairness. Fairness, and also someone who cares about what happens to them. That's my role. That's what makes it worthwhile for me. I like to feel that the fact a judge is concerned, is fair to them, and cares about them, may evoke in them a desire for some form of rehabilitation.

"Each one I want to reach. I tell them, 'Look, you've been given a fair trial, a fair sentencing hearing, this isn't some kangaroo deal. You've had your chance, now, what are you going to do about this? I don't want you back here. I don't want you back in the criminal courts, that's my desire. We're not looking for business here.' And many realize the pain they've caused their families and their victims and they say that. Some don't, of course. They're angry enough that they just don't give a damn, don't care."

Crown Prosecutor Jill Manny: "A kid goes into The Bay and steals a tape or a CD, I don't have any problem with Alternative Measures. But when kids do really serious crimes, it's hard for me to have sympathy. Like the kid who killed his mom and dad." Manny says in some of these cases, lawyers are putting forward 'the abused child syndrome' as a defence. She doesn't buy it. "Sometimes the parent is a monster and (the abuse) is horrible. And the defence is:

'This person deserved to die. Why should we feel badly that this person is dead? Why should we care? This kid did a service, to himself and to society by killing his parents.' But then, you see, you have the danger of that defence becoming so acceptable, that parents are murdered because the kids don't want to obey the rules of the house. The kid who killed his parents, he was waiting at the top of the stairs for his mother to come home. Now, if that's not premeditated murder, then what is?"

Like the staff at the jail, Jill Manny says, no excuses. "There comes a point where you say what else is there but jail? I don't think jail is the answer for these kids. But you have to protect society from these people for a period of time."

For these kids, the ones for whom there is no alternative but a stint in jail, Judge Nosanchuk says: "I don't think it should be for 10 days or 15 days, but for a sufficient period of time so they can become involved in a structured rehabilitation program. Because they (the jails) do have teaching they can do, they can establish relationships, they have professionals there who can help these kids. I think that's most desirable. If they deserve to be away from the community, then they deserve to be away for months, at least, so that something can sink in, so that the experience can be more beneficial to them. To send someone away for five days, I don't see what point there is in that. It's only disruptive to the facility."

"A lot of people don't understand how deep-rooted these kids' problems are," says the jail's director, William B. "I was just at lunch with a woman and she knew of a girl who came into our jail for 30 days. And this woman said 'You didn't help that girl at all.' She's still doing this, that, and the other. And how could I even start, without sounding defensive, to explain it. So you just say 'yah, you're right.' And she is right. Thirty days would not have helped that girl in the long term. No way." Thirty days would barely let the staff begin to know where to begin dealing with the girl's problems. It's not the kind of thing people want to hear if they want to hear about quick fixes.

2. PROBATION AND REHABILITATION

Many of the kids in the jail need help. Extensive, long-term help. As more than one person will tell you who works with these kids, you can't fix in a couple of months problems which were years in the making.

One of the good things about the Young Offenders Act, according to Staff Sgt. Mike Wilson, is that it calls for all kinds of intervention — counselling and treatment — for troubled kids. "The emphasis, without a doubt," says Judge Doug Phillips, "is on the need to rehabilitate and provide assistance for this young person." But the problem, as Mike Wilson will tell you, is that the government never did come through with enough funds to create enough programs and hire enough workers to provide the rehabilitation and assistance The Act calls for. So the kids keep going, untreated, through the revolving door: police station, court, jail, street. "The Juvenile Delinquents Act didn't work, either, but we've got the same problem all over again."

The Young Offenders Act relies heavily on probation orders, particularly for first offenders. Judge Doug Phillips: "The tool that's supposed to be used to provide rehabilitation is to place them under terms of probation and hope the resources of probation are sufficient to address what it is they need. If they have an anger management need, the probation should provide the necessary counselling. If they have an alcohol or substance abuse problem, then probation should make sure they get channelled into the right resource. One would hope those community resources would be sufficient to address the problem

188

and, within a short or medium term, help redirect that person."

It doesn't always work out that way, as Staff Sgt. Mike Wilson will tell you: "The biggest problem is the lack of facilities for mental health treatment for these kids. We'll direct the kids to the Teen Health Centre, but they've got a huge waiting list. Now and then we'll have a kid who's so troubled we'll beg them to take him in, but they'll do it only in extreme emergencies. It's the same with the Regional Children's Centre."

Which is only part of the problem. Probation is a short-term measure. Probation officers usually deal with kids for a few months, perhaps a year, on occasion a couple of years. "But if you've got a more serious and deep-rooted problem," says Judge Phillips, "if there's no parent in the home, or the parent isn't doing the job and doesn't recognize that he or she isn't doing the job, or doesn't want anything to do with the child, then that's a long-term problem. Sometimes you feel you're addressing the short-term problems but that the root problems are still there. Probation won't deal with those. Often times you have the sinking feeling if you send the child out on probation that the young person is just going to be waiting a period of time before they're back before the courts because you can't get to the real problem."

The real problem, as Doug Phillips will tell you, and as most others in the field will tell you, is the parents. But Doug Phillips' hands are tied: "I can't, through the young person, try to rehabilitate the parents. I can't make them 'parent' the youngster. I can only do so much and I sometimes feel that by the time the child gets here (to court), it's probably too late."

It's frustrating for the person on the bench. All the more frustrating because the judge often senses that a youngster needs a fairly long sentence in custody so that professionals can start to give that child the help he or she needs. But a judge can't sentence a youngster to a jail term merely to help that youngster. The Act is quite clear. "You are obliged," says Phillips, "to deal with the offense that's been committed, not the problems which may have contributed to the young person committing the act. My job is to provide the appropriate disposition for the offense which has been committed. But you see all the symptoms which say this person is headed in the wrong direction, hasn't got the structure in the home, may have some other psychiatric or psychological problems, but you're not in a position to say, 'Well, I'm going to fix this youngster, I'm going to put this youngster into a treatment resource which is really what this youngster needs.' If it relates to a minor offense, you can't do that. You can't use the criminal justice system to fix young people and all their host of problems. You have to hope," says the judge, "that those who have responsibility for a young person in need as a result of absent parenting, absent appropriate home, absent appropriate shelter, that all those resources will respond. But sitting where I do, I can see that those resources are not getting the kind of support they should. And I speak of places like the Children's Aid and the Regional Children's Centre. Their funding is not what it should be to deal with these problems."

So, the kids are sent out for treatment and find themselves at the back of the line waiting to get into an over-crowded and under-staffed program which may help them deal with their problems, if they feel like taking part and sticking with it.

The unsettling fact is, the system which is sending kids back out into the community is almost guaranteeing those kids will go untreated, will graduate to more serious and more hurtful crimes, will come back into the court on more serious charges, and will finally be sent to jail, one of the few places which can treat them.

Which begs the question. Which Judge Phillips asks before you can get it out yourself: "Of course, someone who is looking on would say, 'Do we have to wait until the third or fourth time (the young person commits a crime)?' I can certainly appreciate why someone out in the public will be looking at the courts and saying 'If you can sense it, and see it and your instincts are reliable enough, then you should have the power to do what's necessary. If that means sending a person away to a custodial facility for a long time so that the treatment is provided, the youngster is cured and future offenses avoided, great.'

"The difficulty is," says the judge, "that's based on a number of assumptions in which you place an enormous amount of power in trial judges. I think everyone should be very careful, cautious, and wary about how wide the discretion should be for any one person in the system. Judges aren't trained psychologists and they aren't social workers. I think we should be very cautious and careful about how wide the discretion we give to anyone who has the power to take someone's liberty away because, remember, that's what we're doing." But let's suppose, for a moment, that we do give judges this right. "Where's the accountability to ensure that the person who makes the decision gets to monitor how well everything's going along the way while the young person is in the treatment facility? That doesn't necessarily happen. So I have some reservations about the idea we should give judges the carte blanche to determine custodial dispositions on a first crack for all sorts of offenses for the purpose of ensuring it doesn't happen again."

The judge casts a wary eye at this entire argument because the argument is, at bottom, that our court system should be fixing our most troubled kids. We say that because the courts get the kids at the flashpoint. But as the judge says: the courts are there to deal with the crime, not the illness or the problems which led to the crimes. "You can't look to the courts to fill the void" which parents have left in their children's lives, says Judge Doug Phillips. "That's not what the Young Offenders Act is designed to do. And I'm not sure that's what you want the courts to do."

That may very well be the case. But the kids keep going into court and society expects judges to do something about them. And some judges wish they had more help at their disposal. Judge Saul Nosanchuk: "I wish we had more resources, recreational programs and other things in place. As far as choices, I think we're limited to some extent. I think the state should make sure there are facilities in place as options for sentencing people. Places where people could do constructive work, recreational things that people could get into where they could let off some steam. Sometimes we feel we sentence someone for a probation order or a community service order and that maybe there's more that could be done. But I think that's a community problem. Really, you want the kids back in their own neighbourhood, back in their own family if the family is functional. But if the family is dysfunctional, then you have to have something in the community that's functional, that's structured, where they can take their energy and work it off. Places like New Beginnings, residential places, are very valuable for certain kinds of people." Even the jails have been good for some of these kids. "I remember once a woman screamed that her kid was being sent there for fourteen months but after all was said and done and he came back, we found that the kid had done great. He'd flourished. And I think the family realized that. So even sending someone to prison, sending them into closed custody, may be the advisable thing to do. It may be helpful in the long run. But we could always use more resources.

"There's a provision in The Act that we can't force someone into treatment. I think that's somewhat unfortunate. Although, on the other hand, if someone is balking at it, then treatment has a slim chance of success. Myself, I don't think that limitation should be there." The judge thinks if it's obvious a kid needs treatment, then treatment "should be something people ought to be required to undergo, made to have the opportunity to undergo if you want to put it that way. There's a lot of resistance (on the part of the kids) and you just have to cut through the resistance and not just accept this initial 'no.' I think it would be better to require it. These young people have to realize it's no awful thing to be treated, to admit you've got problems. That's the whole thing: if you don't admit it, where do you go from there? If you've got problems and won't admit it, then you're in the worst possible position. You're never going to make any changes."

Why not order kids into treatment? Well, it goes back to the times in which The Act was framed, and the changing attitude about children in our society. Alec Marks, executive director of New Beginnings group homes for young offenders: "The Young Offenders Act starts out by talking about young offenders being responsible for their behaviour." And it has as its starting point the belief that "young offenders are not children, they're not adults, they're something in between, young adults, I guess, or mature children. So it's a different way of looking at the problem."

A flawed way of looking at the problem? "Not necessarily," says Alec Marks, "because it was based on hard research, hard facts. We know that if offenders are going to be successfully rehabilitated, it makes sense for them to be willingly engaged in programs to treat them. And if they are engaged voluntarily, the chances of them being rehabilitated are greater."

The Young Offenders Act states "the young offenders need to be responsible for their behaviour and it's up to the young person to be rehabilitated. So we as a society can offer to help the young person. The way The Act was written would not allow treatment to be forced in most cases. In order to get a young person into treatment, a young person must agree to do treatment, the agency that's going to provide the treatment must agree and the parents, if they're involved, must agree. If at any point, any of those people want the treatment to end, the treatment ends."

Have we all gone down the rabbit hole? "My first reaction is that provision, I think it's Section 13 of the Young Offenders Act, should be subject of change." But no sooner does Judge Doug Phillips say that than he says this: "However, effective treatment only works if those who are the subject of it engage in it and want to work within it. Secondly, if I tell somebody to engage in treatment, I have to be concerned about what kind of treatment. Treatment can sometimes be pretty intrusive. Are we talking about electric shock treatments? To what extent are we talking about treatment that might in any way be so intrusive as to constitute a very serious violation of the civil rights of this person? We don't demand that adults engage in treatment without their express consent. So why treat young persons differently?" Let's suppose we do that because the young people are at a formative age and can still be saved. Well then, says the judge, you'd better know that the treatment you're ordering is going to work. How would he, who is not a psychiatrist, a psychologist, or a social worker, know that? How would he know that he could rely on the recommendations of the people who purport to know? "So, it's easy enough to say, sure, make these young persons engage in treatment even if it's against their will, but I think it's a little more difficult question. I'm not convinced. Of course I don't have to be convinced. It's the lawmakers who have to be convinced."

So far, the lawmakers aren't convinced. No matter how obvious it is that a kid has serious mental problems, treatment remains an option, except for sex offenders. Most kids won't take part in voluntary programs. But even those who do agree to treatment can opt out at any time. It doesn't make a whole lot of sense to psychologist Janet Orchard. "That's the problem with the changes that society made in response to treating children. It's related also in the Child and Family Services Act in which at the age of 12 a child has to sign with the parent to consent to treatment and as of 16 they can sign themselves in and out of treatment."

"We need to be a little more balanced about kids' rights," says the jail's director, William B. "You could ask yourself whether kids should be given as many legal rights as they are." An example? "The Children's Aid will tell you that once a child is over 12, even if the parent wants the Children's Aid to take that child into care because they're not managing and the child needs the help, the child can refuse. Kids over 12. There has to be more recognition of what's in the child's best interest." And a child of 12, a deeply disturbed child of 12, is unlikely to be aware of what's in his or her own best interest. The move to give kids all these rights was well-intentioned — it was designed to protect them from unscrupulous people, including their parents, and to make them shoulder more responsibility for their own actions. But William B. says, flatly, "We've swung far too much in the wrong direction." And the very system which was supposed to help the kids, now gives the kids freedom to avoid the treatment and the programs which could help them, which could, in some cases, save their lives.

"From newborn to age 12," says Judge Doug Phillips, "we have the child protection system. To what extent does society look at the parents and parenting skills in those formative years such that we should know well before the child reaches the age of 12 whether someone has abandoned the parenting function? I'm sure if you went out into the community you'd hear from many who don't like the child protection legislation, who think it gives too many chances to the parents and that we have inadequate resources to help parents do their job. So even before they get to the criminal justice system at age 12, there are other minefields out there, pitfalls and difficulties that revolve around the kind of quality parenting that our children get. If every child got good quality parenting, we'd have an ideal world. But they don't."

Psychologists like Janet Orchard also think the system isn't dealing wisely with youngsters when it allows them to refuse treatment. "The argument can be made that a child in early adolescence is not intellectually or morally able to make that kind of decision, can't think in terms of the long run, about how their life is going to be a decade or 15 years from now. I think that's very true. They can't. And that's a real flaw in the system."

Another flaw. As the jail's social worker Sandra J. says to her kids, "When you start to feel bad, I start to feel good." It means they're getting to the bottom of things. When the kids start feeling guilty and sorry for what they've done, when they start feeling rage at what's been done to them, Sandra and the kids are getting somewhere. No pain, no gain. But often, as soon as things get painful, the kid signs himself out of treatment. Sandra J. shakes her head.

"Treatment can be very uncomfortable," says Alec Marks of New Beginnings. "And many young offenders say 'I'm not gonna do that. I've got three months to do. I'd rather just sit in the jail. I'll do my three months and then I'll go back to what I was doing before.' That's a problem, in my eyes."

But this raises the question: if an unwilling kid is ordered into treatment, can the counsellor make any headway? "There's a debate about that," says Alec Marks. "There's one group that says, no, treatment should not be forced. In psychoanalysis, a person should voluntarily accept treatment and want change for his own reasons. There are others who say that's not true with every type of intervention with an offender. For example, behaviour modification can still be effective when the person is put in the program not by choice but by being put in prison. So there are different perspectives."

Janet Orchard runs mandatory counselling programs for juvenile sexual offenders. Does such treatment work? "Yes and no. Yes I think it can, for some of them. For some it's ridiculous and it can't. If we look at the sex offenders, none of them wants to be in treatment. None. They come because they're forced. And they still benefit. But you have to do a lot of work, and you have to work with their parents to support the treatment. The ones with whom we fail miserably are the ones who go home from treatment and hear from their parents 'they're making a mountain out of a molehill,' 'you don't need to be there,' 'this is stupid, the only reason you have to go is probation.' This can undercut your efforts dramatically. But if the parents can be helped to be supportive of the treatment and the court is saying you have to do it, if you're prepared to be patient trying to wheedle the kids into doing it, I think you can do it. I think so."

"People have been under the impression that the way the Young Offenders Act was written these young offenders were going to be rehabilitated," says Alec Marks. No surprise so many people are disappointed, and want major changes to The Act. Marks, too, would like to see some changes. "We've had nice programs out there that help young offenders, but we don't have enough in the way of treatment, we're not forcing treatment requirements or expectations on these young people. Many of them are going through the system just killing time and if they're doing that, we're not helping them much. We're not helping them at all, in many cases.

"So," says Marks, "what I'm hoping for in some of the changes to the Young Offenders Act is that they're going to look at making treatment more attractive and more available and will have programs geared toward true rehabilitation rather than simply soft programs that are just killing time."

3. PREVENTION

There's no doubt the kids in the jail need treatment of some kind. But there's also no doubt in some minds that if the kids had been reached, and helped, when they were much younger, they might not have wound up hurting someone and being jailed. Kids don't get screwed up overnight. Randy Semeniuk: "The young offender who torched the house, a few of us predicted the year before that he'd kill somebody. He'd been in trouble, having some difficulties and they were going untreated and his mother refused to acknowledge he had a problem. She was a single parent, she was mentally challenged, her son had some problems, she just refused to acknowledge them and sure enough . . .

"We see that quite a bit. We'll say 'this person is going to be major trouble.' " Another example: a young offender assaulted a child. "This young offender had been charged once or twice previously. In one case, he was sitting with a boy and shot him in the leg with a pellet gun, shot him to see what it would feel like to shoot someone. So he comes to court, you can see there's a problem here, and you just know that unless this person gets some help he's going to be back. The parents refused to acknowledge there was a problem. Unless Children's Aid can somehow get involved then from our perspective and the police perspective we have to wait until he does something and then we can hope he's sentenced and something happens. The mother refused to believe this kid had a problem. You shake your head and think, 'You should have to write a test, pass a test, receive a licence and then you can have kids'. Sometimes you think that way, when you get real cynical."

Former youth bureau cop Roger Montchamps: "Help isn't always available. The social agencies that are in place are over-burdened. And in many cases they're hamstrung by the rules and regulations, if not the law itself. A woman called and said 'I have this 15-year-old, he's running away, hitting his sisters, won't do any work around the house' and she's tried to get assistance but they tell her 'well, we can't do anything until he breaks the law'. Meanwhile, life in the house is hell on wheels. And the other kids in the house invariably suffer."

What happens to these kids if they don't get the help they need? "Some of these kids are candidates to kill someone." Randy Semeniuk has seen it many times before. "You know they're going to continue and it's just a matter of time before they go to the pen when they become an adult. The only thing we can do to keep the public safe is to warehouse him as long as we can. So we ask for long sentences. At least if he gets eight years and serves half then he's off the street for four years. That's about all we can do. And if it's a violent crime and you predict he's going to kill someone, you can only hope you're wrong. But we've seen it happen. We've seen it happen too many times. You sit there helplessly. You know there's a problem and there's nothing you can do."

Psychologist Janet Orchard says part of the problem is that it takes the system far too long to get the troubled kids into jail, which is, sadly, about the only place they're likely to get treatment. "And unfortunately, we know who those kids are. I don't think it's hard, in the assessment of a family and a kid by a probation officer or a social worker or a psychologist, to be able to figure out that this is more likely to be the kind of kid who is not going to benefit from probation or community service or coming in with mother and father for therapy because they're just not interested. But unfortunately, you can't sentence a kid to a year in jail just because he's done a B&E and this is the first or second time he's been caught and some professional thinks, 'Oh my gosh, you're on the road toward habitual criminal behaviour.' It just isn't possible to do that, legally."

The system thinks a tough first-offense sentence would violate the kid's rights. Maybe. Maybe not. But are we violating their rights, in a more abstract sense, their rights to be a well-adjusted member of society, if we refuse to deal with them in a way that will help them to deal with their problems, get their act together? Janet Orchard doesn't hesitate a second before answering: "Oh sure."

Crown Prosecutor Jill Manny doesn't think the counselling should be limited to the kids. "I think there should be more avenues whereby parents are given some help, outside the criminal justice system, in parenting skills. There should be some mechanism whereby counsellors who are skilled psychologists, or specially-trained social workers, can sit down with the parents and the kids and work out some of these problems. Because it goes back to the parents. This is acting-out behaviour. The kid is saying, 'My dad doesn't care about me,' 'My mom doesn't care about me.' This kid is saying, 'I don't give a shit about you. I don't give a shit about this, that or the other. I'm going to be with my friends.' In order to change that hostility, anger or whatever it is, you've got to go back to the family, where there are families, and work this out. 'Why can't we cope with this kid?' 'Why isn't this kid responding?' 'Why's he doing what he's doing instead of doing what he's told?' 'What's the matter here?' 'What problems do you have?' And let the kid speak. Sit down and work it out in a much more informal setting than the court."

Ask people what goes wrong in the lives of these kids and, almost invariably, the fingers point at the parents. Ask what all these kids have in common, you'll get this: these kids don't care about other people. Put one and one together.

Long-time youth worker Tom Bromley: "The home's part of the problem. The home's gotta be part of the solution." As Jill Manny says, "There has to be someone who cares, who takes enough interest in this child to do something positive."

This is something the nuns next door think about, and pray about, a good deal. Sister Grace: "These children have misbehaved, okay. I could misbehave as much as they have. But these kids, who have they got to help them get back on the right road? Who's going to take care of them? I mean, once they've made this mistake, the YOA says, okay, you don't have a blot on your name like some other people would who've been to jail. But are there enough people out there who would treat them as a human being who has failed but who maybe deep down wants to come back?" Sister Grace, and all the other sisters, pray this might be so. And, strange as this might sound to secular ears, they believe their prayers will be answered. "Let's say your son has really offended you. You're good and mad at him, but your daughter knows you're upset and she also knows you have a soft spot for her and so she says 'Dad, Jim didn't mean to do that.' And so you feel lenient toward your son because your daughter interceded on his behalf. That's what we do with God. That's the idea. We intercede with God for these children, for all these children, regardless of what they've done."

Why the concern? Sister Gabrielle is almost puzzled by the question. She smiles and softly says: "They're our children. The equivalent of our children." Sister Grace: "Our interest in these children stems from the fact we have made a vow of zeal. It's our special gift. Our gift is a concern for people who are in need. And these children are definitely in need. So we go before God and say 'Oh, Lord, this kid is really in a mess today.' " Which the sisters know, because the staff at the jail will tell them, will phone over and ask that prayers be offered for kids who are especially troubled. "They say

'We have a boy here who is deeply troubled and he's kind of upset today, would you pray for him?' They don't go into much detail. They never give us names. Just initials." But names, as the nuns will tell, don't need to be mentioned. The nuns are confident God does not need to be reminded of names. "And then we put notes on the bulletin board." Please pray for W. Please pray for J. The notes are white, except for Sister Gabrielle's, which are pink. "I use pink so they'll stand out." Then the other sisters read the notes and pray for the child who is mentioned, initial only.

And just what, specifically, do the sisters pray for when they pray for these children? Sister Grace: "I pray that they will have someone come into their life who will lead them to God, get them to know God, and from the caring of that person they will get to know that God cares for them. I pray they will become responsible and lead a good life. Do they even know what a good life is? Have they had nothing but the example of sex, drugs and crime since they were this high? They don't know better, some of them. If they don't have the basics, they can't get anywhere. Everyone knows inside themselves what's good and what's bad. A conscience. The old saying is 'do unto others what you want them to do unto you.' If you don't want someone to punch you, then don't punch anyone. If you don't want to suffer the ill effects of drugs as you have, then don't go out and be a drug pusher. Don't go out there and do the things that have hurt you. I think that's basic Christianity."

Prayers notwithstanding, if these kids do find someone to care for them, teach them, and guide them, in most cases that person won't be a parent. Which enrages Jill Manny: "I think it's absolutely amazing that parents say, 'We don't want him back.' They can be middle class or lower class, economically they're all over the place, and they're saying, 'We don't want this kid back in our home. He's out of control, he won't do what he's told, she won't do what she's told.' I don't think parents should get off the hook. This is your child. You have a responsibility here. No. You're not getting off the hook. You're going to do something for your child."

But then you have the opposite. Janet Orchard: "I see moms who would walk on burning coals for their kids. They're doing it in the wrong direction, often. These are the moms who would fight the system to the ground over their kids, protecting them from the consequences the kids have earned, standing up for them through thick and thin. They're doing that because they love that child. No question about it. But, often because of what they've been through themselves, the way in which that love is expressed is all screwed up. So some of the kids have been rejected left and right, and why shouldn't they be the way they are? But for others, it's been love that's been damaging. It's been love that just hasn't been helpful. And we all know you can do that: you can love people to death. Love can be damaging as hell. And I think that's happened to some of these kids."

Two sad facts. Many parents have cut their kids adrift. And many parents who haven't, don't have what it takes to instill in their kids a sense of values. Some don't have much of value to impart to their kids. "I think society in general is really missing the boat on values." Supervisor Frank M.: "Core values, respect being the main one. Somehow these kids aren't being trained in values from an early age, they're not getting that teaching and that's reflected in how they're choosing to lead their lives."

Want dark vision? Frank M.: "The parents of these kids were damaged, they're having kids and damaging them. These kids are going to go out and have kids and damage them. The cycle is going to continue. Just the logistics of it, you're going to get a population where the majority's going to be damaged. Now, maybe that's a pessimistic way of looking at it, but I think unless there's something done to counteract that, to get the cycle stopped, and get the values injected back into society, it's hard to break out of that dark vision."

"I keep saying to myself, 'Does it not make sense that society is going to topple over on itself eventually?' " To William B., it does make sense. "There seem to be more and more parents who are having kids and who are not parenting them. And these kids are going to be adults and they'll be having kids and they'll be victimizing their own kids. And these kids are going to continue ending up in jail. There's no question about it. And on and on and on."

"Somehow," says Crown Prosecutor Randy Semeniuk, "you have to break the cycle, break the chain." How? If the church has lost its sway over many people, and if parents themselves grew up without these values and are thus incapable of instilling values in their own children, then what?

As much as people in the corrections system are loathe to add another brick onto the teachers' wagon, there's really only one place for the teaching of values to take place.

Barry Clark of the John Howard Society: "I've had this discussion with educators who say don't put it all on the schools. But the point of the matter is, like it or not, we can't avoid this. There is greater secularity, there is greater breakup of the family, there is greater family dysfunction. Granted, ideally we should keep the responsibility within the family. But what I see is that increasingly, the schools — whether they like it or not — are going to have to do it."

Randy Semeniuk: "You have to start with education." The Crown prosecutor takes part in an elementary school program called Values, Influences and Peers (VIP). He goes into the schools and talks to kids about those things, encourages them to toe the line. Successes? "There's no way to measure it. But I've had some kids come up to me and say it's helped. Whether they've been in trouble and stopped, I don't know. But even if you save one or two, it's worth it."

William B. will tell you that in almost every instance, there were signs that the inmates were headed for trouble long before they ever broke a law. "They say, 'Oh, I could have told you when he was four that he'd be trouble.' And I said, well, why didn't we help this child when he was four?" The teachers do see it. They tell their superiors that these kids need help, need to see counsellors, social workers, psychologists. But the kids, invariably, end up on waiting lists. The lists are long because the professionals are few. The professionals are few because money is scarce and money is scarce because preventing trouble is always more obscure, and less popular, than dealing with problems after the fact. Politicians, who dole out the money, can get re-elected for solving problems. Hard to grab headlines, and votes, for preventing them.

William B.: "That's the one thing I'd change if I could. I'd emphasize prevention, rather than punishment." This, from the director of a jail for young offenders.

However, these days, punishment, not prevention, is all the rage. The jail's nurse Cathy B. hears it all the time: "Punish them and then let them out again. There has to be a balance between treating and taking them away for awhile, with an emphasis on treatment, including the family." And Cathy B. sees treatment "as something that has to be ordered. The child needs treatment, and the parents as well" and she knows from having worked with these kids that neither the kids nor their parents will volunteer for such treatment. Especially in those cases where it's needed most.

The sad thing, the really heartbreaking thing, is "a lot of these kids want to change. Some of them are conscious of the fact they're victimizing people. Some of them never feel that, and those are very scary kids. However, many of them don't like what they're doing, but they don't know how to change." Cathy B. isn't convinced stiffer punishment will effect that change. "They've already been punished horrendously."

Bomber Bromley has been working with kids for more years than he cares to remember. And from his vantage point, in a residential treatment centre for troubled adolescents, this is what he sees: "I think there has to be a lot more attention paid in the schools. If the teacher can start identifying problems at a real early stage and they can have an agency right at their disposal, child-care workers in the schools, I think that's one way they'll be able to eliminate a lot of this juvenile delinquency. I'm talking about right when they first start school. You can see kids in the primary grades, somebody who's real fidgety, or a kid who doesn't want to share a toy and he's hitting other kids. People will say that's normal, kids hit each other. But there might be one or two in the class who are always hitting and that might be a signal that there's someone at home who's telling them 'to get what you want, you hit'. And all that does is escalate. The way Bomber Bromley sees it, a little intervention early on in the cycle could do a world of good.

The jail's nurse, Cathy B., would describe early intervention this way: "People need to be planning pregnancies. They have to have pre-natal care and parenting classes. There have to be support services for single moms with children, some place they can go to get help and have someone to talk to. They're so frustrated and who can blame them? They need help before they go over the edge. Then it's the child who suffers."

"When a mother has a baby," says William B., "there have to be a lot more services, more assessment and diagnosis right then and there before that mother gets out of the hospital. The health unit does a superb job, but it's just one tiny program and they haven't been given the authority to follow through." Nor the money. And it's not as though you can't see the need, right there in the maternity ward. "You could go into a hospital and look at those mothers and you could pretty well guess which ones could use help. It doesn't take any training in psychology or in social work, just good common sense."

But the mothers take their babies home "and things are set up so that the abuses have to occur before organizations have the right to move in. For instance, maybe the baby is allowed to lie wet in the crib for a couple of days, or a baby is fed when the mother remembers to feed it or doesn't have her boyfriend over. Or sometimes a boyfriend is allowed to knock the baby around because he can't stand it crying and it's not his baby anyway and the mother doesn't interfere because she doesn't want to lose the boyfriend. We hear stories like that and it's just awful." As William B. and others say, most of the mothers who feature in stories like this went through the same thing when they were kids. Fathers too. And you have to have concerns about people who have endured this having kids of their own. And if we can't do anything about that, then society ought to do something to shore up the rights of the babies before they get thrown against the wall or plopped in tubs of scalding water, in short, before the cycle repeats itself. As William B. will tell you, "There should be an awful lot more services and, somehow, more legal authority for organizations to insist on staying involved with moms." Because if those organizations aren't involved helping the mom, other organizations will be involved later, picking up the pieces.

William B. thinks we need to do much more in the area of teaching mothers and fathers the importance of the first few years of their infants' lives so they can avoid creating the damaged teenagers he and his staff are dealing with day in day out. He thinks parenting training ought to be mandatory for all high school kids.

Hard to hear 'prevention' when most people are yelling 'punishment.' Frank M. says the community itself has to understand "what's happening and try to stop it. It's at the grass-roots level that it breaks down, when these kids are infants. What's going on there? I guess the thing that really ticks me off is the lack of understanding about that concept from the people who have the power, which is government, and I think government in some ways represents society. You can't blame it on the people, because they don't understand it either. They're not clued in to what's really needed. People call for increased sentences. Punishment, punishment, punishment. Don't do any rehabilitation. They're not looking past the crime to see what's behind this and what we can be doing. It's all reactive. There's nothing positive about it. And as a society, we've got to get proactive. That's why we're so vulnerable to all these trends, because everyone's just reactive. They don't do anything until something happens, and even then, they're just reacting to what's happened."

Psychologist Janet Orchard: "I think we have to do some big time preventive work when kids are much younger. We have to deal with the adolescents who are in trouble, that's fair. But in order to prevent them winding up that way, we've got to start way back and look at providing preventive programs in schools and churches and in community settings to try to support parents who are doing a terribly difficult job and often, in our culture, all by themselves. We have to support schools so they will be able to teach values. There's always the big debate from the school saying 'it's not our job to do that.' But that's the best setting in which we can support the kids. That's where they are. The adolescents aren't there, the problem population. Usually by that time they're skipping out more than they're there. But early on, starting out in junior kindergarten, most of the time you've got most of the kids before the problems start interfering with their attendance. And it can be as simple as some of those very basic breakfast programs, feeding kids and feeding parents along with their kids and at the same time talking about 'why is it important to care that you hurt Harry when you do such and such' and 'how do you teach your kids to believe it's better if you help people versus taking from people when you want things.'

"Recently we had a meeting about Zero Tolerance of Violence in Schools. We talked a lot about trying to set up a climate where you teach kids how to solve problems and resolve conflicts in a nonviolent way. That's really important. I think maybe in the years to come we'll see improvements because of that. But we'll see that only in the kids who've started to experience that in the elementary schools, not the kids who are in high schools because their path is set at that point."

William B. thinks the schools need a lot more resources than they're being provided with in order to deal with the troubled kids they're forced to deal with. "Some people will tell you that we need to have more of the type of people who work here (in the jail) in the schools, that teams from places like ours be in the schools, that's where our work is and that's where our offices ought to be. We would be able to see the kids and pick them up at the beginning of it as opposed to letting it go on and on and on." Makes sense to him. And it probably makes sense even to the people who run our schools. But those administrators can't do it for at least two reasons — they haven't got the money, and they are getting pressure.

"My sense is," says William B., "they're being pressured from Queen's Park. It's government philosophy to mainstream everyone. There's this push, push, push to mainstream every kid no matter what the disability. I'm all for mainstreaming many kids, but kids who have severe mental health problems, I'm not so sure it's right to mix them in until they're better. When you've got a kid who's biting other kids, you've got a kid who's mentally disturbed, emotionally disturbed. Not a lot, maybe just a little. But it won't correct itself. You won't outgrow it. And it's not a phase. It's a sign of a disease or a deficit or whatever you want to call it and it's going to get worse unless it's dealt with." And while you're waiting to deal with it, the entire class will be disrupted because the teacher is trying to pry the kid's jaws away from another kid's arm.

As far as William B. is concerned, the school system never has had enough child care workers, social workers and psychologists to deal with these troubled kids. Even in the free-spending days. These days even though the boards are mainstreaming all the troubled kids who turn up at the door "there isn't enough being built in to help the teachers handle these kids." Far from it. In fact, just the opposite. "The school boards are paring their special services, eliminating some social workers and psychologists. I wish it didn't have to go that way."

"We can identify the kids," says Barry Clark. "But we have not put into place the programs that look at the child, dissemble the problems, analyse them and put into place programs to address the problems." Instead, we react to symptoms, not problems. Example: a kid is caught shoplifting, gets arrested, winds up in court. "But we don't realize that they're shoplifting because there are other issues in the home. Maybe there's family breakup. Maybe it's peer pressure. They may be doing this to pay for a drug habit. We have to look at the causes of behaviour, then address those causes. We certainly do this in other systems. If someone has schizophrenia, we don't lock them in a closet and expect them to heal themselves and come out in a year and be better."

The one place we shouldn't be looking, if we're looking to change the lives of these kids, is the court system. Crown Prosecutor Jill Manny says, "I think people turn to the criminal justice system for answers to everything. This system is not designed to change human behaviour. It should be a punishment. You committed a criminal offense. We're going to determine whether you actually did commit the offense, whether we can prove it, and then you're going to get a fit sentence. Now people want the criminal justice system to deal with all the ills of society: wife assault, every goddamn thing, let's go to court. Well, the system is not equipped or skilled to deal with all of that. I don't know why this kid is angry, the one who went out and wrecked the Co-Op building. It bothers me, it really bothers me, this case has stayed with me for weeks. Usually you see so many they just come and go. But this 12-year-old kid, I'm a lawyer, I can't cope with this problem." But someone better deal with it.

"That's right. Because what's he going to do next time? Get a gun and shoot someone? He's going to do something. And you don't have to be a genius, or a psychologist, to know that. But it's not the criminal justice system that has to bear the responsibility for all these things. Let's find some way of dealing with these problems other than turning to the criminal justice system. Jail's not the answer for these kids."

"These are not criminal justice issues," says Barry Clark. "These are social justice issues." And what the John Howard Society official sees here is a need for some major restructuring of society. No easy quick fixes. No quick vote-grabbers. "We have to look at a larger, more holistic approach, a more co-operative, collaborative approach between the systems. We're talking about housing issues, multicultural issues, health, mental health, and education issues. Somewhere in the background is the criminal justice system. And that part should be reserved to the end, not the beginning," of the process of dealing with our troubled kids.

"I think the schools already assume some responsibility in terms of the Values Influences and Peers program." The schools have some good and workable programs in place: teaching kids to solve conflicts non-violently, teaching them to make good choices incorporating good values. But when I asked Barry Clark how we as a society can go further in instilling values in our kids, he paused and looked at me and said: "That's certainly the most difficult question you've asked, because it's a matter that's really beyond strictly the parents or the schools or any single group. If we don't have a culture or society that is fair and just, and is not perceived to be fair and just by identifiable sectors in our society, then I don't think we can expect them to respect the values we have. And we have a system that is unfair."

An example: "Young children who come from minority homes or from different ethnocultural backgrounds, who have known prejudice and inequalities firsthand, when these children get involved with the law they react very indignantly and angrily. I think we have to understand where these children are coming from. And we have to understand that to react with more oppression by applying the letter of the law only creates an angrier individual. That's not to excuse what they do, but to qualify it.

"In terms of instilling values in children," Clark says, "it returns to the first question you asked: where do these problems come from? Very often, they come from the home. And so the question is: Do parents see values as an important issue? Teaching a lesson. Teaching responsibility. Teaching respect for property. Respect for life." Such lessons were once taught in the home, in the church and in the schools. "Traditionally they have done it, they've held the fabric of society together, they gave us goals." But times have changed. And if many families are no longer teaching society's values, and if the churches have lost their sway over many people, then it falls, as others have said, to the schools to do it.

But Barry Clark, like Cathy B., would begin even earlier than elementary school. He would have society deal with expectant mothers and fathers, help them understand the responsibilities they're about to shoulder, help them acquire the skills they need to do the job they're about to undertake. And he would have society offer the supports that those young people need, in the absence of their own family support, so that when they have problems they would also have the resources to solve them.

"What we're talking about is a safe and humane environment for parenting and for children. In the absence of that you create tremendous hurdles at a later date. You say at the age of three children have picked up most of what they need to know to make moral decisions and I would agree. And when you talk of conscienceless individuals, people committing unconscionable crimes, sociopathic personalities, anti-social personality disorders, very frequently what we're looking back to is what has occurred during the first three to five years of life, the kind of attachments that children have made or have not made, or the kind of attachments that have been destroyed on a consistent basis. We create very, very difficult hurdles for these children.

"So," says Barry Clark, "if we're talking about crime prevention, we're really talking about the quality of life. The best crime prevention programs are Big Brothers and Big Sisters, parent groups in schools, community organizations. That's crime prevention. It isn't this little artifact (the jail) that we've created over here that very clinically and antiseptically tries to engineer changes in a child's behaviour in an ersatz environment and then puts them back into the real world. It simply does not and cannot work that way. And hence the ultimate futility of looking to corrections to address what very frankly is not a correctional or a criminal justice problem. I don't think the correctional system works very well. In fact, the 'correctional system' is probably the greatest misnomer in western language because it corrects very little and tends to make things much worse. The best of our efforts, the best of our time and our energy and intelligence should be put into keeping children out of this system."

4. LIFE AFTER JAIL

But at the end of the day, whether or not society chooses to prevent crime rather than deal with it ... there will still be kids in the jail. And those kids, one day, will get out. And when they get out, there needs to be some kind of follow-up, some form of treatment or assistance.

One of the things which strikes you about these kids in the jail is that they're polite, they're friendly and, for the most part, their behaviour is acceptable, if not exemplary. So the question is: if they're so pleasant, then obviously they have the capability to be that way. So why are they doing crime if they can behave otherwise?

Janet Orchard, psychologist: "They can behave otherwise with the kind of support and structure they have in a jail. They can't behave otherwise, some of them, when they're flung out of that setting and into the regular world where there is not that kind of support, structure, routine in which you're supposed to be doing this now and then after that you'll be doing this and this is the rule in this situation and there's always a staff member to say 'Harry ...'. They cue the kids and help them keep their behaviour in line. There are all sorts of immediate incentives to do that. Take them out of that setting and plunk them back into an environment where there hasn't been a kind of nurturance and support, then they flail again. They're right back to the insecurity, the inability to cope; that flings them back into the easiest population of people to associate with, and that's the one where they break all the rules. It's a lot easier to hang out with those people. They don't feel they can fit in with the ones who look like they're more confident, the kids who are doing well academically and socially so they fall back into that group of kids who can't succeed in the more socially appropriate ways. They define for themselves what's successful, and what's successful is 'to hell with all the rules.' I sat with a kid yesterday who said that very thing: 'I can't really do those things that those kids who are doing well are doing. I'm really afraid that's what's going to happen when I go back, I'm going to go right back to hanging out with the kids I got in trouble with. Because I'm not scared of them. I don't feel insecure with them. They're not better than me. And I don't know how to do that other stuff.' And I think that's true. Or take the kid who can't read and who's angry at the school system. And his response, because he's terrified he's going to yet another high school in the fall, he can't read and he knows he's going to screw up, is to say 'I'm going to punch the principal' and he will and it'll be a horrible mess. But that, for him, is related to the fact that he's scared. And he's also scared of some of those kids who go to that school, the kids who are doing well. So that's the other thing that happens. With support and structure they can function in a certain way, but you make that transition back out (into the world) and it's hell on wheels for them."

What they need is support. What the kids often get, as Janet Orchard says, is an overworked probation officer. "Given the huge caseloads, in some cases they meet once a week, a very brief meeting: 'How're you doing? Not breaking any laws? Goodbye.' It's a real problem with the system.I think what we need is some kind of in-the-community, half-way house for the kids to go through before they end up thrust into their regular environment. Otherwise the contrast (between jail and freedom) is just so dramatic they can't make it."

What these kids need, according to Barry Clark, is "a case manager who co-ordinates the various aspects of the individual's return to the community. So there are individuals working one on one with the child in certain key areas: school and other programming and organizations to which the young person could belong upon release." In place of chaos and confusion and isolation, "there'd be some semblance of hope and structure and co-ordination."

The staff at the jail think the kids need a place, perhaps on the grounds, where they could come back to get some of the support they need. Penny B., supervisor: "I know the Salvation Army had a centre where the kids could go to play pool, have coffee and donuts. I think having a place with young staff would help, because young people have a way of reaching young people. I think that would be beneficial. There's a centre over here run by a couple of police officers. I think there needs to be more of that, run by fairly young experienced staff who know how to get across to kids. Because if they pop in for a coffee or a game of pool, you'd be surprised what comes out. They feel comfortable, they like the person, they chat, they ask questions, they seek advice. And some of them will admit 'I don't want to get into trouble but I find myself going in that direction' and some of them can't help themselves. I've run into a kid we've had here, I think, three or four times. He came in when he was 13. Then he went into the Phase 2 system (for older young offenders) and each time we saw him come through here he left a little bit more intact, but he went back to the same environment and got right back into trouble again." It's a familiar story. And it worries Penny B.: "I do worry about them. Some of them I really worry about. There are those you know are going back into their own environment and their old ways. We know that, and it's heartbreaking."

For those kinds of kids, especially, a drop-in centre or a half-way house on the grounds would be a life saver. "A centre which

216

employs some of our staff here," says Penny. "Somebody they're familiar with, somebody they could stay in touch with. They call us, but that's not the same as sitting across from them and having a chat over a cup of coffee, where they feel relaxed. I think these kids would probably hesitate to come to you and dump their problems on you, or want to admit they have problems, but if you're there with them and spending time with them, read their body language, you know that they need to talk.

"I think all the kids we work with, they'd come back, almost all of them would come back if there was a place here where they knew they could talk to the staff. I think it would be ideal. We could continue our work, it would be more like aftercare. While they're in here, we provide the structure they need. They can't get into any serious trouble here." What they need, desperately, is some structure in their lives that will help them stay on the straight and narrow.

"What we need," says Bomber Bromley, "are more half-way homes for these kids, and I don't mean a half-way house where a guy goes in and hangs around and smokes and drinks coffee and plays cards with the guys. Half-way houses where there are professional people with life skills programs. Maybe some of the sentences should be that you have to go to these programs. Like if an adult is convicted of impaired driving, he's got to go to these classes before he gets his licence back. Same thing. I think the whole thing revolves around education, and dollars for that education. Establish these places. Give them the funding. Because when you're always worrying about funding, and Lord knows we do it here, it takes away from the main goal."

"If you really wanted to be effective," says Alec Marks of New Beginnings, "you could shut down half the correctional programs and put that money into after-care to deal with young offenders after they're released. It wouldn't be that expensive, except where you

217

have a residential program. But if you had a program where young offenders had a chance to spend some time with a counsellor, a chance to talk with someone who knows their history and their problems and their goals, it wouldn't be that expensive. You're not talking much overhead. You're not talking mega-bucks.

"To do that, though," he says, "you would vastly improve the crime rate and I think you would vastly improve the quality of life for many people in our society. The offenders, and also the people they affect. They wouldn't be breaking into old ladies' houses and tying them up and robbing them.

"I'm realistic." And a realistic Alec Marks says he realizes money is tight. All the more reason, he thinks, to spend our money wisely. "I think we should put our resources into things we know do work. After-care is a key part of it, and it's being neglected right now."

If everyone knows what these kids need, why not provide it?

Randy Semeniuk: "It'd be an ideal world if there was some follow-up. But there just isn't. I guess the government's argument is, 'there's no money. It'd be nice to provide follow-up treatment, but who's going to provide it and where are we going to get the money to do it?' And then you'd probably get the argument from the police 'why are you giving them more money for follow-up? If you gave us more money for more manpower we could prevent more crime.' In an ideal world you'd have that follow-up. If there are some psychological problems, then you'd have a psychologist or a psychiatrist. If a child gets out and doesn't have the educational skills then the follow-up would be giving them an education. Say they're 17, not interested in school but don't have any vocational skills, you could have follow-up in that area so they could get a job and be a productive member of society. If it's just that a person needs someone to talk to, someone to give him advice, keep him out of trouble, then you could have some kind of counselling."

The kids also need something to do with their time. Randy Semeniuk deals daily with the kids who wind up in serious trouble with the law. And he often thinks about what's needed to prevent other kids from taking the same path. "I think we should give kids something to do, give them more programs, more coaching. I was involved in coaching baseball seven days a week when I was in my 20's. It seems to me when I was growing up everyone was involved in playing sports. We didn't have time to get into trouble. I was out there playing sports from the time the sun came up until the time the sun went down. Most trouble I'd get into was breaking the window of someone's house hitting a baseball. I didn't have time to get into trouble. Kids who aren't involved in these kinds of activities have a lot of idle time and what do they do? They get into trouble."

Janet Orchard: "How can we get him involved in this or that activity so he can feel better about himself? I think we need more activities in the community that these kids can access easily. There are kids who play baseball and there are kids who break the law. There are reasons why these kids don't play baseball any more by the time they're adolescents. Often times a combination of things — money, parents not able to fund some of the sporting activities. Parents who don't have the resources to access what is available for the kids who can't pay those dues for baseball or hockey or whatever, can't buy the scout uniforms." But the parents whose kids most need these activities often don't know how to get their kids involved. "So it's almost like we have to set up a system whereby, in the housing projects, there is funding for there to be an organization that reaches out to kids, follows kids, chases kids, and continues to support their involvement. An organization that looks for funding for them, doesn't rely on the parents to do that. An organization that really almost does that kind of parenting for both the parent and the kid. In the middle-class world we support our kids like crazy in those activities. I mean, the hours that parents in middle-class families spend trucking off to various things, watching their kids, applauding their kids. Nobody has done that for the majority of these kids you see. So there needs to be an organization that we fund and support to do that for them."

Janet Orchard says, "The other thing is that we need, as Canadians, to somehow look at all children as our children so that more people are prepared to give of themselves when the parents can't. I think we have a tendency to lull ourselves and figure 'That's your responsibility and if you're not doing it, too bloody bad.' Then we get really angry at the kids when they break into our houses. Then they're our problem. And then we think, 'throw them in jail and lock the door and don't let them out any more.' We get into this business where people think 'Just make longer sentences.' Longer sentences will not deter these children from committing these crimes. Adolescents are impulsive by nature. We all know that. They're not going to sit outside a store and decide whether or not to vandalize it based on whether they're going to get three, five, six or however many years. It just doesn't work that way."

Kids need an adult in their lives. Coach, teacher. Someone. Someone who, as the nuns say and believe, will care what's going on in their lives. Jail supervisor Frank M.: "A lot of the kids who wind up in here don't have a strong influence from someone you'd call a significant other. Someone who had a very positive influence, someone who could turn them around. I think if we all look back we can identify at least one, possibly two, three or four people we'd consider significant others, or even mentors. Sometimes it's a parent, sometimes a sibling, sometimes a teacher. Someone who really changed us, changed our views, changed our direction. I see a lot of that lacking in the histories of these kids. The significant others have, in most of these cases, been negative influences, either turning them to crime or damaging them psychologically so they're very vulnerable."

Psychologist Janet Orchard: "I've talked about charismatic people who work with these kids. For some of these kids, a Big Brother or a Big Sister who hangs in there through thick and thin and takes them out and supports them and does those kinds of things, can make the difference between night and day that a therapist can't. The reality is that the kid comes to see you during your working day, this is your job. That other person gives of himself or herself from their own life and their own time, takes away from time they could be using to do something else in order to give to you. That kind of thing makes a huge difference." And the kid begins to think, 'if that person is doing this, then I must be worthwhile'? "Exactly. And I hear kids say they feel that way about those people."

Barry Clark says the one common thread through the lives of troubled kids who do well is this: "Someone, a parent or a mentor of some sort, often a coach or a teacher, who's been involved at a critical moment in that child's life, has given the child a sense of mastery over their own life. A sense of empowerment. A sense they can control their own futures, a sense their lives aren't completely hapless. And I think there's a tremendous lesson of hope for us here: you start small intervention in the lives of individual children, and from there great successes will flow. Crime looks monolithic and irreversible. But in fact you can make great strides with individuals."

The key ingredient? "Somebody caring," says Bomber Bromley. Somebody who would run a program in the neighbourhood school after classes. He knows of people who have volunteered their time to do that. "A lot of kids ended up going in there. Any kids from the community, any kids period, who wanted to go in there. They had all kinds of activities, they had couches in there, they had pool tables, they had a gymnasium for basketball, they even talked to us about running anger management programs. They had guest speakers come in, family groups. They had 'no kids hungry on Saturday morning' where any kid who wants can go there and have breakfast. Every community could use that kind of thing."

The west end used to be a very tough part of town. Still tough, but Bomber Bromley, listening to his police scanner, doesn't hear the kinds or numbers of calls to the west end that he used to hear. "And what could be part of that? Part of that could be what these guys have done down here. Part of it could be the Children's Regional Centre right here in the neighbourhood. A big part of it could be the Sandwich Police Patrol." The Windsor police recently opened a sub-station in the west end and assigned officers to the neighbourhood full-time so people would see them as neighbours, with names. "All of a sudden these guys in blue, these big bad boys with badges, the kids are saying, "They're not so bad. I won't say it to anybody right now, but when I hear another guy in the gang say it, then I'll agree with him.' "

I tell Bomber what Janet Orchard said, about all these kids being our kids. Does he buy that? "Big time. All kids are our responsibility. And who's paying attention, Paul? There's kids all over on the streets who have nowhere to go. Why bitch and squabble? Everybody work together and get some of these things going. A couple more community centres where young people are encouraged to go to them. Give them a reason to go. I saw a program on TV the other night about a guy running a midnight basketball program to get kids off the streets. That's the kind of thing that's helpful.

"And get the kids involved who are doing great. You and I are talking right now about a very small percentage of teenagers in this community who are getting into trouble. Very small. And as a professional, you gotta stay on tour. Sometimes, even myself, you can forget there's another 90 percent of kids out there doing great. And

222

if there's some way people could involve those 90 percent as role models, then we're on our way to helping these 'who cares' kids. A lot of times, Paul, these kids over here don't want nothing to do with 'em. 'They're negative, they're trouble.' Maybe it should be 'How can we help?'

The 'who cares' kids are all over the place. "You and I were down there watching a ball game last spring, shooting the breeze, talking real positive about that kid playing third base, and the kid in the outfield. Meanwhile, there's another crowd sitting at a picnic table on the far side of the diamond, smoking and planning nonsense. Who's noticing the kids at the picnic table? Nobody. But somebody better. If we don't get to them now and train 'em and educate 'em, what are they gonna be able to do?"

The answer starts with a capital C. "I'm hearing things now, bats and chains and twenty, thirty kids fighting at a time. You watch. Look what's going on in Toronto. Bats and chains are boring. Now they got bullets flying. Bringing guns to school. Look at other countries, what's happening there. Looking at them, Canada ain't bad. But if people don't get on tour, it's gonna be.

"I think sometimes communities think they're immune, so they don't pay attention." As Bomber can tell you, and as anyone else in the system can tell you, no one's immune. "It's a community problem, it's a provincial problem, it's a whole country's problem. It's everyone's problem."

We could use a much more co-ordinated effort to solve some of the problems. As Bomber said, 'why bitch and squabble'? But there's lots of bitching and squabbling going on behind the scenes as groups vie with each other for power and money.

"There are almost two systems to deal with young offenders," says Alec Marks. "When the Young Offenders Act came into effect, back in the mid-80s, there was a lot of political infighting as to which body of government should be dealing with the service. At that time there were two ministries that had expressed interest in providing young offender service and each ministry said 'we're the most appropriate ministry to be giving this service.' There was a lot of money at stake, coming from the federal government." And, as Alec Marks doesn't add, and doesn't need to, empires thrive on money.

The ministries fought it out to the bitter end and finally the government, like King Solomon, picked up the sword. But in this story, unlike the biblical story, there was no loving mother to let go of the child at the last minute. The government swung the axe, dividing the body in half. "So we have two ministries dealing with young offenders. The Ministry of Community and Social Services deals with the 12 to 15-year-old young offenders and the Ministry of Solicitor General and Correctional Services deals with the older young offenders, the ones 16 and 17 years of age." The ministries got their money and the ministers got their empires. As for the logic?

Leaving logic aside — and only one other province suffers this kind of bureaucratic schizophrenia — there are unhappy side effects. "It's almost like there are two systems," says Alec Marks, "and sometimes we're not very well integrated. It can be wasteful, and we're too overwhelmed with work to have any waste."

It's not just the ministries manoeuvring for money, power and turf. "The whole system of handling kids is piecemeal," says retired youth bureau cop Roger Montchamps. "Everyone's getting their funding from different places and everybody's got a different mandate. There's an old proverb that it takes a community to raise a child, and that's what we need here. We need a community of educators and social workers, child care workers, child welfare workers, children's aid workers, police — everyone who works with these kids to be working all together, not working apart from each other." And, in some instances, against each other and the kids' best interests.

What we need, he thinks, is some kind of Children's Tribunal or Council made up of representatives of all the agencies dealing with children in any community. As soon as a child comes in contact with the police, someone from the council would become involved: arrange counselling if needed, for the kid and the family, arrange help for the family if they needed it, in short plug the kid and the family into what services they needed. We'd stop looking at kids' criminal acts as the problem and start looking at them as the symptom of a problem. And all the agencies in the child-care community would be available to help.

Meanwhile, back in the present tense, fourteen kids are spending their days and their nights in the jail. Some of them are figuring things out and some of them aren't. Some of them are making progress and some of them could care less. And one of these days, later or sooner, the front door will be unlocked and it'll be 'goodbye, good luck' and, as jail director William B. says, "We cross our fingers and send them out the door." For most, there'll be no home to go to. And the friends who welcome them back will be the same friends who helped them get into trouble in the first place.

It's more than a shame, if you ask Barry Clark. And he doesn't buy the argument that we don't have enough money to provide good preventive and after-care programs. "The ministry will be quick to say it's because we don't have the money. It's not that they don't have the money. In fact, they're receiving more money than education or health. But they're misallocating the dollars. There's been a tremendous increase in the use of custody, in dollars flowing into the deep end of corrections, to the custodial end of corrections. And this money has to come from somewhere. When you take dollars and put them into institutional areas, then you deplete dollars that are available for alternatives to custody, for social welfare programs, social

225

development programs, mental health programs, education programs."

A hopeful note: William B. says the Ministry of Community and Social Services is looking at ways to reallocate money into prevention and community-based programs for these youngsters.

It's a much-needed move, according to Alec Marks, executive director of the two New Beginnings group homes for young offenders: "If we're going to make any change, if we're going to help society, we have to look at society itself. We have to look at children and families when children are really young. If we could redirect dollars to working with families who are in poverty, families with poor coping skills, families which are dysfunctional, if we could rebuild positive family relationships, rebuild a sense of community, if we could do things in the community to build up the community, then eventually we'll be spending a lot less on group homes like this one and on jails. This is a very expensive program to run. It's even more expensive to lock someone up in prison."

It costs the taxpayers $1.25 million a year to operate the 20 beds at New Beginnings' two open custody facilities for young offenders. It costs taxpayers another $1.5 million a year to operate 14 beds at the jail, nearly $3 million to take care of troubled kids in three centres. And there are dozens of these facilities in every province in the country. As Alec Marks says: "It really gets expensive." And those costs don't include the financial cost to victims and their insurance companies. And, of course, they don't include the psychological and emotional costs to the victims and to society in a broader sense. "It's very, very expensive," says Alec Marks.

"The name of the game, as far as I'm concerned, is to target programs for kids who aren't doing well in pre-school, for families which are having problems, trying to make corrections at that point. That's true correction. Just in terms of being effective as a society, that would be the most effective route. But unfortunately we can't do that because we don't have the money because we still have to spend money on the people in prisons and open custody. We can't all of a sudden say, 'We won't deal with these people.' "

What we may well have to do is make a short-term, and very large, overlapping expenditure on both correction and prevention in the hope that, down the road, the preventive efforts will reduce the corrections costs. "I think so," says Marks. But he's the first to admit it's not an easy sell, politically. "Especially given the hard times we've been having." And given the hardening of the emotional arteries we seem to be experiencing. "Sure," says Marks. "People feel we should get much tougher with young offenders. There is a perception young offenders are running wild and that the rate of crime among young offenders is doubling every few years. If you did an informal poll you'd get a majority of people on the streets of Windsor saying that." A majority, probably, in every town and city across the land.

Barry Clark, of the John Howard Society: "We can never eliminate crime and I don't think we can ever eliminate the need for jails. What we can do is reduce the number of people in jails." But that means spending money on preventive programs, and spending money on after-care programs to help kids stay legal. Vicious circularity.

And as Staff Sgt. Mike Wilson is quick to remind us, we'll be paying, one way or the other. As he says, 90 percent of the kids out there are terrific kids, causing no problems. But 10 percent are pure trouble. "That 10 percent you'd better take care of. They've got serious psychological problems but we're not getting them the care they need. And you know where they're going: barring a miracle, some of these kids are hellbent for destruction."

Every now and then Randy Semeniuk will see one of his former customers. "You'll see them walking down the street and you say 'there goes the future of Canada' and it scares you. The future of

Canada is the youngsters and a lot of them are vicious criminals. Scary."

6:34 p.m. ───────────────────────────────

While B Group is out in the yard, A Group is inside, in the computer room. George, first in the door, was first to grab the computer disks, shuffle through the pile until he found the game he wanted: The Pirate's Ball, a kind of computerized pinball game. Which is not, according to Norm, the best of the games. He's got that one: David's Midnight Magic, another computerized pinball game.

George, John, Walt, and Norm are all on computers alone. Fred and Mary are working on a computer together. Rick is cooling his heels in South Wing, an area separate from the main wing of the building where staff can keep a close watch on troublemakers, and keep them separate from the group. Rick will spend the remainder of his sentence down there, and out of the group.

Walt isn't happy about the Fred-Mary pairing at the corner computer and he keeps looking over his shoulder at the two of them. Tough to keep your mind on the game when the woman you think is yours is sitting at another computer with another guy. Now and then Mary turns to smirk at Walt.

There are undercurrents. John is saying something to Walt. It's something staff member Sid G. didn't quite hear. "I can't hear what you're saying, John." John turns, and gives him a syrupy smile. "Sorry, Sid."

George, meanwhile, has started hammering the keys indiscriminately, frenetically. "George, you know which keys to use?" George is a little flushed, a little wired. "Yah." "Well, use them. You break the computers, you won't be using them again."

George starts tapping, a little more quietly.

Walt asks for permission to go to the bathroom. Permission granted. Sid follows him out into the hall, and makes sure he goes into the bathroom.

George and John are talking about computer games they'd rather be playing. Satanic pinball is high on George's list. "It's a good game. If you shoot the ball into the dragon's mouth, then you wind up in a graveyard. There's all kinds of gravestones. If you kill them, you get points. There's bats flying around and if you kill them you get more points."

He's saying all this, while hammering the keys. Then John strikes up a conversation with Norm, who's playing the computer beside theirs. Muttered comments. Then Norm turns, grins at John and says: "What're you gonna do, assault me?" Barb: "Norm?" "What?" "Is this necessary?" "He started it." "No he didn't." "Yes he did." "Shut the computer off and have a seat outside." Norm keeps tapping. "Shut the computer off, now, and have a seat outside." Norm stands, shuts off the computer, and smiles his way out of the room, puts his back to the corridor wall and slides to the floor, still smirking at Barb.

Where's Walt? Barb gets up, goes to the door, looks down the hall. Walt is head to head with Sid G.

George, sitting at the computer nearest the door, is now working on a kick-boxing video. One combatant puts the other on the floor. "Hey, I won! Knocked him out." He turns, looks at Barb. "Aggressive behaviour, on the computer." Turns back to the game. Fingers flying. Face flushed.

Mary asks to go to the bathroom.

She and Walt pass each other in the hallway. She says something to him in a near whisper. It's too much for him to take, apparently. Whatever Walt says in return isn't quite whispery enough. Sid hears him. "Walt, take a time-out." Back in the room, Fred has apparently added his two cents worth. Now there are three in the hall. Three's a crowd. Supervisor Frank M. doesn't like the dynamics: "Let's get them into their rooms."

Off go the computers. Down the hall and up the ramp we go. Fred is walking ahead of Walt, who has a very identifiable gait. Fred starts mimicking Walt's rolling side-to-side way of walking. He turns to make sure Walt gets the point. Walt does. So does Sid who is walking at the back of the line. As the group nears the top, Sid tugs at the back of Walt's shirt, to keep him from going through the door. "Wait here." They wait until the rest of the group heads down the hall and Barb can get Fred into his room. Then Sid lets go of Walt's shirt. "All right. Go to your room."

What was happening? Needling was what was happening. Subtle little shots that hit the target. When Walt took a washroom break, Sid G. followed him down the hall and had a chat. Walt told Sid he'd been having trouble with Fred and Mary. The way Walt looked at it, he and Mary were 'dating', which is jail parlance for sitting together when possible: at mealtimes, during recreation periods. He figured Mary was his girl. Then Fred started moving in, or Mary switched allegiance, or both, and Walt found himself on the outside looking in. Looking in, he was getting 'the look' from Mary and from Fred and he didn't like it. Bad enough being on the outside. Worse yet, having it rubbed in his face. Sid asked Walt how he felt he was handling the pressure. Walt said he thought he was doing all right, but there were moments when he felt he could punch someone in the head. Fred, for instance. "He was calm and felt that wouldn't happen because he knew he had a lot to lose (in terms of privileges). But the thought was there. And he said if things weren't resolved he might resort to clobbering someone. There's always the risk that it'll end up in a fight rather than talking it through." And just as Walt was telling

Sid about his feelings, Mary passed by on her way to the washroom and gave him a look. Walt couldn't help himself: he asked her what she was giving him the look for. Time-out, Walt. So, two in the hall at that point. Not comfortable.

But there was more going on here than met the eye. A couple of weeks earlier, Fred had talked to Sid about Walt. They'd been friends, but then Walt had started ignoring him and spent most of his time trying to move in on Mary. So Fred felt slighted. He also felt attracted to Mary. One thing led to another. And Fred isn't above a little pay-back for hurt feelings.

And where does Mary fit in? "I think she's playing both sides, really." And she wasn't above playing computers with Fred in order to isolate Walt.

Now that the kids are all in their rooms, what's next?

"Barb will talk to Walt and then she'll talk to Fred. I'll talk to Mary and we'll get a sense of where everyone's at. We'll try to find out whether they're about to continue with that or whether they're going to give everybody a break and back off and try to work things out without further conflict or potential aggression.

"If you take Fred's comments as being genuine, and Mary's comments as being genuine, there's a need for some sort of honesty or respect for friendships, because there's one guy who's blatantly treating his relationships with women very superficially and doing the same with his buddies. I'm not trying to judge what's going on, but I think it's important for them to hear each other out."

It's one of those days. Before Patricia P. does anything else, she wants to sit down in her office and have a coffee, with the door closed. "I need a break for a few minutes. What is there, a full moon or something?"

Half-way through her coffee, she offers this spin on the happenings of the day: "I think one of the things that the kids have the

231

most difficult times with, and get a lot of help here with, is relationships. How do we learn about relationships? We learn about relationships from our parents and other adults around us when we're young. We learn our roles as males and females. We learn all of those things. Many of these kids come from an environment where the woman is subservient to the male, seen as property, and the male is the dominant one and he calls the shots. And it's okay for him to fool around. Many of them have absent fathers and have a whole slew of other brothers and sisters because dad's been married six times or had six other girlfriends or whatever. And I think it really shows up in how they deal with each other.

"I remember at 15 and 16 being nervous around boys. And I think that's normal for many kids. But you don't see these kids being nervous. These kids, I think, grew up way too quick.

"You have one young boy who has to have a relationship with a girl. Has to. There hasn't been a girl who's walked into this place that he hasn't pursued. One just left and now this one's here and he almost assumes that because he's pursuing, that means she belongs to him. She hasn't said yes or no. But he sent her a letter asking 'will you go out with me' and just because he's doing that it means he's interested and he's pursuing and everybody else back off. And if anybody else even talks with her a little bit, or writes her a letter, he gets angry. I think that's what happened. Fred wrote her a letter, and Walt got angry. Rick has written her a letter as well because Rick likes her. Rick told me today that she answered him back and said she didn't want to go out with him, she just wanted to be friends.

"But you can see how real these emotions are. Walt's genuinely upset Fred would interfere this way. This is his woman, even though she's given him no signs. And I'm sure that's very deliberate on her part. This way, if Fred is still interested, she can keep stringing him along. Rick is writing her. God, what a flattering thing for a teenaged girl, who probably has very low self-esteem and views being valuable in life if men like her. It's wonderful to have all these guys jealous and fighting over her. It's like a little soap opera.

"So she keeps the iron in the fire and they're all kind of flocking around and this one's losing his mind over it. Yah. And unfortunately that's how many of them see relationships. Until we intervene and tell them that's not what relationships are all about. That's why we role model for them. Sometimes when we don't have kitchen staff I'll ask the male staff to work in the kitchen. I'll ask male staff to sew and do laundry. I'll try to get the female staff outside to play basketball and to do activities that are seen as male activities. And you should see the kids' reactions. You think this is a new generation, that they'd be even more liberated than we are. And they're not. They're more old-fashioned than my father."

How serious was this little episode?

"If we hadn't been there, Fred and Walt would have gone after each other. And that's probably what they would have done on the street."

This, despite the fact they've already had it out with each other, verbally. "Walt's way of looking at resolving this is saying 'Back off buddy, she's mine' and Fred's view is 'She doesn't belong to you. I can write to her. I can talk to her.' So in Walt's mind, this isn't resolved. 'He's still treading on my territory.' And so basically, this continues. One of them has to back off. That's the only way of resolving it."

6:58 p.m. ———————————————————————

B Group arrives, fresh and flushed from the baseball diamond, full of comments and questions. "Can I go to the bathroom?" "Can I get a book?" "Can I have a phone call?"

The kids get shepherded into their rooms.

Patricia: "We're going to have to go over the rules with these guys. This is getting out of hand."

The rules are pretty simple. And they're in black and white on the wall:

Task Time

1. All residents go directly to rooms to begin routines.

2. The reasons to be out of your room are:

> *i) to brush teeth, go to the washroom, get materials from closet, get medication.*

> *ii) to make phone call.*

3. No knocking once in your room.

4. No stalling in the hallway.

5. Bed should be neatly made before task time is over.

There are two task times. Three to four in the afternoon, seven to eight at night. During the afternoon, residents can get items from the cart — writing paper, envelopes — or they can get a book or their walkman. During the evening, they can take a book or a walkman. After the evening task time, there's snack time. Then the kids can watch TV until bed time.

Staff unlock the closets so kids can get their toothbrush and pyjamas, housecoats and walkman.

Curt: "Joe, can I get the arms cut off this T-shirt?" He'd like the arms cut off at the body seam. Joe looks at the shirt, thinks about it, and says "I'll see." Later, supervisor Frank M. will say, no, it's not allowed. No muscle shirts. It's not the muscle Curt is concerned about showing off. It's the tattoo, which he reveals by pulling up the arm of his T-shirt.

Closet doors are unlocked. Closet doors are locked. Boys and girls head into their rooms. Silence in the hall. Until someone starts whistling. "Whoever's whistling, please stop." The whistling stops.

"Joe?" Joe holds up a finger, finishes a conversation with one of the kids, then comes down the hall to see Patricia. "Could you go down to the A&P and get a birthday cake for Sandy? Somehow we overlooked her birthday."

Normally, Veronica bakes a cake for the kids on their birthdays. But Sandy, who arrived not that many days ago, got overlooked. And today's The Day.

"Sure," says Joe. "No problem. I'll go right after the environment check."

7:08 p.m.

"Sid?"

Patricia is standing outside George's door. Sid joins her, lifts the curtain, looks inside, drops the curtain.

"He seems to be getting agitated. Can you take him down to the lounge and spend some time with him?"

What started down in the computer room — George getting agitated by the chaos around him — has been intensifying. He's been pacing in his room, unable to get himself settled. And he could be heading for another episode such as the one — swearing, threatening staff, finally having to be put in the time-out room to calm down — that landed him in trouble a few days ago.

Sid opens George's door. "George? Want to come with me?"

Patricia watches them go down the hall and into the lounge at the far end. "George isn't stable right now." Which is a shame, because he's been doing really well: working in the Job Club, earning temporary releases into the community. But soon, he'll be discharged from the jail, and he's unsettled by the prospect. He doesn't know, yet, where he'll live, or what will happen to him. "George doesn't feel safe when things aren't calm, when things aren't going smoothly." It certainly didn't help, today, when things came unglued out in the playpen. Nor did it help when things came apart in the computer room. The last thing George needs is chaos around him when there's so much chaos in his head.

Chaos causes anxiety in most of us. "If you're already upset about something and things around you aren't going well, that doesn't help you to feel better or to calm or relax you at all. One of the things he's gained while he's been here is some of that calmness, some of that predictability, some of that structure with the staff and the environment around him. Because of the structure and the staff and the tight ship we run he gets the benefit of that."

He's recently been acting up, causing problems, which Patricia thinks "may be an effort to tell us 'I'm not really doing as well as everyone thinks I'm doing.' It was a last bid to say 'Maybe I really do need to be here, maybe I'm not ready to leave.' And we see this with many kids when their time is almost up. Especially with the kids who've been here for a long time. He's been here almost a year. And because he's come from a chaotic background and he's been in other residential programs this has been a long solid stay.

"Anybody having seen him when he first came in can tell you that he's miles ahead of where he was then. Some of the things we're seeing now (the flareups, the swearing, the agitation) were constant. He was always unstable. Very agitated. Very hyper. Very anxious about everything. Very untrusting." Patricia also tells you this: "George still sleeps with the curtain up on his door. We'll make exceptions for him, let him read longer at night and keep his light on for him until he goes to sleep. He's come from quite an abusive background, and he's been safe here. When anybody comes from a chaotic situation, very unhealthy situation, and can now be stable and safe and know that nobody's going to hurt him, and learn to trust that, well that's hard to leave.

"It's a struggle sometimes. A lot of people will say 'That's not what you should be doing. This is a jail. And in a jail people are there to be punished and they shouldn't be enjoying it.' But I don't think we make them better people, better children, we don't make them any healthier if we don't work with them in that way. We won't help society or children at all if we don't help them deal with some of those issues and make sure that all of this unhealthiness they had when they came in, or at least some of it, is going to be gone when they go back out again."

Given all this, what does Patricia think about when she thinks about George walking out the door in a few weeks' time? "It's bleak. It's very bleak. To this day, nobody knows where he's going yet when he gets out. There's no home for him to go back to. He's not well enough and not mature enough and not old enough to live on his own." This is just about the worst thing a kid can face when he's so unnerved by instability in the first place. "Absolutely. The problem is, what do you do with him. Who's got the answer? And where are the resources that can pick up where we leave off?"

In an ideal world, what would be there for him? "The goal of the whole team that works with him, his social worker, his probation officer, everyone, is to get him into a treatment program and that's not always easy because there aren't many of them and the spaces are few and far between so you have to make an incredible case for why you need to have this child in treatment and then you wait. And what if there's not a bed? You can't keep him. We can't keep him for another day. This is jail. The day he's out, he's out."

And George, she'd like to remind you, is not alone in this predicament. "So many of the kids don't have a home to go back to.

Actually, George may be more fortunate than many of our kids because he's still young and he's got a Children's Aid worker involved with him, somebody who can follow up with him. Many of our kids who are older who don't have homes to go back to end up on the welfare system in the community, many of the girls getting pregnant as soon as they leave, renting an apartment, not having much of an existence at all. And these are 16-year-old kids. It's just repeating the cycle that we've already seen. They're not going to be fit parents.

"Some of them will have their children taken away from them because they can't take care of them. Children's Aid will step in. Some of them leave the babies for other people to take care of anyway, so that they can go out and do what other teenagers are out doing. Some of the girls will tell you that having a baby is their goal, to have this little thing that will love them unconditionally: they talk about wanting to be the type of parent to the baby that their parents never were to them. For both boys and girls, there's that sense of wanting a family, doing something better than what they had. And they feel they're mature enough to do it. They're not, obviously. They don't see that what makes a healthy parent is a healthy individual. They try to reverse. 'I'll be better, once I have a baby.' 'I'll be responsible once I have a child.' 'My boyfriend's always fooling around, or beating me up, but if I get pregnant and have his baby, the baby will make us a family, the baby will make him responsible.' It's almost like a fairy tale picture. I don't know of many fairy tales that come true. And unfortunately, there's another life involved now. Another person who has to contend with all this. I'll tell you, it scares me to death to think of a baby who could have some of these kids as a mother or a father."

And George? What are his chances? "You know, I honestly believe if he doesn't have this type of structure around him, he won't be very successful in life. He'll get in trouble with the law again. He needs someone to be around, someone to help guide his day. " Could he go to school, on his own? "I think he could, so long as supports were built in for him. I don't think he could just go into a school like quote normal unquote kids do. He'd maybe need a counsellor he could always go talk to. And the teachers would have to understand that maybe he'd have to leave the room from time to time when he got agitated. People would really need to be knowledgeable about him and how he behaves. He's come such a long way here that he can almost tell you, he will admit to you, 'yah, it's too much for me right now. I felt like I was going to lose it. Everything was getting out of control.' That's why I had Sid go talk to him when he got agitated. Normally he can handle that, he can deal with it. But right now he's got his own issues that he's trying to deal with.

"He's a fairly bright boy. I think the thing that comes between him and doing well academically is all of the other stuff, all of the agitation, the not being able to deal with his environment. How can you focus on lessons when you're in that kind of chaos? You can't do your work then.

"And where are the cuts being made in the school system? They're being made in the so-called soft services. What are the soft services? Guidance counsellors. Child-care workers who used to work in classrooms where they have behaviour-problem kids. So what happens if he goes back to school now? Are the resources and services there to help him function? Probably not. So what's going to happen? He's going to get so agitated that he'll tell his teacher where to go. What happens then? He gets kicked out of school, or maybe he gets really pissed off and goes and smashes the teacher's window and gets charged. Or something might happen with a peer.

"Unless those supports are built in for many of these kids, I don't think they're successful when they leave. And unfortunately, many of them don't have much to go back to. I think they can function well here because in many respects it's a very unrealistic environment for them. Many of these kids have never had people around them every day that are taking care of their needs, that are talking to them when they need someone to talk to. I always go back and think: is this what we're supposed to be doing? Are we doing something wrong making them dependent on this type of programming? I don't think we are. I think we're giving them the type of skills they'll need in order to trust other adults. Maybe George's relationship with us will help him trust a teacher, trust his landlord, trust somebody else more quickly than taking a whole year to do that. And he won't have to go through the struggle he's gone through this past year."

7:14 p.m.

Staffer Dwight gets a table set up in the hallway outside the office. He goes from door to door, asking if the kids want to make a phone call. If yes, he asks for the name of the person the kid would like to call. Then he returns to his desk and checks the requested names against the list of people the kids are permitted to call: parents, brothers or sisters, other relatives, guardians.

Dwight dials the first number. "Hello. This is the jail. Will you accept a call from Grant?" The answer is yes. "Wait a minute, please." He goes down the hall, opens Grant's door. Grant follows him down the hall and goes into the lounge, slumps down into the chair. "Hi ma."

7:16 p.m.

Penny hears someone knocking on a wall. She goes from door to door until she's standing outside the room where the knocking's

240

going on. She pulls back the curtain, catches Elizabeth in the act. Elizabeth looks up and smiles. "Oh! I'm sorry."

She should be. She was trying to signal to the boy in the next room. They were involved in the same crime and the judge ruled there's to be no contact between them, verbal or otherwise, which is why they've been put in separate groups and spend all their time in separate rooms. Judge's order or no judge's order, there's no talking through the radiators or knocking on rads or walls. You try, and get caught, and there'll be consequences. "Elizabeth was well aware of that. She chose to knock at an opportune time, she thought everyone was busy, she was waiting for her book and as soon as I caught her she immediately looked up and said 'Oh, I'm sorry'. So she obviously knew."

⦁ Every kid's an individual. Elizabeth? One minute, she's fine. The next, she's bouncing off the walls. "She can be very very extreme one moment," says Penny, "and very caring and affectionate the next and you never know when she's going to flip. And in the matter of a couple of seconds she can. You never know how she's going to respond." So, for safety sake, Penny stands in the hall and keeps Elizabeth's door ajar with her foot. She tells Elizabeth what Elizabeth already knows, that she's been caught doing something she ought not to have been doing. For every action, there are consequences.

"You fucking bitch. You fucking hosebag. I hate you. I'd like to kill you."

"Elizabeth, I want you to sit on your bed. Sit quietly on your bed and then I'll come back and we'll talk about this."

"Why don't you get the fuck out of my face."

Penny repeats the message, then shuts the door.

Elizabeth's voice echoes in the room, rings out into the hall.

"Fucking bitch."

Penny leans against the wall, listening. "Her way of dealing with it is blaming me. Calling me a fucking bitch, a hosebag, she hates me, she wants to kill me. All she can do is say what she's feeling at that moment, a lot of hurtful things to try to get me away, get me out of her face. She wants me away, so that's why I backed away and told her to stay in her room. What I need to see from her is compliance, for her to sit on her bed."

This could take some time.

Meanwhile, there are medications to attend to. Penny heads down the hall. As she approaches Dwight's desk in the hall, Grant drops the receiver into its cradle, a little heavier than is necessary. Mutters "Bitch," and stands up. He heads down the hall toward his room. Penny knows a signal when she hears one. "Grant?" He stops and turns.

The timing of the muttered comment was probably no coincidence. As Penny later says: "Subconsciously it's probably 'Come talk to me. I need someone to talk to.' He's a very talkative one. And he loves one-on-one attachments. He really enjoys talking to staff and trying to figure out his problems. Usually kids who are frustrated, or having problems with their parents will do that after a really frustrating phone call. What I usually try to find out is not who's right or wrong but what the problem is. Because if they do have a problem with a phone call and they don't resolve it then they can cause problems back in the group." So, Penny takes her cue.

"Bad phone call?"

That's one way of describing it. Here's another: "I hate my mother." "What's the problem?" The problem is, he'd asked his mother, during a call last week, if one of his friends could come over when he gets home on a temporary release. The friend is a girl. "She wasn't my girlfriend. She's a friend. She's my best friend, in fact." But the fact she was a girl was a problem for his mother. "She said

242

she'd think about it and tell me in a few days. So I asked her if she'd thought about it and she said she had. And I asked if she'd decided to let her come over and she said she wouldn't do that. "I hate her."

Penny knew Grant had been having problems with Mom and Dad. He doesn't have a lot of contact with them, except by phone, and when Mom does get on the phone "she plays games with him. Mom's there when it comes to phone contacts: who he can and can't talk to, she says yes or no. But then he feels when we need money for shoes or necessities, then she's not there. Very controlling. And he feels she's there only to say no and make decisions that are against him. When he feels he needs something, or needs to be nurtured and taken care of, something positive, he feels that she's not there for him." Mom, or anyone else. Which is why Penny stopped him, called him back, let him vent his frustrations. "Sometimes it can help."

But it doesn't mean Penny can't be honest.

"Your mom doesn't like your friends?" Grant looks up, and grins. "Yah." "Well, from what I've seen in here, that is one of your problems, Grant. You don't always choose very good friends." He looks at her and laughs. "Is there anything I can do? Anything you'd like to talk about Grant?" He looks at her for a second or two, then shakes his head. "No. Thanks. I think I'd just like to go back to my room and think for a while." He turns, again, to go. "If you want to talk, let me know." He smiles. "Thanks, Penny." Then turns and goes to his room.

"Grant is the kind of kid who's sort of between somewhere and nowhere. I think it's important to let him know that I understand about his mom pulling and pushing him because that does happen to him. If they need to talk then I'm there. But I can't pressure them. That doesn't help. They've got to want to talk. And slowly but surely, some of them begin to trust you. Trust is a very difficult thing with these kids because they've been put down, they've been pushed out, they've been lied to, they've tried to trust somebody and everything's fallen apart. So trust is a very very difficult thing with them. They have to earn our trust. But we also have to earn their trust." With Grant, trust doesn't seem to be a problem. "We're kind of like a family for him now because he has no one. I think he sees this as an environment which is very nurturing and caring." Like home? "Yah."

Penny goes in to start arranging the medications.

Joe shows up in the doorway. "Want to do an environment check with me?"

7:27 p.m.

We go down the back stairs. All the way down Joe is looking for things that aren't as they should be. He checks the rad covers to make sure screws haven't been removed, light fixtures to ensure covers are secure. He pushes the door to make sure it's secured, then opens it and walks out into the fenced fire-escape enclosure.

If the fire alarms go off, all the room doors are automatically unlocked, as are the stairwell doors and the doors to the two outside yards: the paved play yard and this one, on the other side of the building. Which is why, at least twice a day, the fences in both yards are thoroughly checked.

Suppose a message gets in from the outside: we'll be cutting the fence at a certain time. You pull the fire alarm, get out into the yard, and you're free. As Joe says: "I'd never put anything past them." No late-night fire-alarm breakouts yet. And the staff don't want to have one.

Joe goes all the way around the yard, checking the bottom of the fence to make sure no one has cut the metal ties; checks the mesh all the way around to make sure no one has cut the chain link.

244

"See that?" He points to a metal plate covering the hole in the wall where there had once been a light fixture. "One of our staff was able to work his way up the fence and then step on the light and get over the top." The light fixture was gone the same day. The fence is unscalable, now. Guaranteed. "We had the most athletic staffers try it. They couldn't scale it."

Joe makes another circuit of the yard, shining a flashlight around the base of the fence to make sure no one has left the residents any 'presents': knives, screwdrivers, saws.

In we go, and he makes the rounds of all the lower-floor rooms: dining room, rec room, honours lounge, bathrooms. He gets down at floor level, checks under the furniture, feels under the open rad covers, checks the waste paper chutes in the bathrooms. "Any place they could hide anything, we check."

Twenty minutes later, he takes me back upstairs, opens the door, and heads off to buy a birthday cake for Sandy.

7:49 p.m.————————————————————

Time to lay down the law.

Patricia goes from door to door, visiting members of B Group. The message is the same at every doorway.

"All this questioning has to stop. All this complaining has to stop."

When the group comes up for task time, they're to go into their rooms. No questions in the hall about bathroom and mail, phone calls, books, and walkmans. No knocking on the doors as soon as they go inside.

No repetitious questions.

"What are you really telling me when you ask me the same question six times?"

245

"That I'm anxious to get my mail."

"What else are you telling me?"

There's silence as Curt thinks about this.

Then, his voice rising into a question mark: "That I don't believe you?"

"Exactly. That you don't believe me and that you don't trust me. Which isn't fair. Do I follow through when I tell you something?"

"Yes. But ..."

There was one time when Curt had asked another staff member for something and the staff member had said it would be taken care of but then forgot. "Well, those things happen once in a while. Maybe he got busy with someone else, or something else came up that was more important or more urgent. But that doesn't mean you can start asking the same question sixteen times."

So. Things will change. The members of the group are going to abide by the rules: no talking on the ramp on the way up from activities, no complaining about food or running shoes or anything else, no questions in the hall before going into the rooms, no calling out from the rooms, no knocking as soon as they go into their rooms.

And if things don't change?

There will be consequences.

"What consequences?"

"Tomorrow, if things don't change, then all the members of the group will stay in their rooms from the beginning of task time until bed time."

No phone calls.

No books.

No walkman in the room.

No time in the TV room.

No trip to the dining room for bed-time snack.

Two and a half hours to contemplate the rules of the house and the need to follow those rules. To the letter.

"Even if I'm not causing the problem?" says Curt.

"Even if you're not causing the problem. It's a group problem. It's a whole bunch of people. Things are getting out of control with the whole group and until it gets settled, then everyone will be in their rooms to think things through. Okay?"

"Okay Patricia."

7:48 p.m. ——————————————————————————

"Penny?"

"Penny!"

Elizabeth's voice echoes in the hallway.

Penny pulls the curtain back. "Yes."

"I'm ready."

Normally when kids are hitting the wall, they take some time to come back to earth. Elizabeth flares like a Roman candle, and snuffs herself out just as quickly. The plaintive voice says it all. She's balancing out.

Penny opens the door. The message hasn't changed. Elizabeth will do a 15-minute time-out, sitting at her desk, and then they'll talk.

"I don't want to sit at my desk. I want to sit on my bed."

Control, control.

"Fine. You can sit on your bed. That's not a problem. But you know what the problem is, Elizabeth? It's the way you go about it. The disrespect you show. Your rudeness. The manipulation."

"Haven't you ever noticed that it's the people I don't like who I don't respect? Haven't you noticed that, Penny? Haven't you noticed that I don't like you? That I hate you? That I can't stand you? That I just want you outta my face?"

"You don't have to like me, Elizabeth. But you do have to show me respect. Now, sit on your bed." Penny closes the door, drops the curtain, lowers the light. Shakes her head.

Talks in whispers: "Normally kids don't de-escalate that fast. She can be very extreme and then turn around, and you saw it, within two or three minutes 'Penny, Penny'." But nothing much had changed, apart from the fact that Elizabeth wanted to get out of her room. She still wanted to control the situation. "She likes to set up a situation where she can gain power, or can get her own way. Which is fine with me if she's being compliant and being appropriate. But it's not fine if she's manipulating. And she's so good at it, too, she's so sneaky, with very subtle words, her body language." She's one of those kids who's saying one thing, but her expression, her body language, her attitude, are saying exactly the opposite.

The key with Elizabeth is to show her the boundary line. "She doesn't have to like me. But she has to respect me." And she can sit in her room for another hour, or two hours, or as long as it takes to get that message across.

Penny has all the time in the world.

8:26 p.m.

Sign on the wall:
Evening Routine
1. Residents move directly into rooms to get changed.
2. Once changed, knock, and staff will let you out of
   your room and into your closet.
3. If staff direct you back into your room, wait
   patiently until all routines are done and all
   meds have been given. Do not knock.
4. When all routines are done, the group will move
   into their designated lounge.

All the routines are done. And all the kids are in their respective lounges at either end of the hall for an hour of TV and cards, then snack-time (and, for Sandy, a birthday cake), then bed.

For the kids on Levels 1 and 2, bedtime is 9:30; those on Levels 3 and 4 go to bed half an hour later; those on Levels 5 and 6, 10:30.

No surprise that Fred, after today's performance, is in his room at 9:30. Given his attitude and his time remaining — a couple of weeks — he won't be moving up the Level ladder.

He pushes his door open, gives Sid the hard stare. He's still staring as the door closes behind him. A moment later, he starts knocking.

Sid: "It's bedtime, Fred"

"I've gotta call my lawyer."

"You know the rules."

"I've gotta call him. Now!"

"You should've called before bedtime."

"I didn't have to call then. I gotta call now."

"You're going to have to call in the morning." Sid drops the curtain, shuts Fred's light. "

Knock, knock, knock.

9:40 p.m. ———————————————————————

The knocking begins again.

"Sid. I gotta call my lawyer."

Sid pulls back the curtain, turns up the light. "It's time for bed."

"I gotta call him."

"You know the rules. You ask to make calls before your bed time. Not after."

249

"Well, I gotta call now. You can't prevent me from calling. I have a right to go to call my lawyer. You can't deny me my rights."

"Fred, it's not making phone calls that's the problem here. You're always trying to create issues after bedtime. And you're always being demanding."

"I want you to call my lawyer. Call him at home. Right now. You can't deny me my right to call my lawyer."

To Be Continued.

9:44 p.m. ————————————————

"Penny ?"

Penny pulls the curtains back and looks into Elizabeth's room. Elizabeth is sitting on the bed. Penny opens the door. "Are you ready to talk?"

Apparently.

Penny props the door open with her foot. She starts talking. Elizabeth is all ears.

Ten minutes later, Penny wraps things up: "Now, I want you to think about all that. And then I'll come back. All right?"

"All right, Penny ."

9:55 p.m. ————————————————

Fred is pounding on his door now.

Sid pulls back the curtain, turns up the light. "What is it, Fred?"

"I want to see Frank (the shift supervisor)."

"He's busy."

"Tell him to come see me."

"He's talking with someone, Fred. As soon as he's done, I'll have him come talk to you."

250

"Whyn't you just let me outta here so I can make a call."

"I'm not going to let you out to make a phone call, Fred. And I want to make it clear you've got to stop creating these issues and trying to manipulate people and you've got to stop being so demanding. And I'll get Frank as soon as you calm down."

"How long I gotta be quiet?"

"Five minutes."

"I'll be counting."

"With no watch?" Sid is smiling. "You're sure you're counting, too?"

10:06 p.m. ───────────────────────────

Penny knocks on Elizabeth's door, then pulls the curtains back. "Come on out, get ready for bed."

Elizabeth emerges.

Penny unlocks her closet, waits until Elizabeth gets her pyjamas, then locks the closet. A few minutes later, Elizabeth comes out into the hall and heads for the bathroom.

On the way back to her room: "Penny, do you think I could get my mail?"

Penny says she'll bring it. "In a few minutes."

"Thanks, Penny." The smile of an angel.

10:10 p.m.───────────────────────────

Frank pulls back the curtain on Fred's door. "What's the problem?"

"I wanna call my lawyer."

"You can call him in the morning."

"I wanna call him now."

251

Frank tells Fred that he supports what Sid has already told him. "Now, it's time for bed. Goodnight." He drops the curtain.

10:21 p.m.

A solitary letter.

Penny pulls back the curtain on Elizabeth's door and holds the letter up so Elizabeth can see it. She opens the door and hands Elizabeth her mail. Elizabeth is all smiles "Thanks, Penny. Thanks a million."

Penny lets the door close, shakes her head, smiles one of those 'can you believe it?' smiles.

Then, down the hall: "Once she relaxed and got started, she was my best friend again. Like you saw there. She switches right back over. And it's a total flip-flop. She comes on very strong to try to back you away and say 'I want it my way' but once you stand up to her and give her limits she falls right into it and flips back over."

And what's this tell Penny about Elizabeth's background? "It's hard to say. I know from her background it's a broken marriage and her sister had a lot of trouble as well. Elizabeth loves attention, she feels she needs it and tries to get it any way she can. Some of her acting-out behaviour comes from 'I want attention any way I can get it, whether it be positive or negative'."

She especially likes to try to manipulate the male staff members: "She's very very seductive with them. And she does it in such a sleek way that sometimes they don't even realize, and we don't even realize until after, what's been going on. She'll try to be very flirty with them, or try to get her own way with them. And that's one of her ways: using her blinking eyes, or 'I'm special aren't I?', anything to get the reaction from them. She goes past those boundaries of staff-resident. And staff have to watch themselves because she could try to set them up very easily. And that's scary, because she is smart enough to plan different things and she's smart enough to try and set things up to harm other people and I wouldn't put it past her at all. The male staff have to be very very careful."

"Good night, Penny ."

Good night, Elizabeth

10:23 p.m.————————————————————————

There's a sticker on Grant's door, one of those cartoon characters with a word balloon: 'Smile Someone Loves You.'

"Like my sticker, Paul?"

Yes, I say. It's a neat sticker.

Grant looks at it and smiles. "Yah. It is."

Sid wonders if it's a sticker he'd like to put in his brag book.

"I don't want a brag book."

"Why not?"

"I don't have any pictures, except my dog."

"You don't have a picture of your mother?"

"I hate my mother. I wouldn't want to have to look at her picture."

We head down the hall toward the lounge.

I've asked William B. for permission to talk with one of the kids. He had suggested Grant. Grant had said 'Sure, why not?'

So, here we are: Grant on the sofa, the tape recorder on the table in front of him. Sid is standing just outside the door, where he can see both of us.

Q: "How long have you been here?"

A: "I've been sentenced here two months so far. But I've did a month's dead time while I was waiting for court. I was here and going to court every week or whatever."

253

Q: "How long to go?"

A: "Ten months."

Q: "Tell me about the trip to the jail. How did you get here?"

A: "Paddy wagon."

Q: "What was that like?"

A: "I just wanted to cry. Because I was, like, leaving everything behind and coming into here. Seeing out the back window, seeing everything I would normally see walking down the street just go by, I just wanted to cry. And I knew I was coming for a long time, so . . ."

Q: "Did you come here straight from court?"

A: "From the police station."

Q: "What else was going on in your head?"

A: "The thought that ran through my head was I wanted to kinda commit suicide because I was so scared. Like I said, I was leaving everything behind. All the holidays I was going to miss. Special occasions, parties, hanging out with my friends."

Q: "A lonely feeling."

A: "Yah. That's what it was, really."

Q: "Anybody else in the paddy wagon with you?"

A: "No. Just by myself."

Q: "Two cops in the front, you in the back?"

A: "Yah. And they were cool cops. They were joking with me. 'Hey, you wanna come ride in the front?' He was really funny."

Q: "What else was going on in your head, on the ride down?"

A: "I was really afraid. Because I'd never been in a secure custody facility before. I guess the thing that was mostly on my mind was having to come into all these rules all of a sudden. And not knowing what to expect, the type of people I'd be working with, how it would be for me. I was kind of being selfish because I was just thinking 'me, me, me.' I was afraid that it was going to be nuts. I was kinda mostly afraid that I wouldn't be able to follow all the rules and I would be getting myself in more trouble. Just drove me nuts, because everything was mixed up inside my head."

Q: "Must have been a very scary time for you."

A: "Yah, it was. Especially being my first time coming into a secure custody facility."

Q: "What did you think this place would look like?"

A: "I expected an ugly building with walls all around on the outside, big brick walls. Like a jail. Even for young offenders, I thought it would be the same type of thing so that we couldn't escape, or whatever."

Q: "What did you think the inside would look like?"

A: "I pictured it not to be so neat, and not comforting. I kind of pictured a jail. Like the county jail. Kind of a range, no lounges on the inside, no TV. I didn't expect none of that kind of things."

Q: "A range, cells, barred doors?"

A: "Yah."

Q: "So then you pulled up here. What'd you think?"

A: "Wow. I thought this wasn't what I was expecting at all. Fences instead of walls. It looked like it was a really nice building. And I kinda said, 'well, here's my home, my new home.' And I just really was afraid to even enter into the building, not knowing what to expect. But once I got into the building, it was another 'wow' what a nice place. Everyone was friendly with me when I came in."

Q: "Tell me about the process you went through once you got inside."

A: "First, the police took the handcuffs off and a supervisor came and they brought me through the front door into a hallway and through another door into another hallway to go to get administrated, whatever. They had to do a search."

Q: "What was involved in that?"

A: "I had to take off all my clothes and turn around for them and they gave me a housecoat to put on and told me I could shower and I showered and they gave me some special shampoo for lice or whatever, in case. And I had to let it sit in my hair for a couple of minutes before I washed it out. And then I got out of the shower and dried off and they gave me some really ugly clothes."

Q: "What were you thinking while all this was happening?"

A: "I was thinking the person who was searching me, I was wondering, I knew it was routine and everything, but I was thinking 'Is this guy gay? He wants to see me turn around naked.' That's all I could think. 'Is he a fruit?' But they explained to me the reasons for having me do all that. I already kind of knew because at the police station it's the same kind of thing."

Q: "They want to make sure you don't have any weapons."

A: "Anything at all."

Q: "What happened after that?"

A: "First, they brought me to a little room. And they said, 'This isn't your room. You'll be upstairs, but this is where you're going to be tonight.' To get administrated into the program, registered, kind of. They brought me some food. I hadn't eaten much that day. Mexican food. Burritos. It was kind of gross, but kind of good."

Q: "And then?"

A: "They read me my rights and told me some of the rules here. And then I was given a book that I had to fill out a bunch of questions. There was questions I had to answer on victimization. And they tell you, 'Be honest, answer the questions to the best of your ability.' So I filled the book out and then I went over it with the staff and then they came and discussed with me a little bit about this program, how I would have to follow all these rules. I was thinking like 'wow, I just ran into a cement wall'. And most of what I was thinking was wow, I've gotta stop doin' all the things I was doin' on the outside. Comin' in, follow all these rules. It was crazy."

Q: "What were some of the rules they told you about that first day?"

A: "That there was no physical contact between the females and the males here. I kinda figured that when I first came here, but I wasn't sure. So they explained it to me. And, if you're on the ramp, going downstairs or coming upstairs, you have to be quiet and show respect to all the staff and the other residents here. And I was just thinking 'wow, these people are crazy, they expect me to follow all these rules?' It's like I have 20 or 30 different bosses now and I wasn't used to having any bosses at all. I was my own boss. And back to the cement wall thing. And ever since I've been here I keep going back to that 'cause I think of things I did on the outside and I want to do it, especially things I really enjoyed doing."

Q: "What do you most miss?"

A: "Partying with my friends. Relationships, like, my girl-friend, being able to spend time with her and her family. Now I can't have anything like that. Actually, I just miss the freedom altogether. But I know that what I did, I deserve to be here. So I gotta live with it."

Q: "Did you know that when you came in?"

A: "Yah. Just I didn't want to be here."

Q: "But did you understand the gravity of what you'd done?"

A: "Yah."

Q: "You mentioned missing your freedom. What does freedom mean to you?"

A: "Doing what I like, to a certain extent. Being able to talk amongst my friends whatever way I want, say things I want to say without being told 'hey, that's inappropriate.' Basically, just being able to do what I want."

Q: "What kinds of things did you like to do that you can't do now?"

A: "Make love. That's one of the main things. I don't know, we do a lot of things here that normally I wouldn't do on the out-side, like getting involved in all the sports and stuff. We do so many things here. I didn't do much on the outside except watch a lot of TV. I was a big couch potato. I miss being able to watch certain shows that I used to look forward to watching during the week, 'cause a lot of TV shows here are inappropriate."

Q: "You've been here a couple of months. I wonder what changes you have felt in yourself in that time."

A: "I feel that I'm learning a lot of self-control since I've been here. It's been really difficult, going through the changes."

Q: "Could you give me an example of a way in which you're able to control yourself now."

A: "Before, if people were to get in my face or tease me or whatever I might have knocked them out or gave them a shot in the head. Now that I'm in here, I find myself holding back even though that's what I want if people get in my face, I just want to cuff 'em and tell 'em 'get outta my face.' Being in here I just totally hold back. Part of the reason is I don't want to end up with a program and lose my Levels and have all those other consequences. But other reasons is because I'm trying to change from doing all the other things that were wrong that I was doing on the outside."

Q: "Why do you want to change?"

A: "Because I don't want to spend the rest of my life in and out of jail. It's depressing. Especially missing special occasions, Christmas, having to spend that holiday in custody, and Easter and my birthday. My birthday just went by. I had to do that in here. It wasn't as bad as I thought. They got a cake for me and everyone sung happy birthday to me, but when I knew my birthday was coming up

I wanted to stay in my room for the whole day, just sleep the whole day, because I couldn't be with my friends, I couldn't do what I wanted, I knew I wasn't going to wake up looking forward to people saying 'Happy birthday, here's a present for you.' But it was good. They gave me a privilege I normally wouldn't have got. I got to call my girlfriend on my birthday and she got to wish me a happy birthday. I talked to her for a couple of minutes. So that really broke my day up. The cake was good."

Q: "You started talking about wanting to change. Tell me more."

A: "It actually kinda started before I got here. I wanted to change. More so I could fit in with my girlfriend's family. My girlfriend, her parents knew a lot of things about me and that was holding them back from like doing other things with me, letting me spend time with my girlfriend. They kinda wanted to keep me away from her. And so I was like 'that ain't right.' I don't have education. I um, been in and out of jail for a certain amount of time and missing all the fun things that I get when I'm free, why don't I just go back to school and get a job and straighten my life out. And after being here a month I started to realize that this place is to my benefit and it's really going to help me to change and make something out of my life."

Q: "Funny way to think of a jail, isn't it?"

A: "It sure is. When I first came here I questioned a lot of the rules and tried to slide by, take the easy way out at first and then I started thinking, why? That's what got me in here. Taking the easy way out. Running away from my problems, not facing responsibility for what I've done."

Q: "What help have you received here, in terms of getting at the things that bugged you in life?"

A: "A lot. Staff here is really supportive. They're always there when you need to talk. And it feels really good because on the outside if I was down or something was going wrong I'd have a beer. And in here, it's good that they're there and they're trying to help me to stay away from having to do that. And they want to talk."

Q: "Do you find that hard? Talking to adults? It couldn't have been easy trusting them.

A: "At first, no. But once I started opening up, or staff started talking to me and I kinda listened to advice from one staff and then I'd go to another and see what they had to say and I'd put it all together. And if something was wrong, I'd kinda want to go back to the same two staff. But lately I've been opening up to other staff and trying to understand how they are and if they are trustworthy but I kinda don't like getting close to anybody."

Q: "Why?"

A: "Because in the past, everybody I've gotten close to never stuck around. It's different in here because they've gotta be here but it's just scary thinking they're not going to be here in ten months, when I get out, they're not going to be there to talk to and support me and to keep me away from my bad habits and what's going to happen when things are going wrong?"

Q: "You concerned about that?"

A: "Yah. In a lot of areas. Am I going to turn back to crime? That's not what I want. That's not what I'm hoping for. But is it going to happen? If things are going wrong am I going to drink that beer or am I going to go to somebody I can trust which, being where I'm at, when I'm on the outside, there's not many people I can trust."

Q: "What most worries you when you think about the day the door opens?"

A: "Where I'm going to be. Where I'm going to live. I don't think that worries me the most, but it does worry me. I know that here they can help me get assistance, get into a good school, get an apartment, which that scares me, independent living, that I'm going to have to do that, because I was always counting on other people to be there for me. And I'm going to be alone."

Q: "Pretty easy to pick up a 12 pack and get yourself in trouble."

A: "Yah. That's just it. I don't know what I'm going to do. I can say a lot of things. I can tell staff 'oh, I'm gonna stay out of trouble, I'm gonna slow down on the drinking, or quit drinking' but I'm afraid when it comes down to it and I'm with my friends, is that really going to happen? My friends don't control me, but the temptation will be there. It's easy to say things, especially here where none of that will ever happen, but what happens when I get out?"

Q: "Tell me more about the help you've been getting in here."

A: "I think they've been helping me have a better outlook on my life, because I used to think there was nowhere I was going to end up, like I'm not going anywhere, I'm just going to end up in the gutter kind of thing. But talking to staff, they really put it into your head that your life's not over, that you can change, and that's what I'm glad about, that they are there for me because no one has ever really been there before and it just seems different. I don't know. The staff, some of them, try to be like a big brother to you or a father figure when they work with you, just to show you 'we care, we care what happens to you.' "

Q: "When you were coming here in the paddy wagon, did it ever cross your mind that you'd be able to say to someone what you just said? I mean, it sounds like you've developed a friendship with some of these people."

A: "A close friendship. Sometimes I get to thinking when I'm having a bad day or whatever that they don't really care, that they're just here to make their money. But then when I really, really think about it, that's not it at all. I know they're here to help and to change us around and that it's not just the money and no I never did think that I would ever say this three months down the road from that first day."

Q: "Have you set goals for yourself, for the rest of your term?"

A: "I've worked with the social worker here and we kinda set goals where I'm gonna do my schooling, since I'm far behind in my schooling. Being here 10 months, there's a whole school year that I'm gonna have completed so I'm gonna have all my credits for one year and that'll help me get into a school for when I get out and finish getting credits and I think I'm going to do some correspondence so I can catch up and be at the grade level I'm supposed to be in."

Q: "What would you like to do, down the road?"

A: "I don't know. I'd kinda thought about going through school and going through university and majoring in computer technology but then after I wrote a story, which I never thought it was a good story, I never thought I'd be able to write, but I kinda started thinking about writing. I wrote based on my ... a true story, but I made it bigger than what it was. I got creative. And everyone tells me they can see I've got good writing skills and I kinda think I'm going to try to follow through on that."

Q: "What about personal goals, in terms of the way you think about the world, the way you act toward other people."

A: (Long pause). "In my relationships, my female relationships, I'm working with the social worker for me to try to be more trustworthy and not so possessive, more honest in my relationships cause in the past I haven't been so honest and stuff. I guess what she says is not go to bed with everyone I'm attracted to because that's what I was telling her, like, in the past I'd be in a relationship and all of a sudden I'd see someone attractive and we'd talk and the next thing I knew, we're in bed. So I'm gonna work on just being friends with girls instead of having to get into a relationship right away. I don't think there are any other personal goals that I've set. At least not yet that I've set for being on the outside. In here I've got goals for while I'm here and those are to be positive, like a role model in my group and not to be so argumentative when given a time-out. I always want to argue right away because I think I'm not wrong, I always think I'm right when it comes to me being consequenced. And I'm working with everybody here to change that around, to not be so defensive and to listen to what they have to say and then afterwards explain myself and admit, yah, maybe I am wrong."

Q: "How are you feeling about yourself now, compared with a year ago?"

A: "I feel pretty good about myself. Not because I did a crime and I'm in here but because before I didn't have much self-control. I always wanted my own way, I still do, but I got my own way a lot of the time and I didn't have such good self-esteem and I didn't interact with people on the outside as well as I do in here. I've gone through a lot of changes since I've been here. I've started to realize that girls aren't everything, and that's what it was for a long time. And, um, everything can't always be my way. I realize that, now. And . . .

Q: "Do you feel better about you?"

A: "Yah. I feel like this place kinda made me a better person. They helped me become a better person in the short time I've been here."

Q: "Do you like yourself more than you liked yourself before you came in here?

A: "Yah. But sometimes I think, I dunno, it's kind of an identity crisis. Sometimes I think 'I don't care. I don't care about nobody. I just care about myself.' And then my mind jumps to, like, you know, why am I acting like that, why am I thinking like that when I know I really do care and I have feelings for other people and I feel really good now because I can tell where I'm wrong, I can see where I'm wrong and I look at a lot of positives in myself now instead of all the negatives."

Q: "Tell me about some of your positives."

A: "I'm good at helping people. I enjoy helping people. I like to get involved in things with everybody, and try to get everybody else involved too and, um, I can change and I have the willpower to change and to follow through with the things that I say in here."

Q: "You know that about yourself now, when you never did before?"

A: "Yah. Because I never really thought about it before."

Q: "Are you less lonely now than you were before?"

A: "In a sense yah I do feel less alone because I know people are here to comfort me and talk with me and I can trust people here. But I feel alone, also, because my girlfriend isn't keeping in touch with me and none of my friends are keeping in touch with me. I'm not getting along with my parents. Well, I haven't been, even before I was in here I wasn't. But now that I'm in here we argue more, it seems like, and it just seems like no one cares anymore, kind of, like, in my background. But I don't feel alone because I know that every-one in here cares."

Q: "But somehow you've got to get yourself to the point where you can survive on the outside."

A: "I have a lot of time to do that. Staff today was telling me, she asked me how much time I had left, I told her and she said, 'We've got a lot of time left to work with you, to work on you, to make some changes.' And I feel that will happen."

Q: "Tell me a little more about your concerns for the future."

A: "I think that I, I hope that I will stay out of trouble. I know it's going to be hard because the pressure's going to be there.

I think that it'll be not as hard to stay away from things because I'll be in school, I'll be working, I'll be living on my own so I'll have a place to go. I think things will work out. I think I can make something of myself."

Q: "When you think about the crime you did that landed you in jail, what do you think?"

A: "A lot of times I just think about, ah, why. How it wasn't worth it. At the time I never, didn't really think, didn't care much. But now whenever I sit down and think about it, which is a lot of the time, whenever I sit down I think why? Why did I do that, and risk throwing a year of my life away? And I always tell myself it wasn't worth it."

Q: "When you ask yourself 'why did I do it?' how do you answer yourself?"

A: "Um, to tell you the truth, I don't really know. A lot of times I think, I just say, for the money or whatever. I don't really know. Kinda, I guess, it would be I thought I was cool, I thought I was fitting in with everybody, I'm getting in trouble and everyone else is getting in trouble so they all liked me 'cause I'm doin' things with them. Um. I guess that's pretty much the main reasons, just because I thought I was cool. Now I know that I was wrong."

Q: "Do you replay that incident in your head a lot?"

A: "Not a lot, but sometimes, yah. It drives me crazy thinking about it."

Q: "Why?"

A: "Just because, I dunno, because I know that I was wrong and I wasn't really cool. I was the dumb one, because I didn't think, I wasn't thinking, I was thinking short-term, what I was going to benefit, I didn't even think of anything like, what if I was put in jail? I hadn't never thought about anything like that."

Q: "And now?"

A: "Now, now I know I would never ever do anything like that again to get myself put in a custody facility, especially for another long term because I respect my freedom, like, and I'd just love to be free, especially holidays. Sometimes I don't think long-term while I'm here but other times, I stop myself from doing something that I know is going to be wrong in here and say, okay, in my head I say what will the consequences be, what will be good, what could I get good out of this for later on? A lot of times that helps."

Q: "At night, lights are out, what do you think about?"

A: "First, I look back on my day and try to figure out where I might have went wrong and lost points, especially days when I'm trying to have a perfect day and earn 50 (points) and have some privilege on the weekend. But I more think about, especially on the weekends, what I would be doing if I was on the outside, who I would be with, where I would be, and then I start to think I wish I would get a letter from at least one friend, my girlfriend, my ex-girlfriend. And I dream at night that I'm hanging around with my friends. I've been having that dream that I've been out with my friends, partying, hanging out. And I wake up in the morning and I'm like, aw, that's where I was, I passed out at the party or something and I wake up and see the four cement walls around me again. Being in my room alone I always go into a deep thought most of the time, about relationships that I had in the past, where I went wrong, how I didn't respect the girl I was with, how I tried to control her. And I think, like, for what? Why? I can't control nobody. I don't own them. Nobody can control me. And then I jump to thinking only 10 months left, then I'll be outta here.' "

Q: "How old are you?"

A. "Sixteen."

The Last Word

Grant and I talked for about half an hour. I've played that tape back three times and each time the tape ends I'm struck by what Grant failed to say at least as much as I'm struck by what he did say.

Not once did he mention a victim. Not once. That surprised me and it may surprise you but not the jail's director, William B. As he'd told me, during our first interview, empathy is a tough one for these kids. Generally speaking, they're as egocentric as four-year-olds. And some of them are absolutely chilling in their inability to feel guilt or any other emotion.

What does it mean when a kid feels nothing for the people he hurts? What does it mean when teenagers don't get the treatment they need and go back out on the street with no appreciable change of heart or mind? What does it mean when we let troubled children slip through the cracks and grow up, without treatment, to become the troubled teenagers of tomorrow?

Pretty obvious, really.

Someone's going to get hurt.

Maybe someone you know.

Maybe you.

What would that be like? A Windsor woman can tell you. Her nine-year-old son was beaten within an inch of his life and left for dead in a field not all that far from my home. She would like to have told me the story directly but she didn't think she could do so without breaking down. It's been more than a year since her son was assaulted.

What follows is an excerpt from the victim impact statement she wrote for use at the trial of the teenager charged with assaulting her son.

"My son suffered a fractured skull, damage to his optic nerve and left ear, multiple cuts and so on. Luckily, Christopher eventually regained vision in his damaged eye. After several months, he also regained movement in that eye (at first, he appeared cross-eyed). Although his vision is improved, he does not see as well as he did prior to the assault.

"Whether or not he sustained brain damage, aside from the optic nerve, is difficult to assess. He was always a very bright child and, thankfully, continues to do well in school. He continues to suffer a memory loss related to the assault itself and has no recollection of the next few days after the injury took place. The doctors speculated this memory loss was due to the severity of the head injury. Although Christopher has made a good physical recovery from this assault, he has had periodic headaches from the time this happened. These headaches were severe and frequent in the first few weeks after the head injury and still occur on a regular basis.

"The assault has also made visible changes in his appearance. He has a noticeable scar on the side of his left eye. As well, his left pupil is more dilated than his right. He is now self-conscious about his appearance. This was made worse by the fact some of his peers made fun of the way he looked when the problem with his eye was more obvious.

"It is very hard for me to talk about the pain this incident has caused Christopher. Luckily he is a very resilient child and has a lot of inner strength. He has recovered amazingly well, considering what happened to him.He sometimes seems nervous when he's around teenagers, but he has not lost his capacity to trust and to be open to those around him. I only hope he can maintain an attitude of trust in the world.

"Although my son does not reveal any obvious emotional problems as a result of this assault, his self-image and self-esteem have suffered. Although most children in his school behaved in a kindly fashion toward him, there were others who were verbally cruel, making fun of his appearance. Even though the eye has recovered and he no longer looks cross-eyed, Christopher is very self-conscious about the way he looks and frequently seeks reassurance that he looks fine.

"Of even greater sorrow to me is what he went through from the time he was assaulted. It is unbelievably hard to put on paper what my son went through that night. Maybe the best way to make it real is to have you imagine what it would be like to be a nine-year-old boy, one minute playing outside without a worry in the world and, the next, being viciously assaulted. I can only imagine how much pain he experienced and how terrified he must have felt. The assault took place between 4 and 5 that afternoon. We didn't find him until 4:15 the next morning at which point he was covered in blood, freezing cold, and in shock. During that 12-hour period, Christopher did not simply lie in one spot unconscious; he was found about a half-mile from where the attack took place. It causes me extreme anguish to think of what he went through during those next twelve hours. Not only would he have been confused and in great pain, but he couldn't see where he was going and he had to feel unbelievably frightened. Because of the many additional wounds on his body, including two deep puncture wounds at the back of his neck, it is highly likely that he fell repeatedly and that he kept reinjuring himself. It must have been like walking through a minefield, feeling both blindfolded and terrified.

"I know it must have been worse than any nightmare imaginable and, considering the condition he was in and how cold he must have been, it must have seemed never-ending. Twelve hours must have felt like an eternity and I can only imagine him screaming out (if only in his mind) for help. I also wonder if he even heard the many people wandering around trying to find him — whether he was too weak to call out to them or whether he called out and simply wasn't heard. Although I am trying my best to say in words what he went through that night, words can't really describe the horror of the situation. I thank God Christopher has no memory of what went on that night, nor of the agony that continued during his hospital stay.

"I wish I could be similarly blessed and that my own memory of that awful evening would disappear. But I remember everything in vivid detail as though watching a film in slow motion. Throughout that night, every breath I took renewed my fear of where my son was, why this person had lured him away. I remember trying extremely hard not to think about what might be happening at each and every moment but the thoughts of what he might be going through tore me apart.

"When the police finally found him at 4:15 in the morning, he was lying on the side of a hill barely conscious. When they radioed his location to the police mobile, no one said whether he was alive or dead — just that he had been found. We were then told he was being rushed to the hospital because of head injuries. When they brought him into the emergency room, I remember how grateful I was that he was still alive and that we had found him before it was too late. While the doctor tried to stitch up the gash in his head, I remember trying to give Christopher whatever comfort I could but I don't know if he even knew who I was.

"The next several days continued to be a nightmare. Not only was it necessary to deal with the possibility that Christopher would be completely blind in one eye, but we had no way of knowing whether he'd be brain damaged, whether the bleeding to his head meant internal damage, what his trauma would do to him emotionally, whether he was sexually as well as physically abused.

"It was terrible to see what Christopher went through the next few days. From being a very loving and very sweet child, he turned into someone who was consumed with rage and who tried to strike out at everyone around him — including his family, the medical staff, the police, and so on. All he wanted to do was die. He begged me repeatedly to kill him — even asking for a knife so he could kill himself. And because I wouldn't comply — because I was often forced to help the nurses in their attempts to care for him — he told me he hated me and did what he could to hurt me physically and emotionally. I knew this wasn't the real Christopher — that this wasn't how he truly felt — but to see him in such pain and to feel that he saw me as an enemy was like a sword twisting inside of me. I don't know how we got through the next few days.

"By the time Christopher was able to come home, he lacked the strength to walk and had to be carried everywhere. Although we tried getting him to walk when he was still in hospital, he had no motivation and refused to try. Luckily, once he got home and began to feel safe, he became my little boy again and started to recover, both emotionally and physically.

"But nothing will negate the horror he was forced to go through."

The teenager accused of beating Christopher was acquitted.

POSTSCRIPT: Bill, the boy who was released in mid-morning on this diary day, was back in jail less than two weeks later, awaiting trial on charges laid the week he was released.

Also by Paul Vasey

Fiction

The Sufferer Kind
Lord, Lord
The Failure of Love
Into Thin Air

Non-Fiction

The Great Train Ride
The Inland Seas
Rivers of North America

Television Drama
The Last Stand